ABOUT THIS PUBLICATION

FOR SERVICE ASSISTANCE

Customer Service Department
704.898.0770

North Carolina General Statues is published by The Muliti-Media Group of Greater Charlotte in Charlotte, North Carolina. Copyright 2015 by the Multi-Media Group of Greater Charlotte. This book or parts thereof may not be reproduced in any form, stored in a retrieval system, or transmitted in any form by any means—electronic, mechanical, photocopy, recording or otherwise—without prior written permission of the publisher, except as provided by United States of America copyright law.

The records required by U.S. Code 2257(a) through (c) and the pertinent regulations 28 C.F.R. Cli. 1, Part 75 with respect to this publication and all materials associated with such records are maintained by The Multi-Media Group of Greater Charlotte, Publisher and available for review by Attorney General.

www.visionbooks.org

Copyright © 2015 by MMGGC
All rights reserved!

TID: 5031730
ISBN (10) digit: 150259868X
ISBN (13) digit: 978-1502598684

123-4-56789-01234-Paperback
123-4-56789-01234-Hardback

First Edition

090520140547

Printed in the United States of America

2015 EDITION

North Carolina Criminal Law And Procedure-Pamphlet # 22

Printed In conjunction with the Administration of the Courts

North Carolina Criminal Law and Procedure
Pamphlet Reference Guide

Chapters	Pamphlet
Chapter 1 Civil Procedure	1
Chapter 1 Civil Procedure (Continue)	2
Chapter 1A Rules of Civil Procedure	2
Chapter 1B Contribution.	2
Chapter 1C Enforcement of Judgments.	2
Chapter 1D Punitive Damages.	2
Chapter 1E Eastern Band of Cherokee Indians.	2
Chapter 1F North Carolina Uniform Interstate Depositions and Discovery Act.	2
Chapter 2 - Clerk of Superior Court [Repealed and Transferred.]	3
Chapter 3 - Commissioners of Affidavits and Deeds [Repealed.]	3
Chapter 4 - Common Law	3
Chapter 5 - Contempt [Repealed.]	3
Chapter 5A - Contempt	3
Chapter 6 - Liability for Court Costs	3
Chapter 7 - Courts [Repealed and Transferred.]	3
Chapter 7A – Judicial Department	3
Chapter 7A – Continuation (Judicial Department)	4
Chapter 7A – Continuation (Judicial Department)	5
Chapter 7B - Juvenile Code	5
Chapter 8 - Evidence	6
Chapter 8A - Interpreters for Deaf Persons [Recodified.]	6
Chapter 8B - Interpreters for Deaf Persons	6
Chapter 8C - Evidence Code	6
Chapter 9 - Jurors	6
Chapter 10 - Notaries [Repealed.]	6
Chapter 10A - Notaries [Recodified.]	6
Chapter 10B - Notaries	6
Chapter 11 - Oaths	6
Chapter 12 - Statutory Construction	6
Chapter 13 - Citizenship Restored	6
Chapter 14 - Criminal Law	7
Chapter 14 –Criminal Law (Continuation)	8
Chapter 15 - Criminal Procedure	9
Chapter 15A - Criminal Procedure Act (Continuation)	10
Chapter 15A - Criminal Procedure Act (Continuation)	11
Chapter 15B - Victims Compensation	11
Chapter 15C - Address Confidentiality Program	11
Chapter 16 - Gaming Contracts and Futures	11
Chapter 17 - Habeas Corpus	11

Chapter 17A - Law-Enforcement Officers [Recodified.]	11
Chapter 17B - North Carolina Criminal Justice Education and Training System [Recodified.] Chapter 17C - North Carolina Criminal Justice Education and Training Standards Commission	11 11
Chapter 17D - North Carolina Justice Academy	11
Chapter 17E - North Carolina Sheriffs' Education and Training Standards Commission	11
Chapter 18 - Regulation of Intoxicating Liquors [Repealed.]	12
Chapter 18A - Regulation of Intoxicating Liquors [Repealed.]	12
Chapter 18B - Regulation of Alcoholic Beverages	12
Chapter 18C - North Carolina State Lottery	12
Chapter 19 - Offenses against Public Morals	12
Chapter 19A - Protection of Animals	12
Chapter 20 - Motor Vehicles	13
Chapter 20 - Motor Vehicles (Continuation)	14
Chapter 20 - Motor Vehicles (Continuation)	15
Chapter 20 - Motor Vehicles (Continuation)	16
Chapter 21 - Bills of Lading	17
Chapter 22 - Contracts Requiring Writing	17
Chapter 22A - Signatures	17
Chapter 22B - Contracts Against Public Policy	17
Chapter 22C - Payments to Subcontractors	17
Chapter 23 - Debtor and Creditor	17
Chapter 24 – Interest	17
Chapter 25 – Uniform Commercial Code	18
Chapter 25 – Uniform Commercial Code (Continuation)	19
Chapter 25A – Retail Installment Sales Act	20
Chapter 25B - Credit	20
Chapter 25C - Sales of Artwork	20
Chapter 26 - Suretyship	20
Chapter 27 - Warehouse Receipts [Repealed.]	20
Chapter 28 - Administration [Repealed.]	20
Chapter 28A - Administration of Decedents' Estates	20
Chapter 28B - Estates of Absentees in Military Service	20
Chapter 28C - Estates of Missing Persons	20
Chapter 29 - Intestate Succession	21
Chapter 30 - Surviving Spouses	21
Chapter 31 - Wills	21
Chapter 31A - Acts Barring Property Rights	21
Chapter 31B - Renunciation of Property and Renunciation of Fiduciary Powers Act	21
Chapter 31C - Uniform Disposition of Community Property Rights at Death Act	21
Chapter 32 - Fiduciaries	21
Chapter 32A - Powers of Attorney	21
Chapter 33 - Guardian and Ward [Repealed and Recodified.]	21

Chapter 33A - North Carolina Uniform Transfers to Minors Act	21
Chapter 33B - North Carolina Uniform Custodial Trust Act	21
Chapter 34 - Veterans' Guardianship Act	22
Chapter 35 - Sterilization Procedures	22
Chapter 35A - Incompetency and Guardianship	22
Chapter 36 - Trusts and Trustees [Repealed.]	22
Chapter 36A - Trusts and Trustees	22
Chapter 36B - Uniform Management of Institutional Funds Act [Repealed.]	22
Chapter 36C - North Carolina Uniform Trust Code	22
Chapter 36D - North Carolina Community Third Party Trusts, Pooled Trusts	23
Chapter 36E - Uniform Prudent Management of Institutional Funds Act	23
Chapter 37 - Allocation of Principal and Income [Repealed.]	23
Chapter 37A - Uniform Principal and Income Act	23
Chapter 38 - Boundaries	23
Chapter 38A - Landowner Liability	23
Chapter 38B - Trespasser Responsibility	23
Chapter 39 - Conveyances	23
Chapter 39A - Transfer Fee Covenants Prohibited	23
Chapter 40 - Eminent Domain [Repealed.]	23
Chapter 40A - Eminent Domain	23
Chapter 41 - Estates	23
Chapter 41A - State Fair Housing Act	23
Chapter 42 - Landlord and Tenant	23
Chapter 42A - Vacation Rental Act	23
Chapter 43 - Land Registration	23
Chapter 44 - Liens	24
Chapter 44A - Statutory Liens and Charges	24
Chapter 45 - Mortgages and Deeds of Trust	24
Chapter 45A - Good Funds Settlement Act	24
Chapter 46 - Partition	24
Chapter 47 - Probate and Registration	25
Chapter 47A - Unit Ownership	25
Chapter 47B - Real Property Marketable Title Act	25
Chapter 47C - North Carolina Condominium Act	25
Chapter 47D - Notice of Settlement Act [Expired.]	25
Chapter 47E - Residential Property Disclosure Act	25
Chapter 47F - North Carolina Planned Community Act	25
Chapter 47G - Option to Purchase Contracts	25
Chapter 47H - Contracts for Deed	25
Chapter 48 - Adoptions +	26
Chapter 48A - Minors	26
Chapter 49 - Bastardy	26
Chapter 49A - Rights of Children	26
Chapter 50 - Divorce and Alimony	26

Chapter 50A - Uniform Child-Custody Jurisdiction and Enforcement Act	26
Chapter 50B - Domestic Violence	26
Chapter 50C - Civil No-Contact Orders	26
Chapter 51 - Marriage	26
Chapter 52 - Powers and Liabilities of Married Persons	27
Chapter 52A - Uniform Reciprocal Enforcement of Support Act [Repealed.]	27
Chapter 52B - Uniform Premarital Agreement Act	27
Chapter 52C - Uniform Interstate Family Support Act	27
Chapter 53 - Banks	27
Chapter 53A - Business Development Corporations and North Carolina Capital Resource Corporations	28
Chapter 53B - Financial Privacy Act	28
Chapter 54 - Cooperative Organizations	28
Chapter 54A - Capital Stock Savings and Loan Associations [Repealed.]	28
Chapter 54B - Savings and Loan Associations	29
Chapter 54C - Savings Banks	29
Chapter 55 - North Carolina Business Corporation Act	30
Chapter 55A - North Carolina Nonprofit Corporation Act	31
Chapter 55B - Professional Corporation Act	31
Chapter 55C - Foreign Trade Zones	31
Chapter 55D - Filings, Names, and Registered Agents for Corporations, Nonprofit Corporations, and Partnerships	31
Chapter 56 - Electric, Telegraph and Power Companies [Repealed.]	31
Chapter 57 - Hospital, Medical and Dental Service Corporations [Recodified.]	31
Chapter 57A - Health Maintenance Organization Act [Recodified.]	31
Chapter 57B - Health Maintenance Organization Act [Recodified.]	31
Chapter 57C - North Carolina Limited Liability Company Act.	31
Chapter 58 - Insurance.	32
Chapter 58 - Insurance (Continuation)	33
Chapter 58 - Insurance (Continuation)	34
Chapter 58 - Insurance (Continuation)	35
Chapter 58 - Insurance (Continuation)	36
Chapter 58 - Insurance (Continuation)	37
Chapter 58 - Insurance (Continuation)	38
Chapter 58A - North Carolina Health Insurance Trust Commission [Recodified.]	38
Chapter 59 - Partnership.	39
Chapter 59B - Uniform Unincorporated Nonprofit Association Act.	39
Chapter 60 - Railroads and Other Carriers [Repealed and Transferred.]	39
Chapter 61 - Religious Societies	39
Chapter 62 - Public Utilities	39

Chapter 62 - Public Utilities (Continuation)	40
Chapter 62A - Public Safety Telephone Service And Wireless Telephone Service	40
Chapter 63 - Aeronautics	40
Chapter 63A - North Carolina Global TransPark Authority	40
Chapter 64 - Aliens	40
Chapter 65 – Cemeteries	40
Chapter 66 - Commerce and Business	41
Chapter 67 - Dogs	41
Chapter 68 - Fences and Stock Law	41
Chapter 69 - Fire Protection	41
Chapter 70 - Indian Antiquities, Archaeological Resources and Unmarked Human Skeletal Remains Protection	42
Chapter 71 - Indians [Repealed.]	42
Chapter 71A - Indians	42
Chapter 72 - Inns, Hotels and Restaurants	42
Chapter 73 - Mills	42
Chapter 74 - Mines and Quarries	42
Chapter 74A - Company Police [Repealed.]	42
Chapter 74B - Private Protective Services Act [Repealed.]	42
Chapter 74C - Private Protective Services	42
Chapter 74D - Alarm Systems	42
Chapter 74E - Company Police Act	42
Chapter 74F - Locksmith Licensing Act	42
Chapter 74G - Campus Police Act	42
Chapter 75 - Monopolies, Trusts and Consumer Protection	42
Chapter 75A - Boating and Water Safety	43
Chapter 75B - Discrimination in Business	43
Chapter 75C - Motion Picture Fair Competition Act	43
Chapter 75D - Racketeer Influenced and Corrupt Organizations	43
Chapter 75E - Unlawful Activities in Connection With Certain Corporate Transactions	43
Chapter 76 - Navigation	43
Chapter 76A - Navigation and Pilotage Commissions	43
Chapter 77 - Rivers, Creeks, and Coastal Waters	43
Chapter 78 - Securities Law [Repealed.]	43
Chapter 78A - North Carolina Securities Act	43
Chapter 78B - Tender Offer Disclosure Act [Repealed.]	43
Chapter 78C - Investment Advisers	43
Chapter 78D - Commodities Act	43
Chapter 79 - Strays [Repealed.]	43
Chapter 80 - Trademarks, Brands, etc.	44
Chapter 81 - Weights and Measures [Recodified.]	44
Chapter 81A - Weights and Measures Act of 1975.	44
Chapter 82 - Wrecks [Repealed.]	44
Chapter 83 - Architects [Recodified.]	44

Chapter 83A - Architects	44
Chapter 84 - Attorneys-at-Law	44
Chapter 84A - Foreign Legal Consultants	44
Chapter 85 - Auctions and Auctioneers [Repealed.]	44
Chapter 85A - Bail Bondsmen and Runners [Recodified.]	44
Chapter 85B - Auctions and Auctioneers	44
Chapter 85C - Bail Bondsmen and Runners [Recodified.]	44
Chapter 86 - Barbers [Recodified.]	44
Chapter 86A - Barbers	44
Chapter 87 - Contractors	44
Chapter 88 - Cosmetic Art [Repealed.]	44
Chapter 88A - Electrolysis Practice Act	44
Chapter 88B - Cosmetic Art	45
Chapter 89 - Engineering and Land Surveying [Recodified.]	45
Chapter 89A - Landscape Architects	45
Chapter 89B - Foresters	45
Chapter 89C - Engineering and Land Surveying	45
Chapter 89D - Landscape Contractors	45
Chapter 89E - Geologists Licensing Act	45
Chapter 89F - North Carolina Soil Scientist Licensing Act	45
Chapter 89G - Irrigation Contractors	45
Chapter 90 - Medicine and Allied Occupations	45
Chapter 90 - Medicine and Allied Occupations (Continuation)	46
Chapter 90 - Medicine and Allied Occupations (Continuation)	47
Chapter 90 - Medicine and Allied Occupations (Continuation)	48
Chapter 90A - Sanitarians and Water and Wastewater Treatment Facility Operators	48
Chapter 90B - Social Worker Certification and Licensure Act	48
Chapter 90C - North Carolina Recreational Therapy Licensure Act	48
Chapter 90D - Interpreters and Transliterators	48
Chapter 91 - Pawnbrokers [Repealed.]	48
Chapter 91A - Pawnbrokers Modernization Act of 1989	48
Chapter 92 - Photographers [Deleted.]	48
Chapter 93 - Certified Public Accountants	48
Chapter 93A - Real Estate License Law	49
Chapter 93B - Occupational Licensing Boards	49
Chapter 93C - Watchmakers [Repealed.]	49
Chapter 93D - North Carolina State Hearing Aid Dealers and Fitters Board.	49
Chapter 93E - North Carolina Appraisers Act	49
Chapter 94 - Apprenticeship	49
Chapter 95 - Department of Labor and Labor Regulations	49
Chapter 95 - Department of Labor and Labor Regulations (Continuation)	50
Chapter 96 - Employment Security	50
Chapter 97 - Workers' Compensation Act	50
Chapter 97 - Workers' Compensation Act (Continuation)	51

Chapter 98 - Burnt and Lost Records	51
Chapter 99 - Libel and Slander	51
Chapter 99A - Civil Remedies for Criminal Actions	51
Chapter 99B - Products Liability	51
Chapter 99C - Actions Relating to Winter Sports Safety and Accidents	51
Chapter 99D - Civil Rights	51
Chapter 99E - Special Liability Provisions	51
Chapter 100 - Monuments, Memorials and Parks	51
Chapter 101 - Names of Persons	51
Chapter 102 - Official Survey Base	51
Chapter 103 - Sundays, Holidays and Special Days	51
Chapter 104 - United States Lands	51
Chapter 104A - Degrees of Kinship	51
Chapter 104B - Hurricanes or Other Acts of Nature	51
Chapter 104C - Atomic Energy, Radioactivity and Ionizing Radiation [Repealed and Recodified.]	51
Chapter 104D - Southern States Energy Compact	51
Chapter 104E - North Carolina Radiation Protection Act	51
Chapter 104F - Southeast Interstate Low-Level Radioactive Waste Management Compact [Repealed]	51
Chapter 104G - North Carolina Low-Level Radioactive Waste Management Authority Act of 1987 [Repealed]	51
Chapter 105 - Taxation	51
Chapter 105 - Taxation (Continuation)	52
Chapter 105 - Taxation (Continuation)	53
Chapter 105 - Taxation (Continuation)	54
Chapter 105A - Setoff Debt Collection Act	55
Chapter 105B - Defaulted Student Loan Recovery Act	55
Chapter 106 - Agriculture	55
Chapter 106 - Agriculture (Continue)	56
Chapter 106 - Agriculture (Continue)	57
Chapter 107 - Agricultural Development Districts [Repealed.]	57
Chapter 108 - Social Services [Repealed and Recodified.]	57
Chapter 108A - Social Services	57
Chapter 108B - Community Action Programs	58
Chapter 108C Medicaid and Health Choice Provider Requirements.	58
Chapter 108D Medicaid Managed Care for Behavioral Health Services.	58
Chapter 109 - Bonds [Recodified.]	58
Chapter 110 - Child Welfare	58
Chapter 111 - Aid to the Blind	58
Chapter 112 - Confederate Homes and Pensions [Repealed.]	58
Chapter 113 - Conservation and Development	58
Chapter 113 - Conservation and Development (Continuation)	59

Chapter 113A - Pollution Control and Environment	59
Chapter 113A - Pollution Control and Environment (Continuation)	60
Chapter 113B - North Carolina Energy Policy Act of 1975	60
Chapter 114 - Department of Justice	60
Chapter 115 - Elementary and Secondary Education [Repealed.]	60
Chapter 115A - Community Colleges, Technical Institutes, and Industrial Education Centers [Repealed.]	60
Chapter 115B - Tuition and Fee Waivers	60
Chapter 115C - Elementary and Secondary Education	60
Chapter 115C - Elementary and Secondary Education (Continuation)	61
Chapter 115C - Elementary and Secondary Education (Continuation)	62
Chapter 115C - Elementary and Secondary Education (Continuation)	63
Chapter 115D - Community Colleges	63
Chapter 115E - Private Educational Facilities Finance Act [Recodified]	63
Chapter 116 - Higher Education	63
Chapter 116 - Higher Education (Continuation)	63
Chapter 116A - Escheats and Abandoned Property [Repealed.]	64
Chapter 116B - Escheats and Abandoned Property	64
Chapter 116C - Continuum of Education Programs	64
Chapter 116D - Higher Education Bonds	64
Chapter 117 - Electrification	64
Chapter 118 - Firemen's and Rescue Squad Workers' Relief and Pension Funds [Recodified.]	64
Chapter 118A - Firemen's Death Benefit Act [Repealed.]	64
Chapter 118B - Members of a Rescue Squad Death Benefit Act [Repealed.]	64
Chapter 119 - Gasoline and Oil Inspection and Regulation	64
Chapter 120 - General Assembly	65
Chapter 120 - General Assembly (Continuation)	66
Chapter 120 - General Assembly (Continuation)	67
Chapter 120C - Lobbying	67
Chapter 121 - Archives and History	67
Chapter 122 - Hospitals for the Mentally Disordered [Repealed.]	67
Chapter 122A - North Carolina Housing Finance Agency	67
Chapter 122B - North Carolina Agricultural Facilities Finance Act [Repealed.]	67
Chapter 122C - Mental Health, Developmental Disabilities, and Substance Abuse Act of 1985	67
Chapter 122C - Mental Health, Developmental Disabilities, and Substance Abuse Act of 1985 (Continuation)	68
Chapter 122D - North Carolina Agricultural Finance Act	68

Chapter 122E - North Carolina Housing Trust and Oil Overcharge Act	68
Chapter 123 - Impeachment	69
Chapter 123A - Industrial Development [Repealed.]	69
Chapter 124 - Internal Improvements	69
Chapter 125 - Libraries	69
Chapter 126 - State Personnel System	69
Chapter 127 - Militia [Repealed.]	69
Chapter 127A - Militia	69
Chapter 127B - Military Affairs	69
Chapter 127C - Advisory Commission on Military Affairs	69
Chapter 128 - Offices and Public Officers	69
Chapter 128 - Offices and Public Officers (Continuation)	70
Chapter 129 - Public Buildings and Grounds	70
Chapter 130 - Public Health [Repealed.]	70
Chapter 130A - Public Health	70
Chapter 130A - Public Health (Continuation)	71
Chapter 130A - Public Health (Continuation)	72
Chapter 130B - Hazardous Waste Management Commission [Repealed.]	72
Chapter 131 - Public Hospitals [Repealed.]	72
Chapter 131A - Health Care Facilities Finance Act	72
Chapter 131B - Licensing of Ambulatory Surgical Facilities [Repealed.]	72
Chapter 131C - Charitable Solicitation Licensure Act [Repealed.]	72
Chapter 131D - Inspection and Licensing of Facilities	72
Chapter 131E - Health Care Facilities and Services	72
Chapter 131E - Health Care Facilities and Services (Continuation)	73
Chapter 131F - Solicitation of Contributions	73
Chapter 132 - Public Records	73
Chapter 133 - Public Works	74
Chapter 134 - Youth Development [Recodified.]	74
Chapter 134A - Youth Services [Repealed.]	74
Chapter 135 - Retirement System for Teachers and State Employees; Social Security; Health Insurance Program for Children	74
Chapter 135 - Retirement System for Teachers and State Employees; Social Security; Health Insurance Program for Children	75
Chapter 136 - Transportation	75
Chapter 136 - Transportation (Continuation)	76
Chapter 137 - Rural Rehabilitation [Repealed.]	76
Chapter 138 - Salaries, Fees and Allowances	76
Chapter 138A - State Government Ethics Act	76
Chapter 139 - Soil and Water Conservation Districts	76

Chapter 140 - State Art Museum; Symphony and Art Societies	76
Chapter 140A - State Awards System	76
Chapter 141 - State Boundaries	76
Chapter 142 - State Debt	76
Chapter 143 - State Departments, Institutions, and Commissions	77
Chapter 143 - State Departments, Institutions, and Commissions (Continuation)	78
Chapter 143 - State Departments, Institutions, and Commissions (Continuation)	79
Chapter 143 - State Departments, Institutions, and Commissions (Continuation)	80
Chapter 143A - State Government Reorganization	80
Chapter 143B - Executive Organization Act of 1973	80
Chapter 143B - Executive Organization Act of 1973 (Continuation)	81
Chapter 143B - Executive Organization Act of 1973 (Continuation)	82
Chapter 143C - State Budget Act	83
Chapter 143D - The State Governmental Accountability and Internal Control Act	83
Chapter 144 - State Flag, Official Governmental Flags, Motto, and Colors	83
Chapter 145 - State Symbols and Other Official Adoptions.	83
Chapter 146 - State Lands	83
Chapter 147 - State Officers	83
Chapter 148 - State Prison System	84
Chapter 149 - State Song and Toast	84
Chapter 150 - Uniform Revocation of Licenses [Repealed.]	84
Chapter 150A - Administrative Procedure Act [Recodified.]	84
Chapter 150B - Administrative Procedure Act	84
Chapter 151 - Constables [Repealed.]	84
Chapter 152 - Coroners	84
Chapter 152A - County Medical Examiner [Repealed.]	84
Chapter 152A - County Medical Examiner [Repealed.] (Continuation)	85
Chapter 153 - Counties and County Commissioners [Repealed.]	85
Chapter 153A - Counties	85
Chapter 153B - Mountain Resources Planning Act	85
Chapter 153C - Uwharrie Regional Resources Act	85
Chapter 154 - County Surveyor [Repealed.]	85
Chapter 155 - County Treasurer [Repealed.]	85
Chapter 156 - Drainage	85
Chapter 156 – Drainage (Continuation)	86

Chapter 157 - Housing Authorities and Projects	86
Chapter 157A - Historic Properties Commissions [Transferred.]	86
Chapter 158 - Local Development	86
Chapter 159 - Local Government Finance	86
Chapter 159 - Local Government Finance (Continuation)	87
Chapter 159A - Pollution Abatement and Industrial Facilities Financing Act [Unconstitutional.]	87
Chapter 159B - Joint Municipal Electric Power and Energy Act	87
Chapter 159C - Industrial and Pollution Control Facilities Financing Act	87
Chapter 159D - The North Carolina Capital Facilities Financing Act	87
Chapter 159E - Registered Public Obligations Act	87
Chapter 159F - North Carolina Energy Development Authority [Repealed.]	87
Chapter 159G - Water Infrastructure	87
Chapter 159H - [Reserved.]	87
Chapter 159I - Solid Waste Management Loan Program and Local Government Special Obligation Bonds	87
Chapter 160 - Municipal Corporations [Repealed And Transferred.]	87
Chapter 160A - Cities and Towns	88
Chapter 160A - Cities and Towns (Continuation)	89
Chapter 160B - Consolidated City-County Act	89
Chapter 160C - Baseball Park Districts [Repealed.]	90
Chapter 161 - Register of Deeds	90
Chapter 162 - Sheriff	90
Chapter 162A - Water and Sewer Systems	90
Chapter 162B Continuity of Local Government in Emergency.	90
Chapter 163 Elections and Election Laws.	90
Chapter 163 Elections and Election Laws. (Continuation)	91
Chapter 164 Concerning the General Statutes of North Carolina.	92
Chapter 165 Veterans.	92
Chapter 166 Civil Preparedness Agencies [Repealed.]	92
Chapter 166A North Carolina Emergency Management Act.	92
Chapter 167 State Civil Air Patrol [Repealed.]	92
Chapter 168 Persons with Disabilities.	92
Chapter 168A Persons With Disabilities Protection Act.	92

Chapter 34

Veterans' Guardianship Act.

§ 34-1. Title.

This Chapter shall be known as "The Veterans' Guardianship Act." (1929, c. 33, s. 1.)

§ 34-2. Definitions.

In this Chapter:

The term "benefits" shall mean all moneys payable by the United States through the Bureau.

The term "Bureau" means the United States Veterans' Bureau or its successor.

The term "Director" means the Director of the United States Veterans' Bureau or his successor.

"Estate" means income on hand and assets acquired partially or wholly with "income."

The term "guardian" as used herein shall mean any person acting as a fiduciary for a ward.

"Income" means moneys received from the Veterans Administration and revenue or profit from any property wholly or partially acquired therewith.

The term "person" includes a partnership, corporation or an association.

The term "ward" means a beneficiary of the Bureau. (1929, c. 33, s. 2; 1945, c. 723, s. 2; 1961, c. 396, s. 1.)

§ 34-2.1. Guardian's powers as to property; validation of prior acts.

Any guardian appointed under the provisions of this Chapter may be guardian of all property, real or personal, belonging to the ward to the same extent as a guardian appointed under the provisions of Chapter 35A of the General Statutes, and the provisions of such Chapter concerning the custody, management and disposal of property shall apply in any case not provided for by this Chapter. All acts heretofore performed by guardians appointed under the provisions of this Chapter with respect to the custody, management and disposal of property of wards are hereby validated where no provision for such acts was provided for by this Chapter, if such acts were performed under and in conformity with the provisions of Chapter 35A of the General Statutes. (1955, c. 1272, s. 1; 1987, c. 550, s. 18.)

§ 34-3. Appointment of guardian for wards entitled to benefits from United States Veterans' Bureau.

Whenever, pursuant to any law of the United States or regulation of the Bureau, the Director requires, prior to payment of benefits, that a guardian be appointed for a ward, such appointment shall be made in the manner hereinafter provided. (1929, c. 33, s. 3.)

§ 34-4. Guardian may not be named for more than five wards; exceptions; banks and trust companies, public guardians, or where wards are members of same family.

It shall be unlawful for any person, other than a public guardian qualified under Article 11, Chapter 35A, General Statutes of North Carolina, to accept appointment as guardian of any United States Veterans Administration ward, if such person shall at the time of such appointment be acting as guardian for five wards. For the purpose of this section, all minors of same family unit shall constitute one ward. In all appointments of a public guardian for United States Veterans Administration wards, the guardian shall furnish a separate bond for each appointment as required by G.S. 34-9. If, in any case, an attorney for the United States Veterans Administration presents a petition under this section alleging that an individual guardian other than a public guardian is acting in a fiduciary capacity for more than five wards and requesting discharge of the guardian for that reason, then the court, upon satisfactory evidence that the individual guardian is acting in a fiduciary capacity for more than five wards, must require a final accounting forthwith from such guardian and shall discharge the guardian in such case. Upon the termination of a public guardian's term of office, he may be permitted to retain any appointments made during his term of office.

This section shall not apply to banks and trust companies licensed to do trust business in North Carolina. (1929, c. 33, s. 4; 1967, c. 564, s. 1; 1987, c. 550, s. 19.)

§ 34-5. Petition for appointment of guardian.

A petition for the appointment of a guardian may be filed in any court of competent jurisdiction by or on behalf of any person who under existing law is entitled to priority of appointment. If there be no person so entitled or if the person so entitled shall neglect or refuse to file such a petition within thirty days after mailing of notice by the Bureau to the last known address of such person indicating the necessity for the same, a petition for such appointment may be filed in any court of competent jurisdiction by or on behalf of any responsible person residing in this State.

The petition for appointment shall set forth the name, age, place of residence of the ward, the names and places of residence of the nearest relative, if known, and the fact that such ward is entitled to receive moneys payable by or through the Bureau and shall set forth the amount of moneys then due and the amount of probable future payments.

The petition shall also set forth the name and address of the person or institution, if any, having actual custody of the ward.

In the case of a mentally incompetent ward the petition shall show that such ward has been rated incompetent on examination by the Bureau in accordance with the laws and regulations governing the Bureau. (1929, c. 33, s. 5.)

§ 34-6. Certificate of Director prima facie evidence of necessity for appointment of guardian of minor.

Where a petition is filed for the appointment of a guardian of a minor ward a certificate of the Director, or his representative, setting forth the age of such minor as shown by the records of the Bureau and the fact that the appointment of a guardian is a condition precedent to the payment of any moneys due the minor by the Bureau, shall be prima facie evidence of the necessity of such appointment. (1929, c. 33, s. 6.)

§ 34-7. Certificate as evidence in regard to guardianship of mentally incompetent wards.

Where a petition is filed for the appointment of a guardian of a mentally incompetent ward a certificate of the Director, or his representative, setting forth the fact that such person has been rated incompetent by the Bureau on examination in accordance with the laws and regulations governing such Bureau; and that the appointment of a guardian is a condition precedent to the payment of any moneys due such person by the Bureau, shall be prima facie evidence of the necessity for such appointment. (1929, c. 33, s. 7.)

§ 34-8. Notice of filing of petition.

Upon the filing of a petition for the appointment of a guardian, under the provisions of this Chapter, the court shall cause such notice to be given as provided by law. (1929, c. 33, s. 8.)

§ 34-9. Qualifications of guardian; surety bond.

Before making an appointment under the provisions of this Chapter the court shall be satisfied that the guardian whose appointment is sought is a fit and proper person to be appointed. Upon the appointment being made the guardian shall execute and file a surety bond to be approved by the court in an amount not less than the sum then due and estimated to become payable during the ensuing year. The said bond shall be in the form and be conditioned as required of guardians appointed under the guardianship laws of this State. The court shall have power from time to time to require the guardian to file an additional bond.

No bond shall be required of the banks and trust companies licensed to do trust business in North Carolina. (1929, c. 33, s. 9.)

§ 34-10. Guardian's accounts to be filed; hearing on accounts.

Every guardian, who shall receive on account of his ward any moneys from the Bureau, shall file with the court annually, on the anniversary date of the appointment, in addition to such other accounts as may be required by the court, a full, true, and accurate account under oath of all moneys so received by him, of all disbursements thereof, and showing the balance thereof in his hands at the date of such account and how invested. A certified copy of each of such accounts filed with the court shall be sent by the guardian to the office of the Bureau having jurisdiction over the area in which such court is located.

At the time such account is filed the clerk of the superior court shall require the guardian to exhibit to the court all investments and bank statements showing cash balance and the clerk of the superior court shall certify on the original account and the certified copy which the guardian sends the Bureau that an examination was made of all investments and cash balance and that same are correctly stated in the account; provided that banks, organized under the laws of North Carolina or the Acts of Congress, engaged in doing a trust and fiduciary business in this State, when acting as guardian, or in other fiduciary capacity, shall be exempt from the requirement of exhibiting such investments and bank statements, and the clerk of the superior court shall not be required to so certify as to the accounts of such banks, except that in addition to the officer verifying the accounts, there shall be added a certificate of another officer of the bank certifying that all assets referred to in the account are held by the guardian or by a clearing corporation for the guardian. If objections are raised to such an accounting, the court shall fix a time and place for the hearing thereon not less than 15 days nor more than 30 days from the date of filing such objections, and notice shall be given by the court to the aforesaid Bureau office and the Department of Military and Veterans Affairs by mail not less than 15 days prior to the date fixed for the hearing. Notice of such hearing shall also be given to the guardian. (1929, c. 33, s. 10; 1933, c. 262, s. 1; 1945, c. 723, s. 2; 1961, c. 396, s. 2; 1967, c. 564, s. 5; 1973, c. 497, s. 6; c. 620, s. 9.)

§ 34-11. Failure to file account cause for removal.

If any guardian shall fail to file any account of the moneys received by him from the Bureau on account of his ward within 30 days after such account is required by either the court or the Bureau, or shall fail to furnish the Bureau a copy of his accounts as required by this Chapter, such failure shall be grounds for removal. (1929, c. 33, s. 11.)

§ 34-12. Compensation at five percent; additional compensation; premiums on bonds.

Compensation payable to guardians shall not exceed five percent (5%) of the income of the ward during any year, except that the court may approve compensation in the accounting in an amount not to exceed twenty-five dollars ($25.00) from an estate where the income for any one year is less than five hundred dollars ($500.00). In the event of extraordinary services rendered by such guardian the court may, upon petition and after hearing thereon, authorize additional compensation therefor, payable from the estate of the ward. Notice of such petition and hearing shall be given the proper office of the Bureau and the Department of Military and Veterans Affairs in the manner provided in G.S. 34-10. No compensation shall be allowed on the corpus of an estate received from a preceding guardian. The guardian may be allowed from the estate of his ward reasonable premiums paid by him to any corporate surety upon his bond. (1929, c. 33, s. 12; 1945, c. 723, s. 2; 1967, c. 564, ss. 2, 5; 1973, c. 620, s. 9.)

§ 34-13. Investment of funds.

Every guardian shall invest the funds of the estate in any of the following securities:

(1) United States government bonds.

(2) State of North Carolina bonds issued since the year 1872.

(3) By loaning the same upon real estate securities in which the guardian has no interest, such loans not to exceed fifty percent (50%) of the actual appraised or assessed value, whichever may be lower, and said loans when

made to be evidenced by a note, or notes, or bond, or bonds, under the seal of the borrower and secured by first mortgage or first deed of trust. Said guardian before making such investment on real estate mortgages shall secure a certificate of title from some reputable attorney certifying that the same is first lien on real estate and also setting forth the tax valuation thereof for the current year: Provided, said guardian may purchase with said funds a home or farm for the sole use of said ward or his dependents upon petition and order of the clerk of superior court, said order to be approved by the resident or presiding judge of the superior court, and provided further that copy of said petition shall be forwarded to said Bureau before consideration thereof by said court. Any guardian may encumber the home or farm so purchased for the entire purchase price or balance thereof to enable the ward to obtain benefits provided in Title 38, U.S. Code, Chapter 37, upon petition to and order of the clerk of superior court of the county of appointment of said guardian and approved by the resident or presiding judge of the superior court. Notice of hearing on such petition, together with copy of the petition, shall be given to the United States Veterans Administration and the Department of Military and Veterans Affairs by mail not less than 15 days prior to the date fixed for the hearing.

(4)   Any form of investment allowed by law to the State Treasurer under G.S. 147-69.1.

(5)   Repealed by Session Laws 1979, c. 467, s. 22.

It shall be the duty of guardians who shall have funds invested other than as provided for in this section to liquidate same within one year from the passage of this law: Provided, however, that upon the approval of the judge of the superior court, either residing in or presiding over the courts of the district, the clerk of the superior court may authorize the guardian to extend from time to time, the time for sale or collection of any such investments; that no extension shall be made to cover a period of more than one year from the time the extension is made.

The clerk of the superior court of any county in the State or any guardian who shall violate any of the provisions of this section shall be guilty of a Class 1 misdemeanor. (1929, c. 33, s. 13; 1933, c. 262, s. 2; 1957, c. 199; 1959, c. 1015, s. 1; 1967, c. 564, ss. 3, 4; 1973, c. 620, s. 9; 1979, c. 467, s. 22; 1993, c. 539, s. 401; 1994, Ex. Sess., c. 24, s. 14(c).)

§ 34-14. Application of ward's estate.

A guardian may apply any income received from the Veterans Administration for the benefit of the ward in the same manner and to the same extent as other income of the estate without the necessity of securing an order of court. A guardian shall not apply any portion of the estate of his ward for the support and maintenance of any person other than his ward, except upon order of the court after a hearing, notice of which has been given the proper officer of the Bureau and the Department of Military and Veterans Affairs in the manner provided in G.S. 34-10. (1929, c. 33, s. 14; 1945, c. 723, s. 2; 1961, c. 396, s. 3; 1967, c. 564, s. 5; 1973, c. 620, s. 9.)

§ 34-14.1. Payment of veterans' benefits to relatives.

(a) It shall be lawful for a guardian or trustee of a mentally disordered or incompetent Veterans Administration beneficiary to pay to or for

(1) The spouse or children or mother or father of the ward, whether or not said spouse or children or mother or father received any part of their maintenance from the ward prior to the appointment of said guardian or trustee, such an amount for support and maintenance as shall be approved by the clerk of the superior court having jurisdiction over such guardian or trustee;

(2) A brother, sister, nephew, niece, uncle, aunt, or any other relative of the ward, who, prior to the appointment of said guardian or trustee, received some part of his or her maintenance from said ward, such an amount for support and maintenance as shall be approved by the clerk of the superior court having jurisdiction over said guardian or trustee and by a superior court judge.

(b) Such approval may be granted upon a duly verified petition filed before the clerk of the superior court having jurisdiction of such guardian or trustees setting forth

(1) The amount of benefits received by the guardian or trustee on behalf of the ward from the Veterans Administration;

(2) The amount of periodic disbursements, if any, made by such guardian or trustee for the maintenance and support of the ward;

(3) The person for whose maintenance and support payment is to be made and the relationship of such person to the ward;

(4) If the person for whose maintenance and support payment is to be made is one described in subsection (a)(2) above, facts showing that prior to the appointment of said guardian or trustee such person received some part of his or her maintenance from said ward;

(5) The amount to be paid and the period when such payments are to be made.

Notice of hearing upon such petition shall be as provided by G.S. 34-14, and no person or persons, other than the guardian or trustees and petitioner, need to be made parties to any such proceeding. If the guardian or trustee is the petitioner, no other parties shall be necessary. (1945, c. 479, ss. 1, 2; 1953, c. 122, s. 1; 1955, c. 1272, s. 2.)

§ 34-15. Certified copy of record required by Bureau to be furnished without charge.

Whenever a copy of any public record is required by the Bureau or the Department of Military and Veterans Affairs to be used in determining the eligibility of any person to participate in benefits made available by such Bureau, the official charged with the custody of such public record shall without charge provide the applicant for such benefits or any person acting on his behalf or the representative of such Bureau or the Department of Military and Veterans Affairs with a certified copy of such record. (1929, c. 33, s. 15; 1945, c. 723, s. 2; 1967, c. 564, s. 5; 1973, c. 620, s. 9.)

§ 34-16. Repealed by Session Laws 1985, c. 589, s. 14, effective January 1, 1986.

§ 34-17. Discharge of guardian.

When a minor ward for whom a guardian has been appointed under the provisions of this Chapter or other laws of this State shall have attained his or her majority, and if incompetent shall be declared competent by the Bureau and by an order of the clerk of the superior court of the county in which such guardian was appointed, and when any incompetent ward, not a minor, shall be declared competent by said Bureau and by an order of the clerk of the superior court of the county in which such guardian was appointed, the guardian shall upon making a satisfactory accounting be discharged upon a petition filed for that purpose. The certificate of the Director, or his representative, setting forth the fact that an incompetent ward has been rated competent by the Bureau on examination in accordance with the laws and regulations governing such Bureau shall be prima facie evidence upon which the court may declare such ward competent. (1929, c. 33, s. 17; 1955, c. 1272, s. 3.)

§ 34-18. Construction of Chapter.

This Chapter shall be construed liberally to secure the beneficial intents and purposes thereof and shall apply only to beneficiaries of the Bureau. (1929, c. 33, s. 18.)

Chapter 35.

Sterilization Procedures.

Article 1.

Definitions.

§§ 35-1 through 35-1.5: Repealed by Session Laws 1987, c. 550, s. 7.

Article 1A.

Guardianship of Incompetent Adults.

Part 1. Legislative Purpose.

§ 35-1.6: Repealed by Session Laws 1987, c. 550, s. 7.

Part 2. Definitions.

§ 35-1.7: Repealed by Session Laws 1987, c. 550, s. 7.

Part 3. Jurisdiction and Venue.

§§ 35-1.8 through 35-1.9: Repealed by Session Laws 1987, c. 550, s. 7.

Part 4. Proceedings before Clerk.

§§ 35-1.10 through 35-1.27: Repealed by Session Laws 1987, c. 550, s. 7.

Part 5. Qualifications, Priorities, Duties, and Liabilities of Guardians.

§§ 35-1.28 through 35-1.40: Repealed by Session Laws 1987, c. 550, s. 7.

Part 6. Testamentary Appointment of Guardians.

§ 35-1.41: Repealed by Session Laws 1987, c. 550, s. 7.

Article 2.

Guardianship and Management of Estates of Incompetents.

§§ 35-2 through 35-9: Repealed by Session Laws 1987, c. 550, s. 7.

Article 3.

Sales of Estates.

§§ 35-10 through 35-13: Repealed by Session Laws 1987, c. 550, s. 7.

Article 4.

Mortgage or Sale of Estates Held by the Entireties.

§§ 35-14 through 35-18: Recodified as §§ 35A-1310 to 35A-1314 by Session Laws 1987, c. 550, s. 2.

Article 5.

Surplus Income and Advancements.

§§ 35-19 through 35-29: Recodified as §§ 35A-1320 through 35A-1330 by Session Laws 1987, c. 550, s. 3.

Article 5A.

Gifts from Income for Certain Purposes.

§§ 35-29.1 through 35-29.4: Recodified as §§ 35A-1335 through 35A-1338 by Session Laws 1987, c. 550, s. 4.

Article 5B.

Gifts from Principal for Certain Purposes.

§§ 35-29.5 through 35-29.10: Recodified as §§ 35A-1340 through 35A-1345 by Session Laws 1987, c. 550, s. 5.

Article 5C.

Declaring Revocable Trust Irrevocable and Making Gift of Incompetent's Life Interest Therein.

§§ 35-29.11 through 35-29.16: Recodified as §§ 35A-1350 through 35A-1355 by Session Laws 1987, c. 550, s. 6.

Article 6.

Detention, Treatment, and Cure of Inebriates.

§§ 35-30 through 35-35.2: Repealed by Session Laws 1963, c. 1184, s. 35.

Article 7.

Sterilization of Persons Mentally Ill and Mentally Retarded.

§§ 35-36 through 35-50: Repealed by Session Laws 2003, c. 13, s. 1, effective April 17, 2003.

§§ 35-51 through 35-57. Repealed by Session Laws 1973, c. 1281.

Article 8.

Temporary Care and Restraint of Inebriates, Drug Addicts and Persons Insane.

§§ 35-58 through 35-60: Repealed by Session Laws 1963, c. 1184, s. 36.

Article 9.

Mental Health Council.

§§ 35-61 through 35-63: Transferred to G.S. 122-105 to 122-107 by Session Laws 1963, c. 1184, s. 13.

Article 10.

Interstate Compact on Mental Health.

§§ 35-64 through 35-69: Transferred to G.S. 122-99 to 122-104 by Session Laws 1963, c. 1184, s. 12.

Article 11.

Medical Advisory Council to State Board of Mental Health.

§§ 35-70 through 35-72: Repealed by Session Laws 1973, c. 476, s. 133.

Article 12.

Council on Mental Retardation and Developmental Disabilities.

§§ 35-73 through 35-77: Repealed by Session Laws 1973, c. 476, s. 170.

Chapter 35A.

Incompetency and Guardianship.

SUBCHAPTER I. PROCEEDINGS TO DETERMINE INCOMPETENCE.

Article 1.

Determination of Incompetence.

§ 35A-1101. Definitions.

When used in this Subchapter:

(1) "Autism" means a physical disorder of the brain which causes disturbances in the developmental rate of physical, social, and language skills; abnormal responses to sensations; absence of or delay in speech or language; or abnormal ways of relating to people, objects, and events. Autism occurs sometimes by itself and sometimes in conjunction with other brain-functioning disorders.

(2) "Cerebral palsy" means a muscle dysfunction, characterized by impairment of movement, often combined with speech impairment, and caused by abnormality of or damage to the brain.

(3) "Clerk" means the clerk of superior court.

(4) "Designated agency" means the State or local human services agency designated by the clerk in the clerk's order to prepare, cause to be prepared, or assemble a multidisciplinary evaluation and to perform other functions as the clerk may order. A designated agency includes, without limitation, State, local, regional, or area mental health, mental retardation, vocational rehabilitation, public health, social service, and developmental disabilities agencies, and diagnostic evaluation centers.

(5) "Epilepsy" means a group of neurological conditions characterized by abnormal electrical-chemical discharge in the brain. This discharge is manifested in various forms of physical activity called seizures, which range from momentary lapses of consciousness to convulsive movements.

(6) "Guardian ad litem" means a guardian appointed pursuant to G.S. 1A-1, Rule 17, Rules of Civil Procedure.

(7) "Incompetent adult" means an adult or emancipated minor who lacks sufficient capacity to manage the adult's own affairs or to make or communicate important decisions concerning the adult's person, family, or property whether the lack of capacity is due to mental illness, mental retardation, epilepsy,

cerebral palsy, autism, inebriety, senility, disease, injury, or similar cause or condition.

(8) "Incompetent child" means a minor who is at least 17 1/2 years of age and who, other than by reason of minority, lacks sufficient capacity to make or communicate important decisions concerning the child's person, family, or property whether the lack of capacity is due to mental illness, mental retardation, epilepsy, cerebral palsy, autism, inebriety, disease, injury, or similar cause or condition.

(9) "Indigent" means unable to pay for legal representation and other necessary expenses of a proceeding brought under this Subchapter.

(10) "Inebriety" means the habitual use of alcohol or drugs rendering a person incompetent to transact ordinary business concerning the person's estate, dangerous to person or property, cruel and intolerable to family, or unable to provide for family.

(11) "Interim guardian" means a guardian, appointed prior to adjudication of incompetence and for a temporary period, for a person who requires immediate intervention to address conditions that constitute imminent or foreseeable risk of harm to the person's physical well-being or to the person's estate.

(12) "Mental illness" means an illness that so lessens the capacity of a person to use self-control, judgment, and discretion in the conduct of the person's affairs and social relations as to make it necessary or advisable for the person to be under treatment, care, supervision, guidance, or control. The term "mental illness" encompasses "mental disease", "mental disorder", "lunacy", "unsoundness of mind", and "insanity".

(13) "Mental retardation" means significantly subaverage general intellectual functioning existing concurrently with deficits in adaptive behavior and manifested before age 22.

(14) "Multidisciplinary evaluation" means an evaluation that contains current medical, psychological, and social work evaluations as directed by the clerk and that may include current evaluations by professionals in other disciplines, including without limitation education, vocational rehabilitation, occupational therapy, vocational therapy, psychiatry, speech-and-hearing, and communications disorders. The evaluation is current if made not more than one year from the date on which it is presented to or considered by the court. The

evaluation shall set forth the nature and extent of the disability and recommend a guardianship plan and program.

(15) "Respondent" means a person who is alleged to be incompetent in a proceeding under this Subchapter.

(16) "Treatment facility" has the same meaning as "facility" in G.S. 122C-3(14), and includes group homes, halfway houses, and other community-based residential facilities.

(17) "Ward" means a person who has been adjudicated incompetent or an adult or minor for whom a guardian has been appointed by a court of competent jurisdiction. (1987, c. 550, s. 1; 1989, c. 473, s. 11; 1997-443, s. 11A.11.)

§ 35A-1102. Scope of law; exclusive procedure.

This Article establishes the exclusive procedure for adjudicating a person to be an incompetent adult or an incompetent child. However, nothing in this Article shall interfere with the authority of a judge to appoint a guardian ad litem for a party to litigation under Rule 17(b) of the North Carolina Rules of Civil Procedure. (1987, c. 550, s. 1; 2003-236, s. 4.)

§ 35A-1103. Jurisdiction; venue.

(a) The clerk in each county shall have original jurisdiction over proceedings under this Subchapter.

(b) Venue for proceedings under this Subchapter shall be in the county in which the respondent resides or is domiciled or is an inpatient in a treatment facility. If the county of residence or domicile cannot be determined, venue shall be in the county where the respondent is present.

(c) If proceedings involving the same respondent are brought under this Subchapter in more than one county in which venue is proper, venue shall be in the county in which proceedings were commenced first.

(d)   If the clerk in the county in which a proceeding under this Subchapter is brought has an interest, direct or indirect, in the proceeding, jurisdiction with respect thereto shall be vested in any superior court judge residing or presiding in the district, and the jurisdiction of the superior court judge shall extend to all things which the clerk might have done. (1987, c. 550, s. 1.)

§ 35A-1104. Change of venue.

The clerk, on motion of a party or the clerk's own motion, may order a change of venue upon finding that no hardship or prejudice to the respondent will result from a change of venue. (1987, c. 550, s. 1.)

§ 35A-1105. Petition before clerk.

A verified petition for the adjudication of incompetence of an adult, or of a minor who is within six months of reaching majority, may be filed with the clerk by any person, including any State or local human services agency through its authorized representative. (1987, c. 550, s. 1; 1989, c. 473, s. 22; 1997-443, s. 11A.12.)

§ 35A-1106. Contents of petition.

The petition shall set forth, to the extent known:

(1)   The name, age, address, and county of residence of the respondent;

(2)   The name, address, and county of residence of the petitioner, and his interest in the proceeding;

(3)   A general statement of the respondent's assets and liabilities with an estimate of the value of any property, including any compensation, insurance, pension, or allowance to which he is entitled;

(4) A statement of the facts tending to show that the respondent is incompetent and the reason or reasons why the adjudication of incompetence is sought;

(5) The name, address, and county of residence of the respondent's next of kin and other persons known to have an interest in the proceeding;

(6) Facts regarding the adjudication of respondent's incompetence by a court of another state, if an adjudication is sought on that basis pursuant to G.S. 35A-1113(1). (1987, c. 550, s. 1.)

§ 35A-1107. Right to counsel or guardian ad litem.

(a) The respondent is entitled to be represented by counsel of his own choice or by an appointed guardian ad litem. Upon filing of the petition, an attorney shall be appointed as guardian ad litem to represent the respondent unless the respondent retains his own counsel, in which event the guardian ad litem may be discharged. Appointment and discharge of an appointed guardian ad litem shall be in accordance with rules adopted by the Office of Indigent Defense Services.

(b) An attorney appointed as a guardian ad litem under this section shall represent the respondent until the petition is dismissed or until a guardian is appointed under Subchapter II of this Chapter. After being appointed, the guardian ad litem shall personally visit the respondent as soon as possible and shall make every reasonable effort to determine the respondent's wishes regarding the incompetency proceeding and any proposed guardianship. The guardian ad litem shall present to the clerk the respondent's express wishes at all relevant stages of the proceedings. The guardian ad litem also may make recommendations to the clerk concerning the respondent's best interests if those interests differ from the respondent's express wishes. In appropriate cases, the guardian ad litem shall consider the possibility of a limited guardianship and shall make recommendations to the clerk concerning the rights, powers, and privileges that the respondent should retain under a limited guardianship. (1987, c. 550, s. 1; 2000-144, s. 33; 2003-236, s. 3.)

§ 35A-1108. Issuance of notice.

(a) Within five days after filing of the petition, the clerk shall issue a written notice of the date, time, and place for a hearing on the petition, which shall be held not less than 10 days nor more than 30 days after service of the notice and petition on the respondent, unless the clerk extends the time for good cause, for preparation of a multidisciplinary evaluation as provided in G.S. 35A-1111, or for the completion of a mediation.

(b) If a multidisciplinary evaluation or mediation is ordered after a notice of hearing has been issued, the clerk may extend the time for hearing and issue a notice to the parties that the hearing has been continued, the reason therefor, and the date, time, and place of the new hearing, which shall not be less than 10 days nor more than 30 days after service of such notice on the respondent.

(c) Subsequent notices to the parties shall be served as provided by G.S. 1A-1, Rule 5, Rules of Civil Procedure, unless the clerk orders otherwise. (1987, c. 550, s. 1; 2005-67, s. 2.)

§ 35A-1109. Service of notice and petition.

Copies of the petition and initial notice of hearing shall be personally served on the respondent. Respondent's counsel or guardian ad litem shall be served pursuant to G.S. 1A-1, Rule 4, Rules of Civil Procedure. A sheriff who serves the notice and petition shall do so without demanding his fees in advance. The petitioner, within five days after filing the petition, shall mail or cause to be mailed, by first-class mail, copies of the notice and petition to the respondent's next of kin alleged in the petition and any other persons the clerk may designate, unless such person has accepted notice. Proof of such mailing or acceptance shall be by affidavit or certificate of acceptance of notice filed with the clerk. The clerk shall mail, by first-class mail, copies of subsequent notices to the next of kin alleged in the petition and to such other persons as the clerk deems appropriate. (1987, c. 550, s. 1; 1989, c. 473, s. 18.)

§ 35A-1110. Right to jury.

The respondent has a right, upon request by him, his counsel, or his guardian ad litem, to trial by jury. Failure to request a trial by jury shall constitute a waiver of the right. The clerk may nevertheless require trial by jury in accordance with G.S. 1A-1, Rule 39(b), Rules of Civil Procedure, by entering an order for trial by jury on his own motion. The jury shall be composed of 12 persons chosen from the county's jury list in accordance with the provisions of Chapter 9 of the General Statutes. (1987, c. 550, s. 1.)

§ 35A-1111. Multidisciplinary evaluation.

(a) To assist in determining the nature and extent of a respondent's disability, or to assist in developing an appropriate guardianship plan and program, the clerk, on his own motion or the motion of any party, may order that a multidisciplinary evaluation of the respondent be performed. A request for a multidisciplinary evaluation shall be made in writing and filed with the clerk within 10 days after service of the petition on the respondent.

(b) If a multidisciplinary evaluation is ordered, the clerk shall name a designated agency and order it to prepare, cause to be prepared, or assemble a current multidisciplinary evaluation of the respondent. The agency shall file the evaluation with the clerk not later than 30 days after the agency receives the clerk's order. The multidisciplinary evaluation shall be filed in the proceeding for adjudication of incompetence, in the proceeding for appointment of a guardian under Subchapter II of this Chapter, or both. Unless otherwise ordered by the clerk, the agency shall send copies of the evaluation to the petitioner and the counsel or guardian ad litem for the respondent not later than 30 days after the agency receives the clerk's order. The evaluation shall be kept under such conditions as directed by the clerk and its contents revealed only as directed by the clerk. The evaluation shall not be a public record and shall not be released except by order of the clerk.

(c) If a multidisciplinary evaluation does not contain medical, psychological, or social work evaluations ordered by the clerk, the designated agency nevertheless shall file the evaluation with the clerk and send copies as required by subsection (b). In a transmittal letter, the agency shall explain why the evaluation does not contain such medical, psychological, or social work evaluations.

(d) The clerk may order that the respondent attend a multidisciplinary evaluation for the purpose of being evaluated.

(e) The multidisciplinary evaluation may be considered at the hearing for adjudication of incompetence, the hearing for appointment of a guardian under Subchapter II of this Chapter, or both. (1987, c. 550, s. 1.)

§ 35A-1112. Hearing on petition; adjudication order.

(a) The hearing on the petition shall be at the date, time, and place set forth in the final notice of hearing and shall be open to the public unless the respondent or his counsel or guardian ad litem requests otherwise, in which event the clerk shall exclude all persons other than those directly involved in or testifying at the hearing.

(b) The petitioner and the respondent are entitled to present testimony and documentary evidence, to subpoena witnesses and the production of documents, and to examine and cross-examine witnesses.

(c) The clerk shall dismiss the proceeding if the finder of fact, whether the clerk or a jury, does not find the respondent to be incompetent.

(d) If the finder of fact, whether the clerk or the jury, finds by clear, cogent, and convincing evidence that the respondent is incompetent, the clerk shall enter an order adjudicating the respondent incompetent. The clerk may include in the order findings on the nature and extent of the ward's incompetence.

(e) Following an adjudication of incompetence, the clerk shall either appoint a guardian pursuant to Subchapter II of this Chapter or, for good cause shown, transfer the proceeding for the appointment of a guardian to any county identified in G.S. 35A-1103. The transferring clerk shall enter a written order authorizing the transfer. The clerk in the transferring county shall transfer all original papers and documents, including the multidisciplinary evaluation, if any, to the transferee county and close his file with a copy of the adjudication order and transfer order.

(f) If the adjudication occurs in any county other than the county of the respondent's residence, a certified copy of the adjudication order shall be sent to the clerk in the county of the ward's legal residence, to be filed and indexed as in a special proceeding of that county.

(g) Except as provided in G.S. 35A-1114(f), a proceeding filed under this Article may be voluntarily dismissed as provided in G.S. 1A-1, Rule 41, Rules of Civil Procedure. (1987, c. 550, s. 1.)

§ 35A-1113. Hearing when incompetence determined in another state.

When the petition alleges that the respondent is incompetent on the basis of an adjudication that occurred in another state, the clerk in his discretion may:

(1) Adjudicate incompetence on the basis of the prior adjudication, if the clerk first finds by clear, cogent, and convincing evidence that:

a. The respondent is represented by an attorney or guardian ad litem; and

b. A certified copy of an order adjudicating the respondent incompetent has been filed in the proceeding; and

c. The prior adjudication was made by a court of competent jurisdiction on grounds comparable to a ground for adjudication of incompetence under this Article; and

d. The respondent, subsequent to the adjudication of incompetence in another state, assumed residence in North Carolina and needs a guardian in this State; or

(2) Decline to adjudicate incompetence on the basis of the other state's adjudication, and proceed with an adjudicatory hearing as in any other case pursuant to this Article. (1987, c. 550, s. 1.)

§ 35A-1114. Appointment of interim guardian.

(a) At the time of or subsequent to the filing of a petition under this Article, the petitioner may also file a verified motion with the clerk seeking the appointment of an interim guardian.

(b) The motion shall set forth facts tending to show:

(1) That there is reasonable cause to believe that the respondent is incompetent, and

(2) One or both of the following:

a. That the respondent is in a condition that constitutes or reasonably appears to constitute an imminent or foreseeable risk of harm to his physical well-being and that requires immediate intervention;

b. That there is or reasonably appears to be an imminent or foreseeable risk of harm to the respondent's estate that requires immediate intervention in order to protect the respondent's interest, and

(3) That the respondent needs an interim guardian to be appointed immediately to intervene on his behalf prior to the adjudication hearing.

(c) Upon filing of the motion for appointment of an interim guardian, the clerk shall immediately set a date, time, and place for a hearing on the motion. The motion and a notice setting the date, time, and place for the hearing shall be served promptly on the respondent and on his counsel or guardian ad litem and other persons the clerk may designate. The hearing shall be held as soon as possible but no later than 15 days after the motion has been served on the respondent.

(d) If at the hearing the clerk finds that there is reasonable cause to believe that the respondent is incompetent, and:

(1) That the respondent is in a condition that constitutes or reasonably appears to constitute an imminent or foreseeable risk of harm to his physical well-being, and that there is immediate need for a guardian to provide consent or take other steps to protect the respondent, or

(2) That there is or reasonably appears to be an imminent or foreseeable risk of harm to the respondent's estate, and that immediate intervention is required in order to protect the respondent's interest,

the clerk shall immediately enter an order appointing an interim guardian.

(e) The clerk's order appointing an interim guardian shall include specific findings of fact to support the clerk's conclusions, and shall set forth the interim guardian's powers and duties. Such powers and duties shall be limited and shall extend only so far and so long as necessary to meet the conditions necessitating the appointment of an interim guardian. In any event, the interim guardianship shall terminate on the earliest of the following: the date specified in the clerk's order; 45 days after entry of the clerk's order unless the clerk, for good cause shown, extends that period for up to 45 additional days; when any guardians are appointed following an adjudication of incompetence; or when the petition is dismissed by the court. An interim guardian whose authority relates only to the person of the respondent shall not be required to post a bond. If the interim guardian has authority related to the respondent's estate, the interim guardian shall post a bond in an amount determined by the clerk, with any conditions the clerk may impose, and shall render an account as directed by the clerk.

(f) When a motion for appointment of an interim guardian has been made, the petitioner may voluntarily dismiss the petition for adjudication of incompetence only prior to the hearing on the motion for appointment of an interim guardian. (1987, c. 550, s. 1; 1989, c. 473, s. 12.)

§ 35A-1115. Appeal from clerk's order.

Appeal from an order adjudicating incompetence shall be to the superior court for hearing de novo and thence to the Court of Appeals. An appeal does not stay the appointment of a guardian unless so ordered by the superior court or the Court of Appeals. The Court of Appeals may request the Attorney General to represent the petitioner on any appeal by the respondent to the Appellate Division of the General Court of Justice, but the Department of Justice shall not be required to pay any of the costs of the appeal. (1987, c. 550, s. 1.)

§ 35A-1116. Costs and fees.

(a) Costs. - Except as otherwise provided herein, costs shall be assessed as in special proceedings. Costs, including any reasonable fees and expenses of counsel for the petitioner which the clerk, in his discretion, may allow, may be taxed against either party in the discretion of the court unless:

(1) The clerk finds that the petitioner did not have reasonable grounds to bring the proceeding, in which case costs shall be taxed to the petitioner; or

(2) The respondent is indigent, in which case the costs shall be waived by the clerk if not taxed against the petitioner as provided above or otherwise paid as provided in subsection (b) or (c).

(b) Multidisciplinary Evaluation. - The cost of a multidisciplinary evaluation order pursuant to G.S. 35A-1111 shall be assessed as follows:

(1) If the respondent is adjudicated incompetent and is not indigent, the cost shall be assessed against the respondent;

(2) If the respondent is adjudicated incompetent and is indigent, the cost shall be borne by the Department of Health and Human Services;

(3) If the respondent is not adjudicated incompetent, the cost may be taxed against either party, apportioned among the parties, or borne by the Department of Health and Human Services, in the discretion of the court.

(c) Witness. - Witness fees shall be paid by:

(1) The respondent, if the respondent is adjudicated incompetent and is not indigent;

(2) The petitioner, if the respondent is not adjudicated incompetent and the clerk finds that there were not reasonable grounds to bring the proceeding;

(2a) The petitioner for any of the petitioner's witnesses, and the respondent for any of the respondent's witnesses, when the clerk finds all of the following:

a. There were reasonable grounds to bring the proceeding.

b. The respondent was not adjudicated incompetent.

c. The respondent is not indigent.

(3) The Administrative Office of the Courts for witness fees for the respondent, if the respondent is indigent.

(c1) Mediator. - Mediator fees and other costs associated with mediation shall be assessed in accordance with G.S. 7A-38.3B.

(c2) Guardian Ad Litem. - The fees of an appointed guardian ad litem shall be paid by:

(1) The respondent, if:

a. The respondent is adjudicated incompetent; and

b. The respondent is not indigent.

(2) The respondent, if:

a. The respondent is not adjudicated incompetent;

b. The clerk finds that there were reasonable grounds to bring the proceeding; and

c. The respondent is not indigent.

(3) The petitioner, if:

a. The respondent is not adjudicated incompetent; and

b. The clerk finds that there were not reasonable grounds to bring the proceedings.

(4) The Office of Indigent Defense Services in all other cases.

(d) The provisions of this section shall also apply to all parties to any proceedings under this Chapter, including a guardian who has been removed from office and the sureties on the guardian's bond. (1987, c. 550, s. 1; 1989, c. 473, s. 15; 1995, c. 235, s. 9; 1997-443, s. 11A.118(a); 2005-67, s. 3; 2009-387, s. 1.)

§§ 35A-1117 through 35A-1119: Reserved for future codification purposes.

Article 2.

Appointment of Guardian.

§ 35A-1120. Appointment of guardian.

If the respondent is adjudicated incompetent, a guardian or guardians shall be appointed in the manner provided for in Subchapter II of this Chapter. (1987, c. 550, s. 1.)

§§ 35A-1121 through 35A-1129. Reserved for future codification purposes.

Article 3.

Restoration to Competency.

§ 35A-1130. Proceedings before clerk.

(a) The guardian, ward, or any other interested person may petition for restoration of the ward to competency by filing a motion in the cause of the incompetency proceeding with the clerk who is exercising jurisdiction therein. The motion shall be verified and shall set forth facts tending to show that the ward is competent.

(b) Upon receipt of the motion, the clerk shall set a date, time, and place for a hearing, which shall be not less than 10 days or more than 30 days from service of the motion and notice of hearing on the ward and the guardian, or on the one of them who is not the petitioner, unless the clerk for good cause directs otherwise. The petitioner shall cause notice and a copy of the motion to be served on the guardian and ward (but not on one who is the petitioner) and any other parties to the incompetency proceeding. Service shall be in accordance with provisions of G.S. 1A-1, Rule 4, Rules of Civil Procedure.

(c) At the hearing on the motion, the ward shall be entitled to be represented by counsel or guardian ad litem, and a guardian ad litem shall be appointed in accordance with rules adopted by the Office of Indigent Defense Services if the ward is indigent and not represented by counsel. Upon motion of any party or the clerk's own motion, the clerk may order a multidisciplinary evaluation. The ward has a right, upon request by him, his counsel, or his guardian ad litem to trial by jury. Failure to request a trial by jury shall constitute a waiver of the right. The clerk may nevertheless require trial by jury in accordance with G.S. 1A-1, Rule 39(b), Rules of Civil Procedure, by entering an order for trial by jury on his own motion. Provided, if there is a jury in a proceeding for restoration to competency, it shall be a jury of six persons selected in accordance with the provisions of Chapter 9 of the General Statutes.

(d) If the clerk or jury finds by a preponderance of the evidence that the ward is competent, the clerk shall enter an order adjudicating that the ward is restored to competency. Upon such adjudication, the ward is authorized to manage his affairs, make contracts, control and sell his property, both real and personal, and exercise all rights as if he had never been adjudicated incompetent.

(e) The filing and approval of final accounts from the guardian and the discharge of the guardian shall be as provided in Subchapter II of this Chapter.

(f) If the clerk or jury fails to find that the ward should be restored to competency, the clerk shall enter an order denying the petition. The ward may appeal from the clerk's order to the superior court for trial de novo. (1987, c. 550, s. 1; 2000-144, s. 34.)

§§ 35A-1131 through 35A-1200: Reserved for future codification purposes.

SUBCHAPTER II. GUARDIAN AND WARD.

Article 4.

Purpose and Scope; Jurisdiction; Venue.

§ 35A-1201. Purpose.

(a) The General Assembly of North Carolina recognizes that:

(1) Some minors and incompetent persons, regardless of where they are living, require the assistance of a guardian in order to help them exercise their rights, including the management of their property and personal affairs.

(2) Incompetent persons who are not able to act effectively on their own behalf have a right to a qualified, responsible guardian.

(3) The essential purpose of guardianship for an incompetent person is to replace the individual's authority to make decisions with the authority of a guardian when the individual does not have adequate capacity to make such decisions.

(4) Limiting the rights of an incompetent person by appointing a guardian for him should not be undertaken unless it is clear that a guardian will give the individual a fuller capacity for exercising his rights.

(5) Guardianship should seek to preserve for the incompetent person the opportunity to exercise those rights that are within his comprehension and judgment, allowing for the possibility of error to the same degree as is allowed to persons who are not incompetent. To the maximum extent of his capabilities, an incompetent person should be permitted to participate as fully as possible in all decisions that will affect him.

(6) Minors, because they are legally incompetent to transact business or give consent for most purposes, need responsible, accountable adults to handle property or benefits to which they are entitled. Parents are the natural guardians of the person of their minor children, but unemancipated minors, when they do not have natural guardians, need some other responsible, accountable adult to be responsible for their personal welfare and for personal decision-making on their behalf.

(b) The purposes of this Subchapter are:

(1) To establish standards and procedures for the appointment of guardians of the person, guardians of the estate, and general guardians for incompetent persons and for minors who need guardians;

(2) To specify the powers and duties of such guardians;

(3) To provide for the protection of the person and conservation of the estate of the ward through periodic accountings and reports; and

(4) To provide for the termination of guardianships. (1987, c. 550, s. 1.)

§ 35A-1202. Definitions.

When used in this Subchapter, unless a contrary intent is indicated or the context requires otherwise:

(1) "Accounting" means the financial or status reports filed with the clerk, designated agency, respondent, or other person or party with whom such reports are required to be filed.

(2) "Clerk" means the clerk of superior court.

(3) "Designated agency" means the State or local human services agency designated by the clerk in an order to prepare, cause to be prepared, or assemble a multidisciplinary evaluation and to perform other functions as the clerk may order. A designated agency includes, without limitation, State, local, regional or area mental health, mental retardation, vocational rehabilitation, public health, social service, and developmental disabilities agencies, and diagnostic evaluation centers.

(4) "Disinterested public agent" means the director or assistant directors of a county department of social services. Except as provided in G.S. 35A-1213(f), the fact that a disinterested public agent provides financial assistance, services, or treatment to a ward does not disqualify that person from being appointed as guardian.

(5) "Estate" means any interest in real property, choses in action, intangible personal property, and tangible personal property, and includes any interest in joint accounts or jointly held property.

(6) "Financial report" means the report filed by the guardian concerning all financial transactions, including receipts and expenditures of the ward's money, sale of the ward's property, or other transactions involving the ward's property.

(7) "General guardian" means a guardian of both the estate and the person.

(8) "Guardian ad litem" means a guardian appointed pursuant to G.S. 1A-1, Rule 17, Rules of Civil Procedure.

(9) "Guardian of the estate" means a guardian appointed solely for the purpose of managing the property, estate, and business affairs of a ward.

(10) "Guardian of the person" means a guardian appointed solely for the purpose of performing duties relating to the care, custody, and control of a ward.

(11) "Incompetent person" means a person who has been adjudicated to be an "incompetent adult" or "incompetent child" as defined in G.S. 35A-1101(7) or (8).

(12) "Minor" means a person who is under the age of 18, is not married, and has not been legally emancipated.

(13) "Multidisciplinary evaluation" means an evaluation that contains current medical, psychological, and social work evaluations as directed by the clerk and that may contain current evaluations by professionals in other disciplines, including without limitation education, vocational rehabilitation, occupational therapy, vocational therapy, psychiatry, speech-and-hearing, and communications disorders. The evaluation is current if made not more than one year from the date on which it is presented to or considered by the court. The evaluation shall set forth the nature and extent of the disability and recommend a guardianship plan and program.

(14) "Status report" means the report required by G.S. 35A-1242 to be filed by the general guardian or guardian of the person. A status report shall include a report of a recent medical and dental examination of the ward by one or more physicians or dentists, a report on the guardian's performance of the duties set forth in this Chapter and in the clerk's order appointing the guardian, and a report on the ward's condition, needs, and development. The clerk may direct that the report contain other or different information. The report may also contain, without limitation, reports of mental health or mental retardation professionals, psychologists, social workers, persons in loco parentis, a member of a multidisciplinary evaluation team, a designated agency, a disinterested public agent or agency, a guardian ad litem, a guardian of the estate, an interim guardian, a successor guardian, an officer, official, employee or agent of the Department of Health and Human Services, or any other interested persons including, if applicable to the ward's situation, group home parents or supervisors, employers, members of the staff of a treatment facility, or foster parents.

(15) "Ward" means a person who has been adjudicated incompetent or an adult or minor for whom a guardian has been appointed by a court of competent jurisdiction. (1987, c. 550, s. 1; 1997-443, s. 11A.13; 2012-151, s. 12(b).)

§ 35A-1203. Jurisdiction; authority of clerk.

(a) Clerks of superior court in their respective counties have original jurisdiction for the appointment of guardians of the person, guardians of the estate, or general guardians for incompetent persons and of related proceedings brought or filed under this Subchapter. Clerks of superior court in their respective counties have original jurisdiction for the appointment of guardians of the estate for minors, for the appointment of guardians of the person or general guardians for minors who have no natural guardian, and of related proceedings brought or filed under this Subchapter.

(b) The clerk shall retain jurisdiction following appointment of a guardian in order to assure compliance with the clerk's orders and those of the superior court. The clerk shall have authority to remove a guardian for cause and shall appoint a successor guardian, following the criteria set forth in G.S. 35A-1213 or G.S. 35A-1224, after removal, death, or resignation of a guardian.

(c) The clerk shall have authority to determine disputes between guardians and to adjust the amount of the guardian's bond.

(d) Any party or any other interested person may petition the clerk to exercise the authority conferred on the clerk by this section.

(e) Where a guardian or trustee has been appointed for a ward under former Chapter 33 or former Chapter 35 of the General Statutes, the clerk, upon his own motion or the motion of that guardian or trustee or any other interested person, may designate that guardian or trustee or appoint another qualified person as guardian of the person, guardian of the estate, or general guardian of the ward under this Chapter; provided, the authority of a guardian or trustee properly appointed under former Chapter 33 or former Chapter 35 of the General Statutes to continue serving in that capacity is not dependent on such motion and designation. (1987, c. 550, s. 1; 2003-13, s. 3.)

§ 35A-1204. Venue.

(a) Venue for the appointment of a guardian for an incompetent person is in the county in which the person was adjudicated to be incompetent unless the clerk in that county has transferred the matter to a different county, in which case venue is in the county to which the matter has been transferred.

(b) Venue for the appointment of a guardian for a minor is in the county in which the minor resides or is domiciled.

(c) Venue for the appointment of an ancillary guardian for a nonresident of the State of North Carolina who is a minor or who has been adjudicated incompetent in another state, and who has a guardian of the estate or general guardian in the state of his residence, is in any county in which is located real estate in which the nonresident ward has an ownership or other interest, or if the nonresident ward has no such interest in real estate, any county in which the nonresident owns or has an interest in personal property. (1987, c. 550, s. 1.)

§ 35A-1205. Transfer to different county.

At any time before or after appointing a guardian for a minor or incompetent person the clerk may, on a motion filed in the cause or on the court's own motion, for good cause order that the matter be transferred to a different county. The transferring clerk shall enter a written order directing the transfer under such conditions as the clerk specifies. The clerk in the transferring county shall transfer all original papers, documents, and orders from the guardianship and the incompetency proceeding, if any, to the clerk of the transferee county, along with the order directing the transfer. The clerk in the transferee county shall docket and file the papers in the estates division as a basis for jurisdiction in all subsequent proceedings. The clerk in the transferring county shall close his file with a copy of the transfer order and any order adjudicating incompetence or appointing a guardian. (1987, c. 550, s. 1.)

§ 35A-1206. Letters of appointment.

Whenever a guardian has been duly appointed and qualified under this Subchapter, the clerk shall issue to the guardian letters of appointment signed by the clerk and sealed with the clerk's seal of office. In all cases, the clerk shall specify in the order and letters of appointment whether the guardian is a guardian of the estate, a guardian of the person, or a general guardian. (1987, c. 550, s. 1.)

§ 35A-1207. Motions in the cause.

(a)   Any interested person may file a motion in the cause with the clerk in the county where a guardianship is docketed to request modification of the order appointing a guardian or guardians or consideration of any matter pertaining to the guardianship.

(b)   The clerk shall treat all such requests, however labeled, as motions in the cause.

(c)   A movant under this section shall obtain from the clerk a time, date, and place for a hearing on the motion, and shall serve the motion and notice of hearing on all other parties and such other persons as the clerk directs as provided by G.S. 1A-1, Rule 5 of the Rules of Civil Procedure, unless the clerk orders otherwise.

(d)   If the clerk finds reasonable cause to believe that an emergency exists that threatens the physical well-being of the ward or constitutes a risk of substantial injury to the ward's estate, the clerk may enter an appropriate ex parte order to address the emergency pending disposition of the matter at the hearing. (1987, c. 550, s. 1.)

§ 35A-1208. Authority for health care decisions.

(a)   A guardian of the person or general guardian of an incompetent adult may petition the Clerk, in accordance with G.S. 32A-22(a), for an order suspending the authority of a health care agent, as that term is defined in G.S. 32A-16(2).

(b)   A guardian of the person or general guardian of an incompetent adult may not revoke a Declaration, as that term is defined in G.S. 90-321. (2007-502, s. 8.)

§ 35A-1209: Reserved for future codification purposes.

Article 5.

Appointment of Guardian for Incompetent Person.

§ 35A-1210. Application before clerk.

Any individual, corporation, or disinterested public agent may file an application for the appointment of a guardian for an incompetent person by filing the same with the clerk. The application may be joined with or filed subsequent to a petition for the adjudication of incompetence under Subchapter I of this Chapter. The application shall set forth, to the extent known and to the extent such information is not already a matter of record in the case:

(1) The name, age, address, and county of residence of the ward or respondent;

(2) The name, address, and county of residence of the applicant, his relationship if any to the respondent or ward, and his interest in the proceeding;

(3) The name, address, and county of residence of the respondent's next of kin and other persons known to have an interest in the proceeding;

(4) A general statement of the ward's or respondent's assets and liabilities with an estimate of the value of any property, including any income and receivables to which he is entitled; and

(5) Whether the applicant seeks the appointment of a guardian of the person, a guardian of the estate, or a general guardian, and whom the applicant recommends or seeks to have appointed as such guardian or guardians. (1987, c. 550, s. 1.)

§ 35A-1211. Service of application, motions, and notices.

(a) Application for appointment of a guardian and related motions and notices shall be served on the respondent, respondent's counsel or guardian ad litem, other parties of record, and such other persons as the clerk shall direct.

(b) When the application for appointment of a guardian is joined with a petition for adjudication of incompetence, the application shall be served with and in the same manner as the petition for adjudication of incompetence. When the application is filed subsequent to the petition for adjudication of incompetence, the applicant shall serve the application as provided by G.S. 1A-1, Rule 5, Rules of Civil Procedure, unless the clerk directs otherwise. (1987, c. 550, s. 1; 1989, c. 473, s. 25.)

§ 35A-1212. Hearing before clerk on appointment of guardian.

(a) The clerk shall make such inquiry and receive such evidence as the clerk deems necessary to determine:

(1) The nature and extent of the needed guardianship;

(2) The assets, liabilities, and needs of the ward; and

(3) Who, in the clerk's discretion, can most suitably serve as the guardian or guardians.

If the clerk determines that the nature and extent of the ward's capacity justifies ordering a limited guardianship, the clerk may do so.

(b) If a current multidisciplinary evaluation is not available and the clerk determines that one is necessary, the clerk, on his own motion or the motion of any party, may order that such an evaluation be performed pursuant to G.S. 35A-1111. The provisions of that section shall apply to such an order for a multidisciplinary evaluation following an adjudication of incompetence.

(c) The clerk may require a report prepared by a designated agency to evaluate the suitability of a prospective guardian, to include a recommendation as to an appropriate party or parties to serve as guardian, or both, based on the nature and extent of the needed guardianship and the ward's assets, liabilities, and needs.

(d) If a designated agency has not been named pursuant to G.S. 35A-1111, the clerk may, at any time he finds that the best interest of the ward would be served thereby, name a designated agency. (1987, c. 550, s. 1; 2003-236, s. 1.)

§ 35A-1212.1. Recommendation of appointment of guardian by will or other writing.

Any parent may by will recommend appointment of a guardian for an unmarried child who has been adjudicated an incompetent person and specify desired limitations on the powers to be given to the guardian. If both parents make such recommendations, the will with the latest date shall, in the absence of other relevant factors, prevail. Such recommendation shall be a strong guide for the clerk in appointing a guardian, but the clerk is not bound by the recommendation if the clerk finds that a different appointment is in the incompetent adult's best interest. If the will specifically so directs, a guardian appointed pursuant to such recommendation may be permitted to qualify and serve without giving bond, unless the clerk finds as a fact that the interest of the incompetent adult would be best served by requiring the guardian to give bond. (2005-333, s. 1.)

§ 35A-1213. Qualifications of guardians.

(a) The clerk may appoint as guardian an adult individual, a corporation, or a disinterested public agent. The applicant may submit to the clerk the name or names of potential guardians, and the clerk may consider the recommendations of the next of kin or other persons.

(b) A nonresident of the State of North Carolina, to be appointed as general guardian, guardian of the person, or guardian of the estate of a North Carolina resident, must indicate in writing his willingness to submit to the jurisdiction of the North Carolina courts in matters relating to the guardianship and must appoint a resident agent to accept service of process for the guardian in all actions or proceedings with respect to the guardianship. Such appointment must be approved by and filed with the clerk, and any agent so appointed must notify the clerk of any change in the agent's address or legal residence. The clerk shall require a nonresident guardian of the estate or a nonresident general guardian to post a bond or other security for the faithful performance of the guardian's duties. The clerk may require a nonresident guardian of the person to post a bond or other security for the faithful performance of the guardian's duties.

(c) A corporation may be appointed as guardian only if it is authorized by its charter to serve as a guardian or in similar fiduciary capacities. A corporation shall meet the requirements outlined in Chapters 55 and 55D of the General Statutes. A corporation will provide a written copy of its charter to the clerk of superior court. A corporation contracting with a public agency to serve as guardian is required to attend guardianship training and provide verification of attendance to the contracting agency. A corporation shall not be appointed as guardian for any individual to whom it provides mental health, developmental disabilities, or substance abuse services for compensation as part of a contractual or other arrangement with a local management entity (LME), including an LME that has been approved to operate the 1915(b)/(c) Medicaid Waiver.

(d) A disinterested public agent who is appointed by the clerk to serve as guardian is authorized and required to do so; provided, if at the time of the appointment or any time subsequent thereto the disinterested public agent believes that his role or the role of his agency in relation to the ward is such that his service as guardian would constitute a conflict of interest, or if he knows of any other reason that his service as guardian may not be in the ward's best interest, he shall bring such matter to the attention of the clerk and seek the appointment of a different guardian. A disinterested public agent who is appointed as guardian shall serve in that capacity by virtue of his office or employment, which shall be identified in the clerk's order and in the letters of appointment. When the disinterested public agent's office or employment terminates, his successor in office or employment, or his immediate supervisor if there is no successor, shall succeed him as guardian without further proceedings unless the clerk orders otherwise.

(e) Notwithstanding any other provision of this section, an employee of a treatment facility, as defined in G.S. 35A-1101(16), may not serve as guardian for a ward who is an inpatient in or resident of the facility in which the employee works; provided, this subsection shall not apply to or affect the validity of any appointment of a guardian that occurred before October 1, 1987.

(f) An individual who contracts with or is employed by an entity that contracts with a local management entity (LME) for the delivery of mental health, developmental disabilities, and substance abuse services may not serve as a guardian for a ward for whom the individual or entity is providing these services, unless the individual is one of the following:

(1)   A parent of that ward.

(2)   A member of the ward's immediate family, a licensed family foster care provider, or a licensed therapeutic foster care provider who is under contract with a local management entity (LME) for the delivery of mental health, developmental disabilities, and substance abuse services and is serving as a guardian as of January 1, 2013. For the purposes of this subsection, the term "immediate family" is defined as a spouse, child, sibling, parent, grandparent, or grandchild. The term also includes stepparents, stepchildren, stepsiblings, and adoptive relationships.

(3)   A biologically unrelated individual who was serving on March 1, 2013, as a guardian without compensation for guardianship services. (1987, c. 550, s. 1; 2004-203, s. 31(a); 2012-151, s. 12(c); 2013-258, ss. 1, 2.)

§ 35A-1214. Priorities for appointment.

The clerk shall consider appointing a guardian according to the following order of priority: an individual recommended under G.S. 35A-1212.1; an individual; a corporation; or a disinterested public agent. No public agent shall be appointed guardian until diligent efforts have been made to find an appropriate individual or corporation to serve as guardian, but in every instance the clerk shall base the appointment of a guardian or guardians on the best interest of the ward. (1987, c. 550, s. 1; 2005-333, s. 2.)

§ 35A-1215. Clerk's order; issuance of letters of appointment.

(a)   When appointing a guardian, the clerk shall enter an order setting forth:

(1)   The nature of the guardianship or guardianships to be created and the name of the person or entity appointed to fill each guardianship; and

(2)   The powers and duties of the guardian or guardians, which shall include, unless the clerk orders otherwise, (i) with respect to a guardian of the person

and general guardian, the powers and duties provided under G.S. 35A, Article 8, and (ii) with respect to a guardian of the estate and general guardian, the powers, and duties provided under G.S. 35A, Article 9 and Subchapter III; and

(3)   The identity of the designated agency if there is one.

(b)   If the clerk orders a limited guardianship as authorized by G.S. 35A-1212(a), the clerk may order that the ward retain certain legal rights and privileges to which the ward was entitled before the ward was adjudged incompetent. Any order of limited guardianship shall include findings as to the nature and extent of the ward's incompetence as it relates to the ward's need for a guardian or guardians.

(c)   The clerk shall issue the guardian or guardians letters of appointment as provided in G.S. 35A-1206. (1987, c. 550, s. 1; 2003-236, s. 2.)

§ 35A-1216. Rule-making power of Secretary of Health and Human Services.

The Secretary of the Department of Health and Human Services shall adopt rules concerning the guardianship responsibilities of disinterested public agents. The rules shall provide, among other things, that disinterested public agents shall undertake or have received training concerning the powers and responsibilities of guardians. (1987, c. 550, s. 1; 1997-443, s. 11A.15.)

§ 35A-1217. Appointment of guardian ad litem for incompetent ward.

The clerk shall appoint a guardian ad litem to represent a ward in a proceeding under this Subchapter if the ward has been adjudicated incompetent under Subchapter I and the clerk determines that the ward's interests are not adequately represented. Appointment and discharge of the guardian ad litem shall be in accordance with rules adopted by the Office of Indigent Defense Services. Nothing herein shall affect the ward's right to retain counsel of his or her own choice. (2009-387, s. 2.)

§ 35A-1218: Reserved for future codification purposes.

§ 35A-1219: Reserved for future codification purposes.

Article 6.

Appointment of Guardian for a Minor.

§ 35A-1220. Absence of natural guardian.

When a minor either has no natural guardian or has been abandoned, and the minor requires services from the county department of social services, the social services director in the county in which the minor resides or is domiciled shall be the guardian of the person of the minor until the appointment of a general guardian or guardian of the person for the minor under this Subchapter or the entry of an order by a court of competent jurisdiction awarding custody of the minor or appointing a general guardian or guardian of the person for the minor. (1987, c. 550, s.1.)

§ 35A-1221. Application before clerk.

Any person or corporation, including any State or local human services agency through its authorized representative, may make application for the appointment of a guardian of the estate for any minor or for the appointment of a guardian of the person or general guardian for any minor who has no natural guardian by filing an application with the clerk. The application shall set forth, to the extent known:

(1)   The minor's name, date of birth, address, and county of residence;

(2)   The names and address of the minor's parents, if living, and of other persons known to have an interest in the application for appointment of a guardian; the name of and date of death of the minor's deceased parent or parents;

(3) The applicant's name, address, county of residence, relationship if any to the minor, and interest in the proceeding;

(4) If a guardian has been appointed for the minor or custody of the minor has been awarded, a statement of the facts relating thereto and a copy of any guardianship or custody order, if available;

(5) A general statement of the minor's assets and liabilities with an estimate of the value of any property, including any income and receivables to which he is entitled;

(6) A statement of the reason or reasons that the appointment of a guardian is sought; whether the applicant seeks the appointment of a guardian of the person, a guardian of the estate, or a general guardian; and whom the applicant recommends or seeks to have appointed as such guardian or guardians; and

(7) Any other information that will assist the clerk in determining the need for a guardian or in appointing a guardian. (1987, c. 550, s. 1; 1989, c. 473, s. 24; 1997-443, s. 11A.16.)

§ 35A-1222. Service of application and notices.

A copy of the application and written notice of the time, date, and place set for a hearing shall be served on each parent, guardian, and legal custodian of the minor who is not an applicant, and on any other person the clerk may direct, including the minor. Service shall be provided by G.S. 1A-1, Rule 4, Rules of Civil Procedure, unless the clerk directs otherwise. When service is made by the sheriff, the sheriff shall make such service without demanding his fees in advance. Parties may waive their right to notice of the hearing and the clerk may proceed to consider the application upon determining that all necessary parties are before the court and agree to have the application considered. (1987, c. 550, s. 1; 1989, c. 473, s. 19.)

§ 35A-1223. Hearing before clerk on appointment of guardian.

The clerk shall receive evidence necessary to determine whether a guardian of the person, a guardian of the estate, or a general guardian is required. If the court determines that a guardian or guardians are required, the court shall receive evidence necessary to determine the minor's assets, liabilities, and needs, and who the guardian or guardians shall be. The hearing may be informal and the clerk may consider whatever testimony, written reports, affidavits, documents, or other evidence the clerk finds necessary to determine the minor's best interest. (1987, c. 550, s. 1.)

§ 35A-1224. Criteria for appointment of guardians.

(a)   The clerk may appoint a guardian of the estate for any minor. The clerk may appoint a guardian of the person or a general guardian only for a minor who has no natural guardian.

(b)   The clerk may appoint as guardian of the person or general guardian only an adult individual whether or not that individual is a resident of the State of North Carolina.

(c)   The clerk may appoint as guardian of the estate an adult individual whether or not that individual is a resident of the State of North Carolina or a corporation that is authorized by its charter to serve as a guardian or in similar fiduciary capacities.

(d)   If the minor's parent or parents have made a testamentary recommendation pursuant to G.S. 35A-1225 for the appointment of a guardian, the clerk shall give substantial weight to such recommendation; provided, such recommendation may not affect the rights of a surviving parent who has not willfully abandoned the minor, and the clerk shall in every instance base the appointment of a guardian or guardians on the minor's best interest.

(e)   Notwithstanding any other provision of this section, an employee of a treatment facility, as defined in G.S. 35A-1101(16), may not serve as guardian for a ward who is an inpatient in or resident of the facility in which the employee works; provided, this subsection shall not apply to or affect the validity of any appointment of a guardian that occurred before October 1, 1987. (1987, c. 550, s. 1; 1989, c. 473, s. 1.)

§ 35A-1225. Testamentary recommendation; guardian for incompetent minor.

(a) Parents are presumed to know the best interest of their children. Any parent may by last will and testament recommend a guardian for any of his or her minor children, whether born at the parent's death or en ventre sa mere, for such time as the child remains under 18 years of age, unmarried, and unemancipated, or for any less time. Such will may be made without regard to whether the testator is an adult or a minor. If both parents make such recommendations, the will with the latest date shall, in the absence of other relevant factors, prevail. In the absence of a surviving parent, such recommendation shall be a strong guide for the clerk in appointing a guardian, but the clerk is not bound by the recommendation if the clerk finds that a different appointment is in the minor's best interest. If the will specifically so directs, a guardian appointed pursuant to such recommendation may be permitted to qualify and serve without giving bond, unless the clerk finds as a fact that the interest of the minor would be best served by requiring the guardian to give bond.

(b) Any person authorized by law to recommend a guardian for a minor by his last will and testament or other writing may direct that the guardian appointed for his incompetent child shall petition the clerk during the six months before the child reaches majority for an adjudication of incompetence and appointment of a guardian under the provisions of this Chapter. If so directed, the guardian shall timely file such a petition unless the minor is no longer incompetent. Notwithstanding the absence of such provision in a will or other writing, the guardian of an incompetent child, or any other person, may file such petition during the six months before the minor reaches majority or thereafter. (1987, c. 550, s. 1.)

§ 35A-1226. Clerk's order; issuance of letters of appointment.

After considering the evidence, the clerk shall enter an appropriate order. If the clerk determines that a guardian or guardians should be appointed, the order may set forth:

(1) Findings as to the minor's circumstances, assets, and liabilities as they relate to his need for a guardian or guardians; and

(2)   Whether there shall be one or more guardians, his or their identity, and if more than one, who shall be guardian of the person and who shall be guardian of the estate. The clerk shall issue the guardian or guardians letters of appointment as provided in G.S. 35A-1206. (1987, c. 550, s. 1.)

§ 35A-1227. Funds owed to minors.

(a)   Certain insurance proceeds or other funds to which a minor is entitled may be paid to and administered by the public guardian or the clerk as provided in G.S. 7A-111.

(b)   A devise of personal property to a minor may be distributed to the minor's parent or guardian with the approval of the clerk as provided in G.S. 28A-22-7.

(c)   A personal representative or collector who holds property due a minor without a guardian may deliver the property to the clerk as provided in G.S. 28A-23-2.

(d)   Inter vivos or testamentary transfers to minors may be made and administered according to the North Carolina Uniform Transfers to Minors Act, Chapter 33A of the General Statutes. (1987, c. 550, s. 1; 1989, c. 473, s. 23; 2011-284, s. 37.)

§ 35A-1228. Guardians of children of servicemen; allotments and allowances.

In all cases where a person serving in the Armed Forces of the United States has made an allotment or allowance to a resident of this State who is his child or other minor dependent as provided by the Wartime Allowances to Service Men's Dependents Act or any other act of Congress, the clerk in the county of the minor's residence may act as temporary guardian, or appoint some suitable person to act as temporary guardian, of the person's minor dependent for purposes of receiving and disbursing allotments and allowance funds for the benefit of the minor dependent, when:

(1)   The other parent of the child or other minor dependent, or other person designated in the allowance or allotment to receive and disburse such moneys

for the benefit of the minor dependent, dies or becomes mentally incompetent; and

(2) The person serving in the Armed Forces of the United States is reported as missing in action or as a prisoner of war and is unable to designate another person to receive and disburse the allotment or allowance to the minor dependent. (1987, c. 550, s. 1; 2011-183, s. 28.)

§ 35A-1229: Reserved for future codification purposes.

Article 7.

Guardian's Bond.

§ 35A-1230. Bond required before receiving property.

Except as otherwise provided by G.S. 35A-1212.1 and G.S. 35A-1225(a), no general guardian or guardian of the estate shall be permitted to receive the ward's property until he has given sufficient surety, approved by the clerk, to account for and apply the same under the direction of the court, provided that if the guardian is a nonresident of this State and the value of the property received exceeds one thousand dollars ($1,000) the surety shall be a bond under G.S. 35A-1231(a) executed by a duly authorized surety company, or secured by cash in an amount equal to the amount of the bond or by a mortgage executed under Chapter 109 of the General Statutes on real estate located in the county, the value of which, excluding all prior liens and encumbrances, shall be at least one and one-fourth times the amount of the bond; and further provided that the nonresident shall appoint a resident agent to accept service of process in all actions and proceedings with respect to the guardianship. The clerk shall not require a guardian of the person who is a resident of North Carolina to post a bond; the clerk may require a nonresident guardian of the person to post a bond or other security for the faithful performance of the guardian's duties. (1987, c. 550, s. 1; 1989, c. 473, s. 2; 2005-333, s. 3.)

§ 35A-1231. Terms and conditions of bond; increase on sale of realty or personal property.

(a)   Before issuing letters of appointment to a general guardian or guardian of the estate the clerk shall require the guardian to give a bond payable to the State. The clerk shall determine the value of all the ward's personal property and the rents and profits of the ward's real estate by examining, under oath, the applicant for guardianship or any other person or persons. The penalty in the bond shall be set as follows:

(1)   Where the bond is executed by personal sureties, the penalty must be at least double the value so determined by the clerk;

(2)   Where the bond is executed by a duly authorized surety company, the penalty may be fixed at not less than one and one-fourth times the value so determined by the clerk;

(3)   Provided, however, the clerk may accept bond in estates where the value determined by the clerk exceeds the sum of one hundred thousand dollars ($100,000), in a sum equal to one hundred and ten percent (110%) of the determined value.

The bond must be secured with two or more sufficient sureties, jointly and severally bound, and must be acknowledged before and approved by the clerk. The bond must be conditioned on the guardian's faithfully executing the trust reposed in him as such and obeying all lawful orders of the clerk or judge relating to the guardianship of the estate committed to him. The bond must be recorded in the office of the clerk appointing the guardian, except, if the guardianship is transferred to a different county, it must be recorded in the office of the clerk in the county where the guardianship is docketed.

(b)   If the court orders a sale of the ward's real property, or if the guardian expects or offers to sell personal property that he knows or has reason to know has a value greater than the value used in determining the amount of the bond posted, the guardian shall, before receiving the proceeds of the sale, furnish bond or increase his existing bond to cover the proceeds if real estate is sold, or to cover the increased value if personal property is sold. The bond, or the increase in the existing bond, shall be twice the amount of the proceeds of any real property sold, or of the increased value of any personal property sold, except where the bond is executed by a duly authorized surety company, in which case the penalty of the bond need not exceed one and one-fourth times the amount of the real property sold or the increased value of the personal property sold. (1987, c. 550, s. 1; 1989, c. 473, s. 9.)

§ 35A-1232. Exclusion of deposited money in computing amount of bond.

(a) When it appears that the ward's estate includes money that has been or will be deposited in an account with a financial institution upon condition that the money will not be withdrawn except on authorization of the court, the court may, in its discretion, order that the money be so deposited or invested and exclude such deposited money from the computation of the amount of the bond or reduce the amount of the bond in respect of such money to such an amount as it may deem reasonable.

(b) The applicant for letters of guardianship, or a general guardian or guardian of the estate, may deliver to any such financial institution any such money in the applicant's or the guardian's possession or may allow such financial institution to retain any such money already deposited or invested with it; in either event, the applicant or guardian shall secure and file with the court a written receipt including the agreement of the financial institution, duly acknowledged by an authorized officer of the financial institution, that the money shall not be allowed to be withdrawn except on authorization of the court. In so receiving and retaining such money from an applicant for letters of guardianship, the financial institution shall be protected to the same extent as though it had received the same from a general guardian or a guardian of the estate.

(c) The term "account with a financial institution" as used in this section means any account in a bank, savings and loan association, credit union, trust company, or registered securities broker or dealer.

(d) The term "money" as used in this section means the principal of the ward's estate and does not include the income earned by the principal, which may be withdrawn without any authorization of the court. (1987, c. 550, s. 1; 2009-309, s. 1.)

§ 35A-1233. Clerk's authority to reduce penalty of bond.

When a guardian has disbursed either income or income and principal of the estate according to law, for the purchase of real estate or the support and maintenance of the ward or the ward and his dependents or any lawful cause, and when the personal assets and income of the estate from all sources in the hands of the guardian have been diminished, the penalty of the guardian's bond may be reduced in the discretion of the clerk to an amount not less than the amount that would be required if the guardian were first qualifying to administer the personal assets and income. (1987, c. 550, s. 1.)

§ 35A-1234. Action on bond.

Any person injured by a breach of the condition of the guardian's bond may prosecute a suit thereon, as in other actions. (1987, c. 550, s. 1.)

§ 35A-1235. One bond sufficient when several wards have estate in common.

When the same person is appointed guardian for two or more minors or incompetent persons possessed of one estate in common, the clerk may take one bond only in such case, upon which each of the wards or their heirs or personal representatives may have a separate action. (1987, c. 550, s. 1.)

§ 35A-1236. Renewal of bond.

Every guardian who is required to post a bond and who does so other than through a duly authorized surety company shall renew his bond before the clerk every three years during the continuance of the guardianship. The clerk shall issue a citation against every such guardian failing to renew his bond, requiring the guardian to renew the bond within 20 days after service of the citation. On return of the citation duly served and failure of the guardian to comply, the clerk shall remove the guardian and appoint a successor. This section shall not apply to a guardian whose bond is executed by a duly authorized surety company. (1987, c. 550, s. 1.)

§ 35A-1237. Relief of endangered sureties.

Any surety of a guardian, who is in danger of sustaining loss by his suretyship, may file a motion in the cause before the clerk where the guardianship is docketed, setting forth the circumstances of his case and demanding relief. The guardian shall have 10 days after service of the motion to answer the motion. If, upon the hearing, the clerk deems the surety entitled to relief, the clerk may order the guardian to give a new bond or to indemnify the surety against apprehended loss, or may remove the guardian from his trust. If the guardian fails to give a new bond or security to indemnify within a reasonable time when required to do so, the clerk must enter a peremptory order for his removal, and his authority as guardian shall cease. (1987, c. 550, s. 1; 1989, c. 473, s. 20.)

§ 35A-1238. Clerk's liability.

(a)   If any clerk commits the estate of a ward to the guardianship of any person without taking good and sufficient bond for the same as required by law, the clerk shall be liable on his official bond, at the suit of the aggrieved party, for all loss and damages sustained for want of sufficient bond being taken; but if the sureties were good at the time of their being accepted, the clerk shall not be liable.

(b)   If any clerk willfully or negligently does, or omits to do, any other act prohibited, or other duty imposed on him by law, by which act or omission the estate of any ward suffers damage, the clerk shall be liable on his official bond, at the suit of the aggrieved party, for all loss and damages sustained from such act or omission. (1987, c. 550, s. 1.)

§ 35A-1239. Health and Human Services bond.

The Secretary of the Department of Health and Human Services shall require or purchase individual or blanket bonds for all disinterested public agents appointed to be guardians, whether they serve as guardians of the estate, guardians of the person, or general guardians, or one blanket bond covering all agents, the bond or bonds to be conditioned upon faithful performance of their duties as guardians and made payable to the State. The premiums shall be paid by the State. (1987, c. 550, s. 1; 1997-443, s. 11A.17.)

Article 8.

Powers and Duties of Guardian of the Person.

§ 35A-1240. Applicability of Article.

This Article applies only to guardians of the person, including general guardians exercising authority as guardian of the person. (1987, c. 550, s. 1.)

§ 35A-1241. Powers and duties of guardian of the person.

(a) To the extent that it is not inconsistent with the terms of any order of the clerk or any other court of competent jurisdiction, a guardian of the person has the following powers and duties:

(1) The guardian of the person is entitled to custody of the person of the guardian's ward and shall make provision for the ward's care, comfort, and maintenance, and shall, as appropriate to the ward's needs, arrange for the ward's training, education, employment, rehabilitation or habilitation. The guardian of the person shall take reasonable care of the ward's clothing, furniture, vehicles, and other personal effects that are with the ward.

(2) The guardian of the person may establish the ward's place of abode within or without this State. In arranging for a place of abode, the guardian of the person shall give preference to places within this State over places not in this State if in-State and out-of-State places are substantially equivalent. The guardian also shall give preference to places that are not treatment facilities. If the only available and appropriate places of domicile are treatment facilities, the guardian shall give preference to community-based treatment facilities, such as group homes or nursing homes, over treatment facilities that are not community-based.

(3) The guardian of the person may give any consent or approval that may be necessary to enable the ward to receive medical, legal, psychological, or other professional care, counsel, treatment, or service; provided that, if the patient has a health care agent appointed pursuant to a valid health care power

of attorney, the health care agent shall have the right to exercise the authority granted in the health care power of attorney unless the Clerk has suspended the authority of that health care agent in accordance with G.S. 35A-1208. The guardian shall not, however, consent to the sterilization of a mentally ill or mentally retarded ward unless the guardian obtains an order from the clerk in accordance with G.S. 35A-1245. The guardian of the person may give any other consent or approval on the ward's behalf that may be required or in the ward's best interest. The guardian may petition the clerk for the clerk's concurrence in the consent or approval.

(b)   A guardian of the person is entitled to be reimbursed out of the ward's estate for reasonable and proper expenditures incurred in the performance of his duties as guardian of the ward's person.

(c)   A guardian of the person, if he has acted within the limits imposed on him by this Article or the order of appointment or both, shall not be liable for damages to the ward or the ward's estate, merely by reason of the guardian's:

(1)   Authorizing or giving any consent or approval necessary to enable the ward to receive legal, psychological, or other professional care, counsel, treatment, or service, in a situation where the damages result from the negligence or other acts of a third person; or

(2)   Authorizing medical treatment or surgery for his ward, if the guardian acted in good faith and was not negligent. (1987, c. 550, s. 1; 2003-13, s. 4; 2007-502, s. 9.)

§ 35A-1242. Status reports for incompetent wards.

(a)   Any corporation or disinterested public agent that is guardian of the person for an incompetent person, within six months after being appointed, shall file an initial status report with the designated agency, if there is one, or with the clerk. Such guardian shall file a second status report with the designated agency or the clerk one year after being appointed, and subsequent reports annually thereafter. The clerk may order any other guardian of the person to file status reports. If a guardian required by this section to file a status report is employed by the designated agency, the guardian shall file any required status report with both the designated agency and the clerk.

(b)   Each status report shall be filed under the guardian's oath or affirmation that the report is complete and accurate so far as he is informed and can determine.

(c)   A clerk or designated agency that receives a status report shall not make the status report available to anyone other than the guardian, the ward, the court, or State or local human resource agencies providing services to the ward. (1987, c. 550)

§ 35A-1243. Duties of designated agency.

(a)   Within 30 days after it receives a status report, the designated agency shall certify to the clerk that it has reviewed the report and shall mail a copy of its certification to the guardian.

(b)   At the same time, the designated agency may:

(1)   Send its written comments on the report to the clerk, the guardian, or any other person who may have an interest in the ward's welfare;

(2)   Notify the guardian that it is able to help the guardian in the performance of his duties;

(3)   Petition the clerk for an order requiring the guardian to perform the duties imposed on him by the clerk or this Article if it appears that the guardian is not performing those duties;

(4)   Petition the clerk for an order modifying the terms of the guardianship or the guardianship program or plan if it appears that such should be modified;

(5)   Petition the clerk for an order removing the guardian from his duties and appointing a successor guardian if it appears that the guardian should be removed for cause;

(6)   Petition the clerk for an adjudication of restoration to competency; or

(7)   Petition the clerk for any other appropriate orders.

(c) If the designated agency files such a petition, it shall cause the petition to be signed and acknowledged by the officer, official, employee, or agent who has personal knowledge of the facts set forth in the petition, and it shall set forth all facts known to it that tend to support the relief sought by the petition.

(d) The clerk shall take appropriate action upon the petition in accordance with other provisions or requirements of this Chapter. (1987, c. 550, s. 1.)

§ 35A-1244. Procedure to compel status reports.

If a guardian of the person fails to file a status report as required, or renders an unsatisfactory report, the clerk shall, on his own motion or the request of an interested party, promptly order the guardian to render a full and satisfactory report within 20 days after service of the order. If, after due service of the order, the guardian does not file such report, or obtain further time in which to file it, on or before the return day of the order, the clerk may remove him from office or may issue an order or notice to show cause for civil or criminal contempt as provided in Chapter 5A of the General Statutes. In such proceedings, the defaulting guardian may be held personally liable for the costs of the proceeding, including the costs of service of all notices or motions incidental thereto, or the amount of the costs of the proceeding may be deducted from any commissions due to the guardian of the person. Where a corporation or disinterested public agent is guardian of the person, the president or director or person or persons having charge of the guardianship for the corporation or agency, or the person to whom the duty of making status reports has been assigned by the corporation or agency, may be proceeded against as herein provided as if he or they were the guardian personally, provided, the corporation or agency itself may also be fined and/or removed as guardian for such failure or omission. (1987, c. 550, s. 1.)

§ 35A-1245. Procedure to permit the sterilization of a mentally ill or a mentally retarded ward in the case of medical necessity.

(a) A guardian of the person shall not consent to the sterilization of a mentally ill or mentally retarded ward unless an order from the clerk has been obtained in accordance with this section.

(b) If a mentally ill or mentally retarded ward needs to undergo a medical procedure that would result in sterilization, the ward's guardian shall petition the clerk for an order to permit the guardian to consent to the procedure. The petition shall contain the following:

(1) A sworn statement from a physician licensed in this State who has examined the ward that the proposed procedure is medically necessary and not for the sole purpose of sterilization or for the purpose of hygiene or convenience.

(2) The name and address of the physician who will perform the procedure.

(3) A sworn statement from a psychiatrist or psychologist licensed in this State who has examined the ward as to whether the mentally ill or mentally retarded ward is able to comprehend the nature of the proposed procedure and its consequences and provide an informed consent to the procedure.

(4) If the ward is able to comprehend the nature of the proposed procedure and its consequences, the sworn consent of the ward to the procedure.

(c) A copy of the petition shall be served on the ward personally. If the ward is unable to comprehend the nature of the proposed procedure and its consequences and is unable to provide an informed consent, the clerk shall appoint an attorney to represent the ward in accordance with rules adopted by the Office of Indigent Defense Services.

(d) Should the ward or the ward's attorney request a hearing, a hearing shall be held. Otherwise, the clerk may enter an order without the appearance of witnesses. If a hearing is held, the guardian and the ward may present evidence.

(e) If the clerk finds the following, the clerk shall enter an order permitting the guardian to consent to the proposed procedure:

(1) The ward is capable of comprehending the procedure and its consequences and has consented to the procedure, or the ward is unable to comprehend the procedure and its consequences.

(2) The procedure is medically necessary and is not solely for the purpose of sterilization or for hygiene or convenience.

(f) The guardian or the ward, the ward's attorney, or any other interested party may appeal the clerk's order to the superior court in accordance with G.S. 1-301.2(e). (2003-13, s. 1(a); 2005-250, s. 5.)

§§ 35A-1246 through 35A-1249: Reserved for future codification purposes.

Article 9.

Powers and Duties of Guardian of the Estate.

§ 35A-1250. Applicability of Article.

(a) This Article applies only to guardians of the estate, including general guardians exercising authority as guardian of the estate. A guardian of the estate or general guardian shall have all the powers and duties under this Article unless those are inconsistent with the clerk's order appointing a guardian, in which case the clerk's order shall prevail.

(b) Nothing contained in this Article shall be construed as authorizing any departure from the express terms or limitations set forth in any court order creating or limiting the guardian's powers and duties. (1987, c. 550, s. 1.)

§ 35A-1251. Guardian's powers in administering incompetent ward's estate.

In the case of an incompetent ward, a general guardian or guardian of the estate has the power to perform in a reasonable and prudent manner every act that a reasonable and prudent person would perform incident to the collection, preservation, management, and use of the ward's estate to accomplish the desired result of administering the ward's estate legally and in the ward's best interest, including but not limited to the following specific powers:

(1) To take possession, for the ward's use, of all the ward's estate, as defined in G.S. 35A-1202(5).

(2) To receive assets due the ward from any source.

(3) To maintain any appropriate action or proceeding to recover possession of any of the ward's property, to determine the title thereto, or to recover damages for any injury done to any of the ward's property; also, to compromise, adjust, arbitrate, sue on or defend, abandon, or otherwise deal with and settle any other claims in favor of or against the ward.

(4) To complete performance of contracts entered into by the ward that continue as obligations of the ward or his estate, or to refuse to complete the contracts, as the guardian determines to be in the ward's best interests, taking into account any cause of action that might be maintained against the ward for failure to complete the contract.

(5) To abandon or relinquish all rights in any property when, in the guardian's opinion, acting reasonably and in good faith, it is valueless, or is so encumbered or is otherwise in a condition that it is of no benefit or value to the ward or his estate.

(5a) To renounce any interest in property as provided in Chapter 31B of the General Statutes, or as otherwise allowed by law.

(6) To vote shares of stock or other securities in person or by general or limited proxy, and to pay sums chargeable or accruing against or on account of securities owned by the ward.

(7) To insure the ward's assets against damage or loss, at the expense of the ward's estate.

(8) To pay the ward's debts and obligations that were incurred prior to the date of adjudication of incompetence or appointment of a guardian when the debt or obligation was incurred for necessary living expenses or taxes; or when the debt or obligation involves a specific lien on real or personal property, if the ward has an equity in the property on which there is a specific lien; or when the guardian is convinced that payment of the debt or obligation is in the best interest of the ward or his estate.

(9) To renew the ward's obligations for the payment of money. The guardian's execution of any obligation for the payment of money pursuant to this subsection shall not be held or construed to be binding on the guardian personally.

(10)   To pay taxes, assessments, and other expenses incident to the collection, care, administration, and protection of the ward's estate.

(11)   To sell or exercise stock subscription or conversion rights; consent, directly or through a committee or other agent, to the reorganization, consolidation, merger, dissolution, or liquidation of a corporation or other business enterprise.

(12)   To expend estate income on the ward's behalf and to petition the court for prior approval of expenditures from estate principal.

(13)   To pay from the ward's estate necessary expenses of administering the ward's estate.

(14)   To employ persons, including attorneys, auditors, investment advisors, appraisers, or agents to advise or assist him in the performance of his duties as guardian.

(15)   To continue any business or venture or farming operation in which the ward was engaged, where that continuation is reasonably necessary or desirable to preserve the value, including goodwill, of the ward's interest in the business.

(16)   To acquire and retain every kind of property and every kind of investment, including specifically, but without in any way limiting the generality of the foregoing, bonds, debentures, and other corporate or governmental obligations; stocks, preferred or common; real estate mortgages; shares in building and loan associations or savings and loan associations; annual premium or single premium life, endowment, or annuity contracts; and securities of any management type investment company or investment trust registered under the Federal Investment Company Act of 1940, as from time to time amended.

(17)   a.   Without a court order to lease any of the ward's real estate for a term of not more than three years, or to sell, lease or exchange any of the ward's personal property including securities, provided that the aggregate value of all items of the ward's tangible personal property sold without court order shall not exceed five thousand dollars ($5,000) per accounting period. When any item of the ward's tangible personal property has a value which when increased by the value of all other tangible personal property previously sold in the estate without a court order would exceed five thousand dollars ($5,000) in the current

accounting period, a guardian may sell the item only as provided in subdivision (17)b.

b. A guardian who is required by subdivision (17)a to do so shall, and any other guardian who so desires may, by motion in the cause, request the court to issue him an order to lease any of the ward's real estate or to sell any item or items of the ward's personal property. Notice of the motion and of the date, time and place of a hearing thereon shall be served, as provided in G.S. 1A-1, Rule 5, Rules of Civil Procedure, upon all parties of record and upon any other persons the clerk may direct, and the court may issue the order after conducting a hearing and upon any conditions that the court may require; provided that:

1. A sale, lease, or exchange under this subdivision may not be subject to Article 29A of Chapter 1 of the General Statutes unless the order so requires; and

2. The power granted in this subdivision shall not affect the power of the guardian to petition the court for prior approval of expenditures from estate principal under subdivision (12) of this section.

(18) To foreclose, as an incident to the collection of any bond, note or other obligation, any mortgage, deed or trust, or other lien securing the bond, note or other obligation, and to bid in the property at a foreclosure sale, or to acquire the property deed from the mortgagor or obligor without foreclosure; and to retain the property so bid in or taken over without foreclosure.

(19) To borrow money for any periods of time and upon the terms and conditions as to rates, maturities, renewals, and security as the guardian shall deem advisable, including the power of a corporate guardian to borrow from its own banking department, for the purpose of paying debts, taxes, and other claims against the ward, and to mortgage, pledge, or otherwise encumber that portion of the ward's estate as may be required to secure the loan or loans; provided, in respect to the borrowing of money on the security of the ward's real property, Subchapter III of this Chapter is controlling.

(20) To execute and deliver all instruments that will accomplish or facilitate the exercise of the powers vested in the guardian.

(21) To expend estate income for the support, maintenance, and education of the ward's minor children, spouse, and dependents, and to petition the court for prior approval of expenditures from estate principal for these purposes;

provided, the clerk, in the original order appointing the guardian or a subsequent order, may require that the expenditures from estate income also be approved in advance. In determining whether and in what amount to make or approve these expenditures, the guardian or clerk shall take into account the ward's legal obligations to his minor children, spouse, and dependents; the sufficiency of the ward's estate to meet the ward's needs; the needs and resources of the ward's minor children, spouse, and dependents; and the ward's conduct or expressed wishes, prior to becoming incompetent, in regard to the support of these persons.

(22) To transfer to the spouse of the ward those amounts authorized for transfer to the spouse pursuant to 42 United States Code § 1396r-5.

(23) To create a trust for the benefit of the ward pursuant to 42 United States Code § 1396p(d)(4), provided that all amounts remaining in the trust upon the death of the ward, other than those amounts which must be paid to a state government and those amounts retained by a nonprofit association as set forth in 42 United States Code § 1396p(d)(4)(C), are to be paid to the estate of the ward.

(24) To petition the court for approval of the exercise of any of the following powers with respect to a revocable trust that the ward, if competent, could exercise as settlor of the revocable trust:

a. Revocation of the trust.

b. Amendment of the trust.

c. Additions to the trust.

d. Direction to dispose of property of the trust.

e. The creation of the trust, notwithstanding the provisions of G.S. 36C-4-402(a)(1) and (2).

The exercise of the powers described in this subdivision (i) shall not alter the designation of beneficiaries to receive property on the ward's death under that ward's existing estate plan but may incorporate tax planning or public benefits planning into the ward's existing estate plan, which may include leaving beneficial interests in trust rather than outright, and (ii) shall be subject to the provisions of Articles 17, 18, and 19 of this Chapter concerning gifts. (1987, c.

550, s. 1; 1989, c. 473, ss. 3, 13; 1995, c. 235, ss. 6, 8; 1999-270, s. 9; 2004-199, s. 15; 2007-106, s. 52; 2008-87, s. 1; 2013-91, s. 3(e).)

§ 35A-1252. Guardian's powers in administering minor ward's estate.

In the case of a minor ward, a general guardian or guardian of the estate has the power to perform in a reasonable and prudent manner every act that a reasonable and prudent person would perform incident to the collection, preservation, management, and use of the ward's estate to accomplish the desired result of administering the ward's estate legally and in the ward's best interest, including but not limited to the following specific powers:

(1)   To take possession, for the ward's use, of all the ward's estate, as defined in G.S. 35A-1202(5).

(2)   To receive assets due the ward from any source.

(3)   To maintain any appropriate action or proceeding to obtain support to which the ward is legally entitled, to recover possession of any of the ward's property, to determine the title thereto, or to recover damages for any injury done to any of the ward's property; also, to compromise, adjust, arbitrate, sue on or defend, abandon, or otherwise deal with and settle any other claims in favor of or against the ward.

(4)   To abandon or relinquish all rights in any property when, in the guardian's opinion, acting reasonably and in good faith, it is valueless, or is so encumbered or is otherwise in such condition that it is of no benefit or value to the ward or his estate.

(4a)   To renounce any interest in property as provided in Chapter 31B of the General Statutes, or as otherwise allowed by law.

(5)   To vote shares of stock or other securities in person or by general or limited proxy, and to pay sums chargeable or accruing against or on account of securities owned by the ward.

(6)   To insure the ward's assets against damage or loss, at the expense of the ward's estate.

(7) To pay taxes, assessments, and other expenses incident to the collection, care, administration, and protection of the ward's estate.

(8) To sell or exercise stock subscription or conversion rights; consent, directly or through a committee or other agent, to the reorganization, consolidation, merger, dissolution, or liquidation of a corporation or other business enterprise.

(9) To expend estate income on the ward's behalf and to petition the court for prior approval of expenditures from estate principal; provided, neither the existence of the estate nor the guardian's authority to make expenditures therefrom shall be construed as affecting the legal duty that a parent or other person may have to support and provide for the ward.

(10) To pay from the ward's estate necessary expenses of administering the ward's estate.

(11) To employ persons, including attorneys, auditors, investment advisors, appraisers, or agents to advise or assist him in the performance of his duties as guardian.

(12) To continue any business or venture or farming operation in which the ward was engaged, where such continuation is reasonably necessary or desirable to preserve the value, including goodwill, of the ward's interest in such business.

(13) To acquire and retain every kind of property and every kind of investment, including specifically, but without in any way limiting the generality of the foregoing bonds, debentures, and other corporate or governmental obligations; stocks, preferred or common; real estate mortgages; shares in building and loan associations or savings and loan associations; annual premium or single premium life, endowment, or annuity contracts; and securities of any management type investment company or investment trust registered under the Federal Investment Company Act of 1940, as from time to time amended.

(14) a. Without a court order to lease any of the ward's real estate for a term of not more than three years, or to sell, lease or exchange any of the ward's personal property including securities, provided that the aggregate value of all items of the ward's tangible personal property sold without court order shall not exceed five thousand dollars ($5,000) per accounting period. When any item

of the ward's tangible personal property has a value which when increased by the value of all other tangible personal property previously sold in the estate without a court order would exceed five thousand dollars ($5,000) in the current accounting period, a guardian may sell the item only as provided in subdivision (14)b.

b. A guardian who is required by subdivision (14)a to do so shall, and any other guardian who so desires may, by motion in the cause, request the court to issue him an order to lease any of the ward's real estate or to sell any item or items of the ward's personal property. Notice of the motion and of the date, time and place of a hearing thereon shall be served, as provided in G.S. 1A-1, Rule 5, Rules of Civil Procedure, upon all parties of record and upon such other persons as the clerk may direct, and the court may issue the order after hearing and upon such conditions as the court may require; provided that:

1. A sale, lease, or exchange under this subdivision may not be subject to Article 29A of Chapter 1 of the General Statutes unless the order so requires; and

2. The power granted in this subdivision shall not affect the power of the guardian to petition the court for prior approval of expenditures from estate principal under subdivision (9) of this section.

(15) To foreclose, as an incident to the collection of any bond, note or other obligation, any mortgage, deed of trust, or other lien securing such bond, note or other obligation, and to bid in the property at such foreclosure sale, or to acquire the property by deed from the mortgagor or obligor without foreclosure; and to retain the property so bid in or taken over without foreclosure.

(16) To borrow money for such periods of time and upon such terms and conditions as to rates, maturities, renewals, and security as the guardian shall deem advisable, including the power of a corporate guardian to borrow from its own banking department, for the purpose of paying debts, taxes, and other claims against the ward, and to mortgage, pledge, or otherwise encumber such portion of the ward's estate as may be required to secure such loan or loans; provided, in respect to the borrowing of money on the security of the ward's real property, Subchapter III of this Chapter is controlling.

(17) To execute and deliver all instruments that will accomplish or facilitate the exercise of the powers vested in the guardian. (1987, c. 550, s. 1; 1989, c. 473, s. 4; 1995, c. 235, s. 7; 2008-87, s. 2.)

§ 35A-1253. Specific duties of guardian of estate.

In addition to any other duties imposed by law or by order of the clerk, a general guardian or guardian of the estate shall have the following specific duties:

(1)   To take possession, for the ward's use, of all his estate.

(2)   To diligently endeavor to collect, by all lawful means, all bonds, notes, obligations, or moneys due his ward.

(3)   To pay income taxes, property taxes, or other taxes or assessments owed by the ward, out of the ward's estate, as required by law. If any guardian allows his ward's lands to be sold for nonpayment of taxes or assessments, he shall be liable to his ward for the full value thereof.

(4)   To observe the standard of judgment and care under the circumstances then prevailing that an ordinarily prudent person of discretion and intelligence, who is a fiduciary of the property of others, would observe as such fiduciary in acquiring, investing, reinvesting, exchanging, retaining, selling, and managing the ward's property. If the guardian has special skills or is named as guardian on the basis of representations of special skills or expertise, to use those skills.

(5)   To obey all lawful orders of the court pertaining to the guardianship and to comply with the accounting requirements of this Subchapter.

Nothing in this section shall be construed as broadening the powers granted in G.S. 35A-1251 or G.S. 35A-1252. (1987, c. 550, s. 1.)

§§ 35A-1254 through 35A-1259: Reserved for future codification purposes.

Article 10.

Returns and Accounting.

§ 35A-1260. Applicability.

This Article applies only to general guardians and guardians of the estate. (1987, c. 550, s. 1.)

§ 35A-1261. Inventory or account within three months.

Every guardian, within three months after his appointment, shall file with the clerk an inventory or account, upon oath, of the estate of his ward; but the clerk may extend such time not exceeding six months, for good cause shown. (1987, c. 550, s. 1; 1989, c. 473, s. 26.)

§ 35A-1262. Procedure to compel inventory or account.

(a)   In cases of default to file the inventory or account required by G.S. 35A-1261, the clerk must issue an order requiring the guardian to file the inventory or account within the time specified in the order, or to show cause why he should not be removed from office or held in civil contempt, or both. If after due service of the order, the guardian does not, within the time specified in the order, file such inventory or account, or obtain further time to file the same, the clerk may remove him from office, hold him in civil contempt as provided in Article 2 of Chapter 5A, or both.

(b)   The guardian shall be personally liable for the costs of any proceeding incident to his failure to file the inventory or account required by G.S. 35A-1261. Such costs shall be taxed against him by the clerk and may be collected by deduction from any commissions that may be found due the guardian upon final settlement of the estate. (1987, c. 550, s. 1; 1989, c. 473, s. 27.)

§ 35A-1263. Repealed by Session Laws 1989, c. 473, s. 28.

§ 35A-1263.1. Supplemental inventory.

Whenever any property not included in the original inventory report becomes known to the guardian or whenever the guardian learns that the valuation or description of any property or interest therein indicated in the original inventory is erroneous or misleading, he shall prepare and file with the clerk a supplementary inventory in the same manner as prescribed for the original inventory. The clerk shall record the supplemental inventory with the original inventory. A guardian who fails to file a supplementary inventory as required by this section shall be subject to the enforcement provisions of G.S. 35A-1262. (1989, c. 473, s. 29.)

§ 35A-1264. Annual accounts.

Every guardian shall, within 30 days after the expiration of one year from the date of his qualification or appointment, and annually, so long as any of the estate remains in his control, file in the office of the clerk an inventory and account, under oath, of the amount of property received by him, or invested by him, and the manner and nature of such investment, and his receipts and disbursements for the past year in the form of debit and credit. The guardian shall produce vouchers for all payments or verified proof for all payments in lieu of vouchers. The clerk may examine on oath such accounting party, or any other person, concerning the receipts, disbursements or any other matter relating to the estate; and having carefully revised and audited such account, if he approve the same, he must endorse his approval thereon, which shall be deemed prima facie evidence of correctness. (1987, c. 550, s. 1.)

§ 35A-1265. Procedure to compel accounting.

(a) If any guardian omits to account, as directed in G.S. 35A-1264, or renders an insufficient and unsatisfactory account, the clerk shall forthwith order such guardian to render a full and satisfactory account, as required by law, within 20 days after service of the order. Upon return of the order, duly served, if the guardian fails to appear or refuses to exhibit such account, the clerk may issue an attachment against him for contempt and commit him until he exhibits such account, and may likewise remove him from office. In all proceedings hereunder the defaulting guardian will be liable personally for the costs of the said proceedings, including the costs of service of all notices or writs incidental to, or thereby acquiring, and also including reasonable attorney fees and expenses incurred by a successor guardian or other person in bringing any such proceeding, or other proceedings deemed reasonable and necessary to discover or obtain possession of assets of the ward in the possession of the defaulting guardian or which the defaulting guardian should have discovered or which the defaulting guardian should have turned over to the successor guardian. The amount of the costs and attorney fees and expenses of such proceeding may be deducted from any commissions which may be found due said guardian on settlement of the estate.

(b) Where a corporation is guardian, the president, cashier, trust officer or the person or persons having charge of the particular estate for the corporation, or the person to whom the duty of making reports of said estate has been assigned by the officers or directors of the corporation, may be proceeded against and committed to jail as herein provided as if he or they were the guardian or guardians personally: Provided, it is found as a fact that the failure or omission to file such account or to obey the order of the court in reference thereto is willful on the part of the officer charged therewith: Provided further, the corporation itself may be fined and/or removed as such guardian for such failure or omission. (1987, c. 550, s. 1; 1989, c. 473, s. 16.)

§ 35A-1266. Final account and discharge of guardian.

Within 60 days after a guardianship is terminated under G.S. 35A-1295, the guardian shall file a final account for the period from the end of the period of his most recent annual account to the date of that event. If the clerk, after review of the guardian's account, approves the account, the clerk shall enter an order discharging the guardian from further liability. (1987, c. 550, s. 1; 1989, c. 473, s. 32.)

§ 35A-1267. Expenses and disbursements credited to guardian.

Every guardian may charge in his annual account all reasonable disbursements and expenses; and if it appear that he has really and bona fide disbursed more in one year than the profits of the ward's estate, for his education and maintenance, the guardian shall be allowed and paid for the same out of the profits of the estate in any other year; but such disbursements must, in all cases, be suitable to the degree and circumstances of the estate of the ward. (1987, c. 550, s. 1.)

§ 35A-1268. Guardian to exhibit investments and bank statements.

At the time the accounts required by this Article and other provisions of law are filed, the clerk shall require the guardian to exhibit to the court all investments and bank statements showing cash balance, and the clerk shall certify on the original account that an examination was made of all investments and the cash balance, and that the same are correctly stated in the account: Provided, such examination may be made by the clerk in the county in which such guardian resides or the county in which such securities are located and, when the guardian is a duly authorized bank or trust company, such examination may be made by the clerk in the county in which such bank or trust company has its principal office or in which such securities are located; the certificate of the clerk of such county shall be accepted by the clerk of any county in which such guardian is required to file an account; provided that banks organized under the laws of North Carolina or the acts of Congress, engaged in doing a trust and fiduciary business in this State, when acting as guardian or in other fiduciary capacity, shall be exempt from the requirements of this section, when a certificate executed by a trust examiner employed by a governmental unit, by a bank's internal auditors who are responsible only to the bank's board of directors or by an independent certified public accountant who is responsible only to the bank's board of directors is exhibited to the clerk and when said certificate shows that the securities have been examined within one year and that the securities were held at the time of the examination by the fiduciary or by a clearing corporation for the fiduciary and that the person making such certification has no reason to believe said securities are not still so held. Nothing herein contained shall be construed to abridge the inherent right of the clerk to require the production of securities, should he desire to do so. (1987, c. 550, s. 1.)

§ 35A-1269. Commissions.

The clerk shall allow commissions to the guardian for his time and trouble in the management of the ward's estate, in the same manner and under the same rules and restrictions as allowances are made to executors, administrators and collectors under the provisions of G.S. 28A-23-3 and G.S. 28A-23-4. (1987, c. 550, s. 1; 1989, c. 473, s. 21.)

Article 11.

Public Guardians.

§ 35A-1270. Appointment; term; oath.

There may be in every county a public guardian, to be appointed by the clerk for a term of eight years. The public guardian shall take and subscribe an oath or affirmation faithfully and honestly to discharge the duties imposed upon him; the oath or affirmation so taken and subscribed shall be filed in the office of the clerk. (1987, c. 550, s. 1.)

§ 35A-1271. Bond of public guardian; increasing bond.

The public guardian shall enter into bond with three or more sureties, approved by the clerk in the penal sum of six thousand dollars ($6,000), payable to the State of North Carolina, conditioned faithfully to perform the duties of his office and obey all lawful orders of the superior or other courts touching said guardianship of all wards, money or estate that may come into his hands. Whenever the aggregate value of the real and personal estate belonging to his several wards exceeds one-half the bond herein required the clerk shall require him to enlarge his bond in amount so as to cover at least double the aggregate amount under his control as guardian. (1987, c. 550, s. 1.)

§ 35A-1272. Powers, duties, liabilities, compensation.

The powers and duties of said public guardian shall be the same as other guardians, and he shall be subject to the same liabilities as other guardians under the existing laws, and shall receive the same compensation as other guardians. (1987, c. 550, s. 1.)

§ 35A-1273. When letters issue to public guardian.

The public guardian shall apply for and obtain letters of guardianship in the following cases:

(1) When a period of six months has elapsed from the discovery of any property belonging to any minor or incompetent person without guardian.

(2) When any person entitled to letters of guardianship shall request in writing the clerk to issue letters to the public guardian; but it is lawful and the duty of the clerk to revoke said letters of guardianship at any time after issuing the same upon application in writing by any person entitled to qualify as guardian, setting forth a sufficient cause for such revocation. (1987, c. 550, s. 1.)

§§ 35A-1274 through 35A-1279: Reserved for future codification purposes.

Article 12.

Nonresident Ward Having Property in State.

§ 35A-1280. Appointment of ancillary guardian.

(a) A clerk may appoint an ancillary guardian whenever it appears by petition or application and due proof to the satisfaction of the clerk that:

(1) There is in the county of the clerk's jurisdiction real or personal property in which a nonresident of the State of North Carolina has an ownership or other interest; and

(2) The nonresident is incompetent or is a minor and a guardian of the estate or general guardian, or a comparable fiduciary, has been appointed and is still serving for the nonresident in the state of his or her residence; and

(3) That the nonresident ward has no guardian in the State of North Carolina.

(b) Except as otherwise ordered by the clerk or provided herein, an ancillary guardian shall have all the powers, duties, and responsibilities with respect to the nonresident ward's estate in the State of North Carolina as guardians otherwise appointed have. An ancillary guardian shall annually make an accounting to the court in this State and remit to the guardian in the state of the ward's residence any net rents of the real estate or any proceeds of sale.

(c) A certified or exemplified copy of letters of appointment or other official record of a court of record appointing a guardian for a nonresident in the state of his residence shall be conclusive proof of the fact of the ward's minority or incompetence and of the appointment of the guardian in the state of the ward's residence; provided, that the letters of appointment or other record shall show that the guardianship is still in effect in the state of the ward's residence and that the ward's incompetence or minority still exists.

(d) Upon the appointment of an ancillary guardian under this Article, the clerk shall notify the appropriate court in the county of the ward's residence and the guardian in the state of the ward's residence. (1987, c. 550, s. 1.)

§ 35A-1281. Removal of ward's personalty from State.

(a) For purposes of this section, the term "personal estate" means:

(1) Personal property;

(2) Personal property substituted for realty by decree of court;

(3) Any money arising from the sale of real estate, whether the same be in the hands of any guardian residing in this State; or in the hands of any executor, administrator, or other person holding for the ward; or, if not being adversely held and claimed, not in the lawful possession or control of any person.

(b) Where any ward residing in another state or territory, or in the District of Columbia, or Canada, or other foreign country, is entitled to any personal estate in this State, the ward's guardian or trustee duly appointed at the place where such ward resides, or, in the event no guardian or trustee has been appointed, the court or officer of the court authorized by the laws of such place to receive moneys belonging to any ward when no guardian or trustee has been appointed, may apply to have such estate removed to the residence of the ward by petition filed before the clerk in the county in which the property or some portion thereof is situated. Such petition shall be proceeded with as in other cases of special proceedings.

(c)   The petitioner must show to the court a copy of his appointment as a guardian or trustee and bond duly authenticated, and must prove to the court that the bond is sufficient, in the ability of the sureties as well as in amount, to secure all the estate of the ward wherever situated: Provided, that in all cases where a banking institution, resident and doing business in a foreign state, is a guardian or trustee of any person and is not required to execute a bond to qualify as guardian or trustee under the laws of the state in which such guardian or trustee qualified and was appointed, and no sureties are or were required by the state in which said banking institution qualified as guardian or trustee, and this fact affirmatively appears to the court, then the personal estate of the ward may be removed from this State without the finding of a court with reference to any sureties, and the court in which the petition for the removal of the property of the ward is filed may order the transfer and removal of the property of the ward and the payment and delivery of the same to the nonresident guardian or trustee without regard to whether a nonresident guardian or trustee has filed a bond with sureties; and the finding of the court that the said guardian or trustee is a banking institution and has duly qualified and been appointed guardian or trustee under the laws of the state where the ward is resident shall be sufficient. Any person may be made a party defendant to the proceeding who may be made a party defendant in civil actions under the provisions of Chapter 1A of the General Statutes. (1987, c. 550, s. 1.)

§§ 35A-1282 through 35A-1289: Reserved for future codification purposes.

Article 13.

Removal or Resignation of Guardian; Successor Guardian; Estates Without Guardians; Termination of Guardianship.

§ 35A-1290. Removal by Clerk.

(a)   The clerk has the power and authority on information or complaint made to remove any guardian appointed under the provisions of this Subchapter, to appoint successor guardians, and to make rules or enter orders for the better management of estates and the better care and maintenance of wards and their dependents.

(b)   It is the clerk's duty to remove a guardian or to take other action sufficient to protect the ward's interests in the following cases:

(1)   The guardian wastes the ward's money or estate or converts it to his own use.

(2)   The guardian in any manner mismanages the ward's estate.

(3)   The guardian neglects to care for or maintain the ward or his dependents in a suitable manner.

(4)   The guardian or his sureties are likely to become insolvent or to become nonresidents of the State.

(5)   The original appointment was made on the basis of a false representation or a mistake.

(6)   The guardian has violated a fiduciary duty through default or misconduct.

(7)   The guardian has a private interest, whether direct or indirect, that might tend to hinder or be adverse to carrying out his duties as guardian.

(c)   It is the clerk's duty to remove a guardian or to take other action sufficient to protect the ward's interests in the following cases:

(1)   The guardian has been adjudged incompetent by a court of competent jurisdiction and has not been restored to competence.

(2)   The guardian has been convicted of a felony under the laws of the United States or of any state or territory of the United States or of the District of Columbia and his citizenship has not been restored.

(3) The guardian was originally unqualified for appointment and continues to be unqualified, or the guardian would no longer qualify for appointment as guardian due to a change in residence, a change in the charter of a corporate guardian, or any other reason.

(4) The guardian is the ward's spouse and has lost his rights as provided by Chapter 31A of the General Statutes.

(5) The guardian fails to post, renew, or increase a bond as required by law or by order of the court.

(6) The guardian refuses or fails without justification to obey any citation, notice, or process served on him in regard to the guardianship.

(7) The guardian fails to file required accountings with the clerk.

(8) The clerk finds the guardian unsuitable to continue serving as guardian for any reason.

(9) The guardian is a nonresident of the State and refuses or fails to obey any citation, notice, or process served on the guardian or the guardian's process agent. (1987, c. 550, s. 1; 2004-203, s. 31(b).)

§ 35A-1291. Emergency removal; interlocutory orders on revocation.

The clerk may remove a guardian without hearing if the clerk finds reasonable cause to believe that an emergency exists that threatens the physical well-being of the ward or constitutes a risk of substantial injury to the ward's estate. In all cases where the letters of a guardian are revoked, the clerk may, pending the resolution of any controversy in respect to such removal, make such interlocutory orders and decrees as the clerk finds necessary for the protection of the ward or the ward's estate or the other party seeking relief by such revocation. (1987, c. 550, s. 1; 2004-203, s. 31(c).)

§ 35A-1292. Resignation.

(a) Any guardian who wishes to resign shall file a motion with the clerk setting forth the circumstances of the case. If a general guardian or guardian of the estate, at the time of making the application, also exhibits his final account for settlement, and if the clerk is satisfied that the guardian has fully accounted, the clerk may accept the resignation of the guardian and discharge him and appoint a successor guardian. The guardian so discharged and his sureties are still liable in relation to all matters connected with the guardianship before the discharge and shall continue to ensure that the ward's needs are met until the clerk officially appoints a successor. The guardian shall attend the hearing to modify the guardianship, if physically able.

(b) A general guardian who wishes to resign as guardian of the estate of the ward but continue as guardian of the person of the ward may apply for the partial resignation by petition as provided in subsection (a) of this section. If the general guardian also exhibits his final account as guardian of the estate for settlement, and if the clerk is satisfied that the general guardian has fully accounted as guardian of the estate, the clerk may accept the resignation of the general guardian as guardian of the estate, discharge him as guardian of the estate, and issue to him letters of appointment as guardian of the person, but the general guardian so discharged as guardian of the estate and his sureties are still liable in relation to all matters connected with the guardianship of the estate before the discharge. (1987, c. 550, s. 1; 2012-151, s. 12(d).)

§ 35A-1293. Appointment of successor guardian.

Upon the removal, death, or resignation of a guardian, the clerk shall appoint a successor guardian following the same criteria that would apply to the initial appointment of a guardian. (1987, c. 550, s. 1.)

§ 35A-1294. Estates without guardians.

(a) Whenever a general guardian or guardian of the estate is removed, resigns, or stops serving without making a full and proper accounting, the successor guardian, or the clerk if there is no successor guardian, shall initiate a proceeding to compel an accounting. The surety or sureties on the previous guardian's bond shall be served with notice of the proceeding.

(b) If no successor guardian has been appointed, the clerk may act as receiver or appoint some discreet person as a receiver to take possession of the ward's estate, to collect all moneys due the ward, and to secure, lend, invest, or apply the same for the benefit and advantage of the ward, under the direction of the clerk until a successor guardian is appointed. The accounts of the receiver shall be returned, audited, and settled as the clerk may direct. The receiver shall be allowed such amounts for his time, trouble, and responsibility as seem to the clerk reasonable and proper. Such receivership may continue until a suitable guardian can be appointed.

(c) When another guardian is appointed, he may apply by motion, on notice, to the clerk for an order directing the receiver to pay over all the money, estate, and effects of the ward. If no such guardian is appointed, the ward shall have the same remedy against the receiver on becoming age 18 or otherwise emancipated if the ward is a minor or on being restored to competence if the ward is an incompetent person. In the event of the ward's death, his executor, administrator, or collector, and the heir or personal representative of the ward shall have the same remedy against the receiver. (1987, c. 550, s. 1.)

§ 35A-1295. Termination of guardianship.

(a) Every guardianship shall be terminated and all powers and duties of the guardian provided in Article 9 of this Chapter shall cease when the ward:

(1) Ceases to be a minor as defined in G.S. 35A-1202(12),

(2) Is adjudicated to be restored to competency pursuant to the provisions of G.S. 35A-1130, or

(3) Dies.

(b) Notwithstanding subsection (a), a guardian of the estate or a general guardian is responsible for all accountings required by Article 10 of this Chapter until the guardian is discharged by the clerk. (1989, c. 473, s. 31.)

§§ 35A-1296 through 35A-1300: Reserved for future codification purposes.

SUBCHAPTER III. MANAGEMENT OF WARD'S ESTATE.

Article 14.

Sale, Mortgage, Exchange or Lease of Ward's Estate.

§ 35A-1301. Special proceedings to sell, exchange, mortgage, or lease.

(a) Whenever used herein, the word "guardian" shall be construed to include general guardian, guardian of the estate, ancillary guardian, next friend, guardian ad litem, or commissioner of the court acting pursuant to this Article, but not a guardian who is guardian of the person only; and the word "mortgage" shall be construed to include deeds of trust.

(b) A guardian may apply to the clerk, by verified petition setting forth the facts, to sell, mortgage, exchange, or lease for a term of more than three years, any part of his ward's real estate, and such proceeding shall be conducted as in other cases of special proceedings. The clerk, in his discretion, may direct that the next of kin or presumptive heirs of the ward be made parties to such proceeding. The clerk may order a sale, mortgage, exchange, or lease to be made by the guardian in such way and on such terms as may be most advantageous to the interest of the ward, upon finding by satisfactory proof that:

(1) The ward's interest would be materially promoted by such sale, mortgage, exchange, or lease, or

(2) The ward's personal estate has been exhausted or is insufficient for his support and the ward is likely to become chargeable on the county, or

(3) A sale, mortgage, exchange, or lease of any part of the ward's real estate is necessary for his maintenance or for the discharge of debts unavoidably incurred for his maintenance, or

(4) Any part of the ward's real estate is required for public purposes, or

(5) There is a valid debt or demand against the estate of the ward; provided, when an order is entered under this subdivision, (i) it shall authorize

the sale of only so much of the real estate as may be sufficient to discharge such debt or demand, and (ii) the proceeds of sale shall be considered as assets in the hands of the guardian for the benefit of creditors, in like manner as assets in the hands of a personal representative, and the same proceedings may be had against the guardian with respect to such assets as might be taken against an executor, administrator or collector in similar cases.

The order shall specify particularly the property thus to be disposed of, with the terms of leasing or sale or exchange or mortgage, and shall be entered at length on the records of the court. The guardian may not mortgage the property of his ward for a term of years in excess of the term fixed by the court in its order.

(c) In the case of a ward who is a minor, no sale, mortgage, exchange, or lease under this Article shall be made until approved by the superior court judge, nor shall the same be valid, nor any conveyance of the title made, unless confirmed and directed by the judge, and the proceeds of the sale, mortgage, exchange, or lease shall be exclusively applied and secured to such purposes and on such trusts as the judge shall specify.

(d) All petitions filed under this section wherein an order is sought for the sale, mortgage, exchange, or lease of the ward's real estate shall be filed in the county in which all or any part of the real estate is situated.

(e) The procedure for a sale pursuant to this section shall be as provided by Article 29A of Chapter 1 of the General Statutes.

(f) Nothing herein contained shall be construed to divest the court of the power to order private sales as heretofore ordered in proper cases.

(g) On and after June 1, 1973, no sales of property belonging to minors or incompetent persons prior to that date by next friend, guardian ad litem, or commissioner of the court regular in all other respects shall be declared invalid nor shall any claim or defense be asserted on the grounds that said sale was not made by a duly appointed guardian as provided herein or on the grounds that said minor or incompetent person was not represented by a duly appointed guardian. (1987, c. 550, s. 1; 1989, c. 473, s. 6.)

§ 35A-1302. Procedure when real estate lies in county in which guardian does not reside.

In all cases where a guardian is appointed under the authority of Chapter 35A and such guardian applies to the court for an order to sell, mortgage, or exchange all or part of his ward's real estate, and such real estate is situated in a county other than the county in which the guardian is appointed and qualified, the guardian shall first apply to the clerk of the county in which he was appointed and qualified for an order showing that the sale, mortgage, or exchange of his ward's real estate is necessary or that the ward's interest would be materially promoted thereby. The clerk to whom such application is made shall hear and pass upon the same and enter his findings and order as to whether said sale, mortgage, or exchange is necessary or would materially promote the ward's interest, and said order and findings shall be certified to the clerk of the county in which the ward's land, or some part of it, is located and before whom any petition or application is filed for the sale, mortgage, or exchange of said land. Such findings and orders so certified shall be considered by the court along with all other evidence and circumstances in passing upon the petition in which an order is sought for the sale, mortgage, or exchange of said land. In the case of a ward who is a minor, before such findings and orders shall become effective the same shall be approved by the superior court judge holding the courts of the district or by the resident judge. (1987, c. 550, s. 1.)

§ 35A-1303. Fund from sale has character of estate sold and subject to same trusts.

Whenever, in consequence of any sale under G.S. 35A-1301, the real or personal property of the ward is saved from demands to which in the first instance it may be liable, the final decree shall declare and set apart a portion of the personal or real estate thus saved, of value equal to the real and personal estate sold, as property exchanged for that sold; and in all sales by guardians whereby real is substituted by personal, or personal by real property, the beneficial interest in the property acquired shall be enjoyed, alienated, or devised and shall descend and be distributed, as by law the property sold might and would have been had it not been sold, until it be reconverted from the character thus impressed upon it by some act of the owner and restored to its character proper. (1987, c. 550, s. 1; 2011-284, s. 38.)

§ 35A-1304: Repealed by Session Laws 1989, c. 473, s. 7.

§ 35A-1305. When timber may be sold.

In case the land cannot be rented for enough to pay the taxes and other dues thereof, and there is not money sufficient for that purpose, the guardian, with the consent of the clerk, may annually dispose of or use so much of the lightwood, and box or rent so many pine trees, or sell so much of the timber on the same, as may raise enough to pay the taxes and other duties thereon, and no more. In addition, the guardian, with the consent of the clerk, may annually dispose of, use, or sell so much of the timber as is necessary to maintain good forestry practices. (1987, c. 550, s. 1.)

§ 35A-1306. Abandoned incompetent spouse.

(a) A guardian of a married person found incompetent who has been abandoned, whether the guardian was appointed before or after the abandonment, may initiate a special proceeding before the clerk having jurisdiction over the ward requesting the issuance of an order authorizing the sale of the ward's separate real property without the joinder of the abandoning spouse.

(b) The ward's spouse shall be served with notice of the special proceeding in accordance with G.S. 1A-1, Rule 4.

(c) If the clerk finds:

(1) That the spouse of the ward has willfully and without just cause abandoned the ward for a period of more than one year; and

(2) That the spouse of the ward has knowledge of the guardianship, or that the guardian has made a reasonable attempt to notify the spouse of the guardianship; and

(3) That an order authorizing the sale of the separate real property of the ward is in the best interest of the ward;

the clerk may issue such an order thereby barring the abandoning spouse from all right, title and interest in any of the ward's separate real property sold pursuant to such an order. (1987, c. 550, s. 1.)

§ 35A-1307. Spouse of incompetent husband or wife entitled to special proceeding for sale of real property.

Every married person whose husband or wife is adjudged incompetent and is confined in a mental hospital or other institution in this State, and who was living with the incompetent spouse at the time of commitment shall, if he or she be in needy circumstances, have the right to bring a special proceeding before the clerk to sell the real property of the incompetent spouse, or so much thereof as is deemed expedient, and have the proceeds applied for support: Provided, that said proceeding shall be approved by the judge of the superior court holding the courts of the superior court district or set of districts as defined in G.S. 7A-41.1 where the said property is situated. When the deed of the commissioner appointed by the court, conveying the lands belonging to the incompetent spouse is executed, probated, and registered, it conveys a good and indefeasible title to the purchaser. (1987, c. 550, s. 1; 1987 (Reg. Sess., 1988), c. 1037, s. 83; 1989, c. 473, s. 8.)

§§ 35A-1308 through 35A-1309: Reserved for future codification purposes.

Article 15.

Mortgage or Sale of Estates Held by the Entireties.

§ 35A-1310. Where one spouse or both incompetent; special proceeding before clerk.

In all cases where a husband and wife shall be seized of property as an estate by the entireties, and the wife or the husband or both shall be or become mentally incompetent to execute a conveyance of the estate so held, and the interest of said parties shall make it necessary or desirable that such property be mortgaged or sold, it shall be lawful for the mentally competent spouse and/or the guardian of the mentally incompetent spouse, and/or the guardians of both (where both are mentally incompetent) to file a petition with the clerk of the superior court in the county where the lands are located, setting forth all facts relative to the status of the owners, and showing the necessity or desirability of the sale or mortgage of said property, and the clerk, after first finding as a fact that either the husband or wife, or both, are mentally incompetent, shall have power to authorize the interested parties and/or their guardians to execute a mortgage, deed of trust, deed, or other conveyance of such property, provided it shall appear to said clerk's satisfaction that same is necessary or to the best advantage of the parties, and not prejudicial to the interest of the mentally incompetent spouse. All petitions filed under the authority of this section shall be filed in the office of the clerk of the superior court of the county where the real estate or any part of same is situated. (1935, c. 59, s. 1; 1945, c. 426, s. 5; c. 1084, s. 5.; 1987, c. 550, s. 2.)

§ 35A-1311. General law applicable; approved by judge.

The proceedings herein provided for shall be conducted under and shall be governed by laws pertaining to special proceedings, and it shall be necessary for any sale or mortgage or other conveyance herein authorized to be approved by a superior court judge who has jurisdiction pursuant to G.S. 7A-47.1 or G.S. 7A-48 in the district or set of districts as defined in G.S. 7A-41.1 wherein the property or any part of same is located. (1935, c. 59, s. 2; 1945, c. 426, s. 6; 1987, c. 550, s. 2; 1987 (Reg. Sess., 1988), c. 1037, s. 84.)

§ 35A-1312. Proceeding valid in passing title.

Any mortgage, deed, or deed of trust executed under authority of this Article by a regularly conducted special proceeding as provided shall have the force and effect of passing title to said property to the same extent as a deed executed jointly by husband and wife, where both are mentally capable of executing a conveyance. (1935, c. 59, s. 3; 1987, c. 550, s. 2.)

§ 35A-1313. Clerk may direct application of funds; purchasers and mortgagees protected.

In all cases conducted under this Article it shall be competent for the court, in its discretion, to direct the application of funds arising from a sale or mortgage of such property in such manner as may appear necessary or expedient for the protection of the interest of the mentally incompetent spouse: Provided, however, this section shall not be construed as requiring a purchaser or any other party advancing money on the property to see to the proper application of such money, but such purchaser or other party shall acquire title unaffected by the provisions of this section. (1935, c. 59, s. 4; 1987, c. 550, s. 2.)

§ 35A-1314. Prior sales and mortgages validated.

Any and all special proceedings under which estates by the entireties have been sold or mortgaged prior to March 5, 1935, under circumstances contemplated in this Article are hereby in all respects ratified and confirmed, provided that such proceeding or proceedings are otherwise regular and conformable to law. (1935, c. 59, s. 5; 1987, c. 550, s. 2.)

§§ 35A-1315 through 35A-1319: Reserved for future codification purposes.

Article 16.

Surplus Income and Advancements.

§ 35A-1320: Repealed by Session Laws 1989, c. 473, s. 14.

§ 35A-1321. Advancement of surplus income to certain relatives.

When any incompetent person, of full age, and not having made a valid will, has children or grandchildren (such grandchildren being the issue of a deceased child), and is possessed of an estate, real or personal, whose annual income is more than sufficient abundantly and amply to support himself, and to support, maintain and educate the members of his family, with all the necessaries and suitable comforts of life, it is lawful for the clerk of the superior court for the county in which such person has his residence to order from time to time, and so often as may be judged expedient, that fit and proper advancements be made, out of the surplus of such income, to any such child, or grandchild, not being a member of his family and entitled to be supported, educated and maintained out of the estate of such person. Whenever any incompetent person of full age, not being married and not having issue, be possessed, or his guardian be possessed for him, of any estate, real or personal, or of an income which is more than sufficient amply to provide for such person, it shall be lawful for the clerk of the superior court for the county in which such person resided prior to incompetency to order from time to time, and so often as he may deem expedient, that fit and proper advancements be made, out of the surplus of such estate or income, to his or her parents, brothers and sisters, or grandparents to whose support, prior to his incompetency, he contributed in whole or in part. (R.C., c. 57, s. 9; Code, s. 1677; Rev., s. 1900; C.S., s. 2296; Ex. Sess. 1924, c. 93; 1971, c. 528, s. 32; 1977, c. 725, s. 5; 1987, c. 550, s. 3.)

§ 35A-1322. Advancement to adult child or grandchild.

When such incompetent person is possessed of a real or personal estate in excess of an amount more than sufficient to abundantly and amply support himself with all the necessaries and suitable comforts of life and has no minor children nor immediate family dependent upon him for support, education or maintenance, such advancements may be made out of such excess of the principal of his estate to such child or grandchild of age for the better promotion or advancement in life or in business of such child or grandchild: Provided, that the order for such advancement shall be approved by the resident or presiding judge of the district who shall find the facts in said order of approval. (1925, c. 136, s. 1; 1977, c. 725, s. 5; 1987, c. 550, s. 3.)

§ 35A-1323. For what purpose and to whom advanced.

Such advancements shall be ordered only for the better promotion in life of such as are of age, or married, and for the maintenance, support and education of such as are under the age of 21 years and unmarried; and in all cases the sums ordered shall be paid to such persons as, in the opinion of the clerk, will most effectually execute the purpose of the advancement. (R.C., c. 57, s. 10; Code, s. 1678; Rev., s. 1901; C.S., s. 2297; 1987, c. 550, s. 3.)

§ 35A-1324. Distributees to be parties to proceeding for advancements.

In every application for such advancements, the guardian of the incompetent person and all such other persons shall be parties as would at that time be entitled to a distributive share of his estate if he were then dead. (R.C., c. 57, s. 11; Code, s. 1679; Rev., s. 1902; C.S., s. 2298; 1977, c. 725, s. 5; 1987, c. 550, s. 3.)

§ 35A-1325. Advancements to be equal; accounted for on death.

The clerk, in ordering such advancements, shall, as far as practicable, so order the same as that, on the death of the incompetent person, his estate shall be distributed among his distributees in the same equal manner as if the advancements had been made by the person himself; and on his death every sum advanced to a child or grandchild shall be an advancement, and shall bear interest from the time it may be received. (R.C., c. 57, s. 12; Code, s. 1680; Rev., s. 1903; C.S., s. 2299; 1977, c. 725, s. 5; 1987, c. 550, s. 3.)

§ 35A-1326. Advancements to those most in need.

When the surplus aforesaid or advancement from the principal estate is not sufficient to make distribution among all the parties, the clerk may select and decree advancement to such of them as may most need the same, and may apportion the sum decreed in such amounts as are expedient and proper. (R.C., c. 57, s. 13; Code, s. 1681; Rev., s. 1904; C.S., s. 2300; 1925, c. 136, s. 2; 1987, c. 550, s. 3.)

§ 35A-1327. Advancements to be secured against waste.

It is the duty of the clerk to withhold advancements from such persons as will probably waste them, or so to secure the same, when they may have families, that it may be applied to their support and comfort; but any sum so advanced shall be regarded as an advancement to such persons. (R.C., c. 57, s. 14; Code, s. 1682; Rev., s. 1905; C.S., s. 2301; 1987, c. 550, s. 3.)

§ 35A-1328. Appeal; removal to superior court.

Any person made a party may appeal from any order of the clerk; or may, when the pleadings are finished, require that all further proceedings shall be had in the superior court. (R.C., c. 57, s. 15; Code, s. 1683; Rev., s. 1906; C.S., s. 2302; 1987, c. 550, s. 3.)

§ 35A-1329. Advancements only when incompetence permanent.

No such application shall be allowed under this Article but in cases of such permanent and continued incompetence as that the incompetent person shall be judged by the clerk to be incapable, notwithstanding any lucid intervals, to make advancements with prudence and discretion. (R.C., c. 57, s. 16; Code, s. 1684; Rev., s. 1907; C.S., s. 2303; 1987, c. 550, ss. 3, 3.1.)

§ 35A-1330. Orders suspended upon restoration of competence.

Upon such incompetent person's being restored to competence, every order made for advancements shall cease to be further executed, and his estate shall be discharged of the same. (R.C., c. 57, s. 17; Code, s. 1685; Rev., s. 1908; C.S., s. 2304; 1987, c. 550, ss. 3, 3.2.)

§§ 35A-1331 through 35A-1334: Reserved for future codification purposes.

Article 17.

Gifts from Income for Certain Purposes.

§ 35A-1335. Gifts authorized with approval of judge of superior court.

With the approval of the resident judge of the superior court of the district in which the guardian was appointed, upon a duly verified petition the guardian of a person judicially declared to be incompetent may, from the income of the incompetent, make gifts to the State of North Carolina, its agencies, counties or municipalities, or to the United States or its agencies or instrumentalities, or for religious, charitable, literary, scientific, historical, medical or educational purposes, or to individuals including the guardian. References in this Article to the "guardian" include any Trustee appointed by the court under prior law as fiduciary for the incompetent ward's estate. (1963, c. 111, s. 1; 1987, c. 550, s. 4; 1999-270, s. 1.)

§ 35A-1336. Prerequisites to approval by judge of gifts for governmental or charitable purposes.

The judge shall not approve gifts from income for governmental or charitable purposes unless it appears to the judge's satisfaction that all of the following apply:

(1)   After making the gifts and the payment of federal and State income taxes, the remaining income of the incompetent will be reasonable and adequate to provide for the support, maintenance, comfort and welfare of the incompetent and those legally entitled to support from the incompetent in order to maintain the incompetent and those dependents in the manner to which the incompetent and those dependents are accustomed and in keeping with their station in life.

(2)   Each donee is a donee to which a competent donor could make a gift, without limit as to amount, without incurring federal or State gift tax liability.

(3)   Each donee is a donee qualified to receive tax deductible gifts under federal and State income tax laws.

(4)   The aggregate of the gifts does not exceed the percentage of income fixed by federal law as the maximum deduction allowable for the gifts in

computing federal income tax liability. (1963, c. 111, s. 2; 1987, c. 550, s. 4; 1999-270, s. 2.)

§ 35A-1336.1. Prerequisites to approval by judge of gifts to individuals.

The judge shall not approve gifts from income to individuals unless it appears to the judge's satisfaction that both the following requirements are met:

(1)   After making the gifts and paying federal and State income taxes, the remaining income of the incompetent will be reasonable and adequate to provide for the support, maintenance, comfort, and welfare of the incompetent and those legally entitled to support from the incompetent in order to maintain the incompetent and those dependents in the manner to which the incompetent and those dependents are accustomed and in keeping with their station in life;

(2)   The judge determines that either:

a.   The incompetent, prior to being declared incompetent, executed a paper-writing with the formalities required by the laws of North Carolina for the execution of a valid will, including a paper-writing naming as beneficiary a revocable trust created by the incompetent, and each donee is entitled to one or more specific devises, or distributions of specific amounts of money, income, or property under the paper-writing or the revocable trust or both or is a residuary devisee or beneficiary designated in the paper-writing or revocable trust or both; or

b.   That so far as is known the incompetent has not, prior to being declared incompetent, executed a will which could be probated upon the death of the incompetent, and each donee is a person who would share in the incompetent's estate, if the incompetent died contemporaneously with the signing of the order of the approval of the gifts; or

c.   The donee is the spouse, parent, descendent of the incompetent, or descendant of the incompetent's parent, and the gift qualifies either for the federal annual gift tax exclusion under section 2503(b) of the Internal Revenue Code or is a qualified transfer for tuition or medical expenses under section 2503(e) of the Internal Revenue Code.

The judge may order that the gifts be made in cash or in specific assets and may order that the gifts be made outright, in trust, under the North Carolina Uniform Transfers to Minors Act, under the North Carolina Uniform Custodial Trust Act, or otherwise. The judge may also order that the gifts be treated as an advancement of some or all of the amount the donee would otherwise receive at the incompetent's death. (1999-270, s. 3; 2011-284, s. 39; 2013-91, s. 3(c).)

§ 35A-1337. Fact that incompetent had not previously made similar gifts.

The judge shall not withhold his approval merely because the incompetent, prior to becoming incompetent, had not made gifts to the same donees or other gifts similar in amount or type. (1963, c. 111, s. 3; 1987, c. 550, s. 4.)

§ 35A-1338. Validity of gift.

A gift made with the approval of the judge under the provisions of this Article shall be deemed a gift by the incompetent and shall be as valid in all respects as if made by a competent person. (1963, c. 111, s. 4; 1987, c. 550, s. 4.)

§ 35A-1339: Reserved for future codification purposes.

Article 18.

Gifts from Principal for Certain Purposes.

§ 35A-1340. Gifts authorized with approval of judge of superior court.

With the approval of the resident judge of the superior court of the district in which the guardian was appointed upon a duly verified petition, the guardian of a person judicially declared to be incompetent may, from the principal of the incompetent's estate, make gifts to the State of North Carolina, its agencies, counties or municipalities, or the United States or its agencies or instrumentalities, or for religious, charitable, literary, scientific, historical, medical or educational purposes, or to individuals including the guardian. The incompetent's estate shall consist of all assets owned by the incompetent, including nonprobate assets. For purposes of this Article, nonprobate assets are those which would not be distributable in accordance with the incompetent's valid probated will or the provisions of Chapter 29 at the incompetent's death. The incompetent's nonprobate estate would include nonprobate assets only. References in this Article to the "guardian" include any Trustee appointed by the court under prior law as fiduciary for the incompetent ward's estate. (1963, c. 112, s. 1; 1987, c. 550, s. 5; 1999-270, s. 4.)

§ 35A-1341. Prerequisites to approval by judge of gifts for governmental or charitable purposes.

The judge shall not approve any gifts from principal for governmental or charitable purposes unless it appears to the judge's satisfaction all of the following requirements are met:

(1) The making of the gifts will not leave the incompetent's remaining principal estate insufficient to provide reasonable and adequate income for the support, maintenance, comfort and welfare of the incompetent and those legally entitled to support from the incompetent in order to maintain the incompetent and these dependents in the manner to which the incompetent and those dependents are accustomed and in keeping with their station in life.

(2) Each donee is a donee to which a competent donor could make a gift, without limit as to amount, without incurring federal or State gift tax liability.

(3) Each donee is a donee qualified to receive tax deductible gifts under federal and State income tax laws.

(4) The making of the gifts will not jeopardize the rights of any creditor of the incompetent.

(5) It is improbable that the incompetent will recover competency during his or her lifetime.

(5a) Sufficient credible evidence is presented to the court that the proposed gift is of a nature which the incompetent would have approved prior to being declared incompetent.

(6) Either a. or b. applies:

a. All of the following apply:

1. The incompetent, prior to being declared incompetent, executed a paper-writing with the formalities required by the laws of North Carolina for the execution of a valid will, including a paper-writing naming as beneficiary a revocable trust created by the incompetent.

2. Specific devises, or nondiscretionary distributions of specific amounts of money, income or property included in the paper-writing or revocable trust or both, will not be jeopardized by making the gifts.

3. All residuary devisees and beneficiaries designated in the paper-writing or revocable trust or both, who would take under the paper-writing or revocable trust or both, if the incompetent died contemporaneously with the signing of the order of approval of the gifts and the paper-writing was probated as the incompetent's will and the spouse, if any, of the incompetent have been given at least 10 days' written notice that approval for the gifts will be sought and that objection may be filed with the clerk of superior court of the county in which the guardian was appointed, within the 10-day period.

b. Both of the following apply:

1. That so far as is known the incompetent has not prior to being declared incompetent, executed a will which could be probated upon the death of the incompetent; and

2. All persons who would share in the incompetent's intestate estate, if the incompetent died contemporaneously with the signing of the order of approval, have been given at least 10 days' written notice that approval for the gifts will be sought and that objection may be filed with the clerk of the superior court, of the county in which the guardian was appointed, within the 10-day period.

(7) If the gift for which approval is sought is of a nonprobate asset, all persons who would share in that nonprobate asset if the incompetent died contemporaneously with the signing of the order of approval have been given at

least 10 days' written notice that approval for the gifts will be sought and that objection may be filed with the clerk of superior court of the county in which the guardian was appointed within the 10-day period. This notice requirement shall be in addition to the notice requirements contained in G.S. 35A-1341(6)a.3. and (6)b.2. (1963, c. 112, s. 2; 1987, c. 550, s. 5; 1999-270, s. 5; 2011-284, s. 40.)

§ 35A-1341.1. Prerequisites to approval by judge of gifts to individuals.

The judge shall not approve gifts from principal to individuals unless it appears to the judge's satisfaction that all of the following requirements have been met:

(1) Making the gifts will not leave the incompetent's remaining principal estate insufficient to provide reasonable and adequate income for the support, maintenance, comfort, and welfare of the incompetent in order to maintain the incompetent and any dependents legally entitled to support from the incompetent in the manner to which the incompetent and those dependents are accustomed and in keeping with their station in life.

(2) The making of the gifts will not jeopardize the rights of any existing creditor of the incompetent.

(3) It is improbable that the incompetent will recover competency during his or her lifetime.

(4) The judge determines that either a., b., c., or d. applies.

a. All of the following apply:

1. The incompetent, prior to being declared incompetent, executed a paper-writing with the formalities required by the laws of North Carolina for the execution of a valid will, including a paper-writing naming as beneficiary a revocable trust created by the incompetent.

2. Each donee is entitled to one or more specific devises, or distributions of specific amounts of money, income, or property under either the paper-writing or revocable trust or both or is a residuary devisee or beneficiary designated in the paper-writing or revocable trust or both.

3. The making of the gifts will not jeopardize any specific devise, or distribution of specific amounts of money, income, or property.

b. That so far as is known the incompetent has not, prior to being declared incompetent, executed a will which could be probated upon the death of the incompetent, and each donee is a person who would share in the incompetent's intestate estate, if the incompetent died contemporaneously with the signing of the order of approval of the gifts.

c. The donee is a person who would share in the incompetent's nonprobate estate, if the incompetent died contemporaneously with the signing of the order of approval.

d. The donee is the spouse, parent, descendant of the incompetent, or descendant of the incompetent's parent, and the gift qualifies either for the federal annual gift tax exclusion under section 2503(b) of the Internal Revenue Code or is a qualified transfer for tuition or medical expenses under section 2503(e) of the Internal Revenue Code.

(5) If the incompetent, prior to being declared incompetent, executed a paper-writing with the formalities required by the laws of North Carolina for the execution of a valid will, including a paper-writing naming as beneficiary a revocable trust created by the incompetent; then all residuary devisees and beneficiaries designated in the paper-writing or revocable trust or both, who would take under the paper-writing or revocable trust or both if the incompetent died contemporaneously with the signing of the order of approval of the gifts and the paper-writing was probated as the incompetent's will, the spouse, if any, of the incompetent and all persons identified in G.S. 35A-1341.1(7) have been given at least 10 days' written notice that approval for the gifts will be sought and that objection may be filed with the clerk of superior court of the county in which the guardian was appointed, within the 10-day period.

(6) If so far as is known, the incompetent has not, prior to being declared incompetent, executed a will which could be probated upon the death of the incompetent, all persons who would share in the incompetent's estate, if the incompetent died contemporaneously with the signing of the order of approval, have been given at least 10 days' written notice that approval for the gifts will be sought and that objection may be filed with the clerk of the superior court of the county in which the guardian was appointed, within the 10-day period.

(7) If the gift for which approval is sought is of a nonprobate asset, all persons who would share in that nonprobate asset if the incompetent died contemporaneously with the signing of the order of approval have been given at least 10 days' written notice that approval for the gifts will be sought and that objection may be filed with the clerk of the superior court of the county in which the guardian was appointed within the 10-day period. This notice requirement shall be in addition to the notice requirements contained in G.S. 35A-1341.1(5) and (6) above.

The judge may order that the gifts be made in cash or in specific assets and may order that the gifts be made outright, in trust, under the North Carolina Uniform Transfers to Minors Act, under the North Carolina Uniform Custodial Trust Act, or otherwise. The judge may also order that the gifts be treated as an advancement of some or all of the amount the donee would otherwise receive at the incompetent's death. (1999-270, s. 6; 2011-284, s. 41; 2013-91, s. 3(d).)

§ 35A-1342. Who deemed specific and residuary devisees of incompetent under § 35A-1341.

For purposes of G.S. 35A-1341(6)a and G.S. 35A-1341.1(4) and (5), if the paper-writing provides for the residuary estate to be placed in trust for a term of years, or if the paper-writing names as beneficiary a revocable trust created by the incompetent, and the trust or trusts include dispositive provisions which provide that assets continue in trust for a term of years with stated amounts of income payable to designated beneficiaries during the term and stated amounts payable to designated beneficiaries upon termination of the trust or trusts, the designated beneficiaries shall be deemed to be specific devisees and beneficiaries and those taking the remaining income of the trust or trusts and, at the end of the term, the remaining principal shall be deemed to be residuary devisees and beneficiaries who would take under the paper-writing or revocable trust or both if the incompetent died contemporaneously with the signing of the order of approval of the gifts. In no case shall any prospective executor or trustee be considered either a specific or residuary devisee or beneficiary on the sole basis of prospective service as executor or trustee. (1963, c. 112, s. 3; 1987, c. 550, s. 5; 1999-270, s. 7; 2011-284, s. 42.)

§ 35A-1343. Notice to minors and incompetents under § 35A-1341 and § 35A-1341.1.

If any person, to whom notice must be given under the provisions of G.S. 35A-1341 and G.S. 35A-1341.1 is a minor or is incompetent, or is an unborn or unascertained beneficiary, then the notice shall be given to his duly appointed guardian or other duly appointed representative: Provided, that if a minor, incompetent, unborn, or unascertained beneficiary has no guardian or representative, then a guardian ad litem shall be appointed by the judge and the guardian ad litem shall be given the notice herein required. (1963, c. 112, s. 4; 1987, c. 550, s. 5; 1999-270, s. 8.)

§ 35A-1344. Objections to proposed gift; fact that incompetent had previously made similar gifts.

If any objection is filed by one to whom notice has been given under the terms of this Article, the clerk shall bring it to the attention of the judge, who shall hear the same, and determine the validity and materiality of such objection and make his order accordingly. If no such objection is filed, the judge shall include a finding to that effect in such order as he may make. The judge shall not withhold his approval merely because the incompetent, prior to becoming incompetent, had not made gifts to the same donees or other gifts similar in amount or type. (1963, c. 112, s. 5; 1987, c.550, s. 5.)

§ 35A-1345. Validity of gift.

A gift made with the approval of the judge under the provisions of this Article shall be deemed to be a gift made by the incompetent, and shall be as valid in all respects as if made by a competent person. (1963, c. 112, s. 6; 1987, c. 550, s. 5.)

§§ 35A-1346 through 35A-1349: Reserved for future codification purposes.

Article 19.

Declaring Revocable Trust Irrevocable and Making Gift of Incompetent's Life Interest Therein.

§ 35A-1350. Declaration and gift for certain purposes authorized with approval of judge of superior court.

When a person has created a revocable trust, reserving the income for life, and thereafter has been judicially declared to be incompetent, the guardian or trustee of such incompetent, with the approval of the resident judge of the superior court of the district in which he was appointed, upon a duly verified petition may declare the trust to be irrevocable and make a gift of the life interest of the incompetent to the State of North Carolina, its agencies, counties or municipalities, or to the United States or its agencies or instrumentalities, or for religious, charitable, literary, scientific, historical, medical or educational purposes. (1963, c. 113, s. 1; 1987, c. 550, s. 6.)

§ 35A-1351. Prerequisites to approval of gift.

The judge shall not approve the gift unless it appears to the judge's satisfaction that:

(1)   It is improbable that the incompetent will recover competency during his or her lifetime;

(2)   The estate of the incompetent, after making the gift and after payment of any gift taxes which may be incurred by reason of the declaration of irrevocability, will be sufficient to provide reasonable and adequate income for the support, maintenance, comfort and welfare of the incompetent and those legally entitled to support from the incompetent in order to maintain the incompetent and such dependents in the manner to which the incompetent and such dependents are accustomed and in keeping with their station in life (and in no event less than twice the average, for the five calendar years preceding the calendar year of such gift, of expenditures for the incompetent's support, maintenance, comfort and welfare);

(3) Each donee of any part of the life interest is a donee to which a competent donor could make a gift, without limit as to amount, without incurring federal or State gift tax liability;

(4) Each donee of any part of the life interest is a donee qualified to receive tax deductible gifts under federal and State income tax laws.

(5) Either:

a. 1. The incompetent, prior to being declared incompetent, executed a paper-writing, with the formalities required by the laws of North Carolina for the execution of a valid will;

2. Specific devises of specific amounts of money, income or property included in such paper-writing, will not be jeopardized by making such gifts;

3. All residuary devisees designated in such paper-writing, who would take under the paper-writing if the incompetent died contemporaneously with the signing of the order of approval of such gifts, and such paper-writing was probated as the incompetent's will and the spouse, if any, of such incompetent have been given at least 10 days' written notice that approval for such gifts will be sought and that objection may be filed with the clerk of superior court, of the county in which the guardian or trustee was appointed, within the 10-day period; or

b. 1. That so far as is known the incompetent has not prior to being declared incompetent, executed a will which could be probated upon the death of the incompetent; and

2. All persons who would share in the incompetent's estate, if the incompetent died contemporaneously with the signing of the order of approval, have been given at least 10 days' written notice that approval for such gifts will be sought and that objection may be filed with the clerk of the superior court, of the county in which the guardian or trustee was appointed, within the 10-day period. (1963, c. 113, s. 2; 1987, c. 550, s. 6; 2011-284, s. 43.)

§ 35A-1352. Who deemed specific and residuary devisees of incompetent under § 35A-1351.

For purposes of G.S. 35A-1351(5)a. of this Article, if such paper-writing provides for the residuary estate to be placed in trust for a term of years, with stated amounts of income payable to designated beneficiaries during the term and stated amounts payable to designated beneficiaries upon termination of the trust, such designated beneficiaries shall be deemed to be specific devisees and those taking the remaining income of the trust and, at the end of the term, the remaining principal shall be deemed to be residuary devisees who would take under the paper-writing if the incompetent died contemporaneously with the signing of the order of approval of such gifts. In no case shall any prospective executor or trustee be considered either a specific or residuary devisee. (1963, c. 113, s. 3; 1987, c. 550, s. 6; 2011-284, s. 44.)

§ 35A-1353. Notice to minors and incompetents under § 35A-1351.

If any person, to whom notice must be given under the provisions of G.S. 35A-1351(5) of this Article, is a minor or is incompetent, then the notice shall be given to his duly appointed guardian or other duly appointed representative: Provided, that if a minor or incompetent has no such guardian or representative, then a guardian ad litem shall be appointed by the judge and such guardian ad litem shall be given the notice herein required. (1963, c. 113, s. 4; 1987, c. 550, s. 6.)

§ 35A-1354. Objections to proposed declaration and gift; fact that incompetent had not previously made similar gifts.

If any objection is filed by one to whom notice has been given under the terms of this Article, the clerk shall bring it to the attention of the judge, who shall hear the same, and determine the validity and materiality of such objection and make his order accordingly. If no such objection is filed, the judge shall include a finding to that effect in such order as he may make. The judge shall not withhold his approval merely because the incompetent, prior to becoming incompetent, had not made gifts to the same donees or other gifts similar in amount or type. (1963, c. 113, s. 5; 1987, c. 550, s. 6.)

§ 35A-1355. Validity of declaration and gift.

Such declaration and gift, when made with the approval of the judge and under the provisions of this Article, shall be deemed to be the declaration and gift of the incompetent and shall be as valid in all respects as if made by a competent person. (1963, c. 113, s. 6; 1987, c. 550, s. 6.)

§§ 35A-1356 through 35A-1359: Reserved for future codification purposes.

Article 20.

Guardians' Deeds Validated When Seal Omitted.

§ 35A-1360. Deeds by guardians omitting seal, prior to January 1, 1944, validated.

All deeds executed prior to the first day of January, 1944, by any guardian, acting under authority obtained by him from the superior court as required by law, in which the guardian has omitted to affix his seal after his signature and/or has omitted to affix the seal after the signature of his ward shall be good and valid, and shall pass the title to the land which the guardian was authorized to convey: Provided, however, this section shall not apply to any pending litigation. (1947, c. 531; 1987, c. 550, s. 9.)

§ 35A-1361. Certain private sales validated.

All private sales of real and personal property made by a guardian under Article 4 of this Chapter before June 1, 1985, that, under G.S. 1-339.36, should have been conducted as public sales because an upset bid was submitted, are validated to the same extent as if the guardian had complied with the procedures for a public sale. (1985, c. 654, s. 1(2); 1987, c. 550, s. 9).

§§ 35A-1362 through 35A-1369. Reserved for future codification purposes.

SUBCHAPTER IV. STANDBY GUARDIANS FOR MINOR CHILDREN.

Article 21.

Standby Guardianship.

§ 35A-1370. Definitions.

For purposes of this Article:

(1)   "Alternate standby guardian" means a person identified in either a petition or designation to become the guardian of the person or, when appropriate, the general guardian of a minor child, pursuant to G.S. 35A-1373 or to G.S. 35A-1374, when the person identified as the standby guardian and the designator or petitioner has identified an alternate standby guardian.

(2)   "Attending physician" means the physician who has primary responsibility for the treatment and care of the parent or legal guardian. When more than one physician shares this responsibility, or when a physician is acting on the primary physician's behalf, any such physician may act as the attending physician pursuant to this section. When no physician has this responsibility, a physician who is familiar with the petitioner's medical condition may act as the attending physician pursuant to this Article.

(3)   "Debilitation" means a chronic and substantial inability, as a result of a physically debilitating illness, disease, or injury, to care for one's minor child.

(4)   "Designation" means a written document voluntarily executed by the designator pursuant to this Article.

(5)   "Designator" means a person who suffers from a progressive chronic illness or an irreversible fatal illness and who is the biological or adoptive parent, the guardian of the person, or the general guardian of a minor child. A designation under this Article may be made on behalf of a designator by the guardian of the person or the general guardian of the designator.

(6)   "Determination of debilitation" means a written determination made by the attending physician which contains the physician's opinion to a reasonable

degree of medical certainty regarding the nature, cause, extent, and probable duration of the debilitation of the petitioner or designator.

(7)   "Determination of incapacity" means a written determination made by the attending physician which contains the physician's opinion to a reasonable degree of medical certainty regarding the nature, cause, extent, and probable duration of the incapacity of the petitioner or designator.

(8)   "Incapacity" means a chronic and substantial inability, as a result of mental or organic impairment, to understand the nature and consequences of decisions concerning the care of one's minor child, and a consequent inability to make these decisions.

(9)   "Minor child" means an unemancipated child or children under the age of 18 years.

(10)   "Petitioner" means a person who suffers from a progressive chronic illness or an irreversible fatal illness and who is the biological parent, the adoptive parent, the guardian of the person, or the general guardian of a minor child. A proceeding under this Article may be initiated and pursued on behalf of a petitioner by the guardian of the person, the general guardian of the petitioner, or by a person appointed by the clerk of superior court pursuant to Rule 17 of the Rules of Civil Procedure as guardian ad litem for the purpose of initiating and pursuing a proceeding under this Article on behalf of a petitioner.

(11)   "Standby guardian" means a person appointed pursuant to G.S. 35A-1373 or designated pursuant to G.S. 35A-1374 to become the guardian of the person or, when appropriate, the general guardian of a minor child upon the death of a petitioner or designator, upon a determination of debilitation or incapacity of a petitioner or designator, or with the consent of a petitioner or designator.

(12)   "Triggering event" means an event stated in the designation executed or order entered under this Article which empowers the standby guardian, or the alternate standby guardian, if one is identified and the standby guardian is unwilling or unable to serve, to assume the duties of the office, which event may be the death of a petitioner or designator, incapacity of a petitioner or designator, debilitation of a petitioner or designator with the petitioner's or designator's consent, or the consent of the petitioner or designator, whichever occurs first. (1995, c. 313, s. 1.)

§ 35A-1371. Jurisdiction; limits.

Notwithstanding the provisions of Subchapter II of this Chapter, the clerk of superior court shall have original jurisdiction for the appointment of a standby guardian for a minor child under this Article. Provided that the clerk shall have no jurisdiction, no standby guardian may be appointed under this Article, and no designation may become effective under this Article when a district court has assumed jurisdiction over the minor child in an action under Chapter 50 of the General Statutes or in an abuse, neglect, or dependency proceeding under Subchapter I of Chapter 7B of the General Statutes, or when a court in another state has assumed such jurisdiction under a comparable statute. (1995, c. 313, s. 1; 1998-202, s. 13(g).)

§ 35A-1372. Standby guardianship; applicability.

This Article provides two methods for appointing a standby guardian: by petition pursuant to G.S. 35A-1373 or by designation pursuant to G.S. 35A-1374. If a standby guardian is unwilling or unable to serve as a standby guardian and the designator or petitioner has identified an alternate standby guardian, then the alternate standby guardian shall become the standby guardian, upon the same conditions as set forth in this Article. (1995, c. 313, s. 1.)

§ 35A-1373. Appointment by petition of standby guardian; petition, notice, hearing, order.

(a) A petitioner shall commence a proceeding under this Article for the appointment of a standby guardian of a minor child by filing a petition with the clerk of superior court of the county in which the minor child resides or is domiciled at the time of filing. A petition filed by a guardian of the person or a general guardian of the minor child who was appointed under this Chapter shall be treated as a motion in the cause in the original guardianship, but the provisions of this section shall otherwise apply.

(b) A petition for the judicial appointment of a standby guardian of a minor child shall:

(1) Identify the petitioner, the minor child, the person designated to be the standby guardian, and the person designated to be the alternate standby guardian, if any;

(2) State that the authority of the standby guardian is to become effective upon the death of the petitioner, upon the incapacity of the petitioner, upon the debilitation of the petitioner with the consent of the petitioner, or upon the petitioner's signing of a written consent stating that the standby guardian's authority is in effect, whichever occurs first;

(3) State that the petitioner suffers from a progressively chronic illness or an irreversible fatal illness, and the basis for such a statement, such as the date and source of a medical diagnosis, without requiring the identification of the illness in question;

(4) State whether there are any lawsuits, in this or any other jurisdiction, involving the minor child and, if so, identify the parties, the case numbers, and the states and counties where filed; and

(5) Be verified by the petitioner in front of a notary public or another person authorized to administer oaths.

(c) A copy of the petition and written notice of the time, date, and place set for a hearing shall be served upon any biological or adoptive parent of the minor child who is not a petitioner, and on any other person the clerk may direct, including the minor child. Service shall be made pursuant to Rule 4 of the Rules of Civil Procedure, unless the clerk directs otherwise. When service is made by the sheriff, the sheriff shall make such service without demanding his fees in advance. Parties may waive their right to notice of the hearing and the clerk may proceed to consider the petition upon determining that all necessary parties are before the court and agree to have the petition considered.

(d) If at or before the hearing any parent entitled to notice under subsection (c) of this section presents to the clerk a written claim for custody of the minor child, the clerk shall stay further proceedings under this Article pending the filing of a complaint for custody of the minor child under Chapter 50 of the General Statutes and, upon the filing of such a complaint, shall dismiss the petition. If no such complaint is filed within 30 days after the claim is presented, the clerk shall conduct a hearing and enter an order as provided for in this section.

(e) The petitioner's appearance at the hearing shall not be required if the petitioner is medically unable to appear, unless the clerk determines that the petitioner is able with reasonable accommodation to appear and that the interests of justice require that the petitioner be present at the hearing.

(f) At the hearing, the clerk shall receive evidence necessary to determine whether the requirements of this Article for the appointment of a standby guardian have been satisfied. If the clerk finds that the petitioner suffers from a progressive chronic illness or an irreversible fatal illness, that the best interests of the minor child will be promoted by the appointment of a standby guardian of the person or general guardian, and that the standby guardian and the alternate standby guardian, if any, are fit to serve as guardian of the person or general guardian of the minor child, the clerk shall enter an order appointing the standby guardian named in the petition as standby guardian of the person or standby general guardian of the minor child and shall issue letters of appointment to the standby guardian. The order may also appoint the alternate standby guardian named in the petition as the alternate standby guardian of the person or alternate general guardian of the minor child in the event that the person named as standby guardian is unwilling or unable to serve as standby guardian and shall provide that, upon a showing of that unwillingness or inability, letters of appointment will be issued to the alternate standby guardian.

(g) Letters of appointment issued pursuant to this section shall state that the authority of the standby guardian or alternate standby guardian of the person or the standby guardian or alternate standby general guardian is effective upon the receipt by the guardian of a determination of the death of the petitioner, upon receipt of a determination of the incapacity of the petitioner, upon receipt of a determination of the debilitation of the petitioner and the petitioner's consent, whichever occurs first, and shall also provide that the authority of the standby guardian may earlier become effective upon written consent of the petitioner pursuant to subsection (l) of this section.

(h) If at any time prior to the commencement of the authority of the standby guardian the clerk, upon motion of the petitioner or any person entitled to notice under subsection (c) of this section and after hearing, finds that the requirements of subsection (f) of this section are no longer satisfied, the clerk shall rescind the order.

(i) Where the order provides that the authority of the standby guardian is effective upon receipt of a determination of the death of the petitioner, the standby guardian's authority shall commence upon the standby guardian's receipt of proof of death of the petitioner such as a copy of a death certificate or a funeral home receipt. The standby guardian shall file the proof of death in the office of the clerk who entered the order within 90 days of the date of the petitioner's death or the standby guardian's authority may be rescinded by the clerk.

(j) Where the order provides that the authority of the standby guardian is effective upon receipt of a determination of the incapacity of the petitioner, the standby guardian's authority shall commence upon the standby guardian's receipt of a copy of the determination of incapacity made pursuant to G.S. 35A-1375. The standby guardian shall file a copy of the determination of incapacity in the office of the clerk who entered the order within 90 days of the date of the receipt of such determination, or the standby guardian's authority may be rescinded by the clerk.

(k) Where the order provides that the authority of the standby guardian is effective upon receipt of a determination of the debilitation of the petitioner, the standby guardian's authority shall commence upon the standby guardian's receipt of a copy of the determination of debilitation made pursuant to G.S. 35A-1375, as well as a written consent signed by the petitioner. The standby guardian shall file a copy of the determination of debilitation and the written consent in the office of the clerk who entered the order within 90 days of the date of the receipt of such determination, or the standby guardian's authority may be rescinded by the clerk.

(l) Notwithstanding subsections (i), (j), and (k) of this section, a standby guardian's authority shall commence upon the standby guardian's receipt of the petitioner's written consent to such commencement, signed by the petitioner in the presence of two witnesses who are at least 18 years of age, other than the standby guardian or the alternate standby guardian, who shall also sign the writing. Another person may sign the written consent on the petitioner's behalf and at the petitioner's direction if the petitioner is physically unable to do so, provided such consent is signed in the presence of the petitioner and the two witnesses. The standby guardian shall file the written consent in the office of the clerk who entered the order within 90 days of the date of such written consent, or the standby guardian's authority may be rescinded by the clerk.

(m) The petitioner may revoke a standby guardianship created under this section by executing a written revocation, filing it in the office of the clerk who entered the order, and promptly providing the standby guardian with a copy of the revocation.

(n)   A person appointed standby guardian pursuant to this section may at any time before the commencement of the person's authority renounce the appointment by executing a written renunciation and filing it with the clerk who entered the order and promptly providing the petitioner with a copy of the renunciation. Upon the filing of a renunciation, the clerk shall issue letters of appointment to the alternate standby guardian, if any. (1995, c. 313, s. 1.)

§ 35A-1374. Appointment by written designation; form.

(a)   A designator may designate a standby guardian by means of a written designation, signed by the designator in the presence of two witnesses at least 18 years of age, other than the standby guardian or alternate standby guardian, who shall also sign the writing. Another person may sign the written designation on the behalf of and at the direction of the designator if the designator is physically unable to do so, provided that the designation is signed in the presence of the designator and the two witnesses.

(b)   A designation of a standby guardian shall identify the designator, the minor child, the person designated to be the standby guardian, and the person designated to be the alternate standby guardian, if any, and shall indicate that the designator intends for the standby guardian or the alternate standby guardian to become the minor child's guardian in the event that the designator either:

(1)   Becomes incapacitated;

(2)   Becomes debilitated and consents to the commencement of the standby guardian's authority;

(3)   Dies prior to the commencement of a judicial proceeding to appoint a guardian of the person or general guardian of a minor child; or

(4)   Consents to the commencement of the standby guardian's authority.

(c)   The authority of the standby guardian under a designation shall commence upon the same conditions as set forth in G.S. 35A-1373(i) through (l).

(d) The standby guardian or, if the standby guardian is unable or unwilling to serve, the alternate standby guardian shall commence a proceeding under this Article to be appointed guardian of the person or general guardian of the minor child by filing a petition with the clerk of superior court of the county in which the minor child resides or is domiciled at the time of filing. The petition shall be filed after receipt of either:

(1) A copy of a determination of incapacity made pursuant to G.S. 35A-1375;

(2) A copy of a determination of debilitation made pursuant to G.S. 35A-1375 and a copy of the designator's written consent to such commencement;

(3) A copy of the designator's written consent to such commencement, made pursuant to G.S. 35A-1373(l); or

(4) Proof of death of the designator, such as a copy of a death certificate or a funeral home receipt.

(e) The standby guardian shall file a petition pursuant to subsection (d) of this section within 90 days of the date of the commencement of the standby guardian's authority under this section, or the standby guardian's authority shall lapse after the expiration of those 90 days, to recommence only upon filing of the petition.

(f) A petition filed pursuant to subsection (d) of this section shall:

(1) Append the written designation of such person as standby guardian; and

(2) Append a copy of either (i) the determination of incapacity of the designator; (ii) the determination of debilitation of the designator and the written consent of the designator; (iii) the designator's consent; or (iv) proof of death of the designator, such as a copy of a death certificate or a funeral home receipt; and

(3) If the petition is by a person designated as an alternate standby guardian, state that the person designated as the standby guardian is unwilling or unable to act as standby guardian, and the basis for that statement; and

(4) State whether there are any lawsuits, in this State or any other jurisdiction, involving the minor child and, if so, identify the parties, the case numbers, and the states and counties where filed; and

(5) Be verified by the standby guardian or alternate standby guardian in front of a notary public or another person authorized to administer oaths.

(g) A copy of the petition and written notice of the time, date, and place set for a hearing shall be served upon any biological or adoptive parent of the minor child who is not a designator, and on any other person the clerk may direct, including the minor child. Service shall be made pursuant to Rule 4 of the Rules of Civil Procedure, unless the clerk directs otherwise. When service is made by the sheriff, the sheriff shall make such service without demanding his fees in advance. Parties may waive their right to notice of the hearing and the clerk may proceed to consider the petition upon determining that all necessary parties are before the court and agree to have the petition considered.

(h) If at or before the hearing any parent entitled to notice under subsection (c) of this section presents to the clerk a written claim for custody of the minor child, the clerk shall stay further proceedings under this Article pending the filing of a complaint for custody of the minor child under Chapter 50 of the General Statutes and, upon the filing of such a complaint, shall dismiss the petition. If no such complaint is filed within 30 days after the claim is presented, the clerk shall conduct a hearing and enter an order as provided for in this section.

(i) At the hearing, the clerk shall receive evidence necessary to determine whether the requirements of this section have been satisfied. The clerk shall enter an order appointing the standby guardian or alternate standby guardian as guardian of the person or general guardian of the minor child if the clerk finds that:

(1) The person was duly designated as a standby guardian or alternate standby guardian;

(2) That (i) there has been a determination of incapacity; (ii) there has been a determination of debilitation and the designator has consented to the commencement of the standby guardian's authority; (iii) the designator has consented to that commencement; or (iv) the designator has died, such information coming from a document, such as a copy of a death certificate or a funeral home receipt;

(3) That the best interests of the minor child will be promoted by the appointment of the person designated as standby guardian or alternate standby guardian as guardian of the person or general guardian of the minor child;

(4) That the standby guardian or alternate standby guardian is fit to serve as guardian of the person or general guardian of the minor child; and

(5) That, if the petition is by a person designated as an alternate standby guardian, the person designated as standby guardian is unwilling or unable to serve as standby guardian.

(j) The designator may revoke a standby guardianship created under this section by:

(1) Notifying the standby guardian in writing of the intent to revoke the standby guardianship prior to the filing of the petition under this section; or

(2) Where the petition has already been filed, by executing a written revocation, filing it in the office of the clerk with whom the petition was filed, and promptly providing the standby guardian with a copy of the written revocation. (1995, c. 313, s. 1.)

§ 35A-1375. Determination of incapacity or debilitation.

(a) If requested by the petitioner, designator, or standby guardian, an attending physician shall make a determination regarding the incapacity or debilitation of the petitioner or designator for purposes of this Article.

(b) A determination of incapacity or debilitation shall:

(1) Be made by the attending physician to a reasonable degree of medical certainty;

(2) Be in writing; and

(3) Contain the attending physician's opinion regarding the cause and nature of the incapacity or debilitation, as well as its extent and probable duration.

(c) The attending physician shall provide a copy of the determination of incapacity or debilitation to the standby guardian, if the standby guardian's identity is known to the physician.

(d) The standby guardian shall ensure that the petitioner or designator is informed of the commencement of the standby guardian's authority as a result of a determination of incapacity or debilitation and of the possibility of a future suspension of the standby guardian's authority pursuant to G.S. 35A-1376. (1995, c. 313, s. 1.)

§ 35A-1376. Restoration of capacity or ability; suspension of guardianship.

In the event that the authority of the standby guardian becomes effective upon the receipt of a determination of incapacity or debilitation and the petitioner or designator is subsequently restored to capacity or ability to care for the child, the authority of the standby guardian based on that incapacity or debilitation shall be suspended. The attending physician shall provide a copy of the determination of restored capacity or ability to the standby guardian, if the identity of the standby guardian is known to the attending physician. If an order appointing the standby guardian as guardian of the person or general guardian of the minor child has been entered, the standby guardian shall, and the petitioner or designator may, file a copy of the determination of restored capacity or ability in the office of the clerk who entered the order. A determination of restored capacity or ability shall:

(1) Be made by the attending physician to a reasonable degree of medical certainty;

(2) Be in writing; and

(3) Contain the attending physician's opinion regarding the cause and nature of the parent's or legal guardian's restoration to capacity or ability.

Any order appointing the standby guardian as guardian of the person or general guardian of the minor child shall remain in full force and effect, and the authority of the standby guardian shall recommence upon the standby guardian's receipt of a subsequent determination of the petitioner's or designator's incapacity, pursuant to G.S. 35A-1373(j), or upon the standby guardian's receipt of a subsequent determination of debilitation pursuant to G.S. 35A-1373(k), or upon the receipt of proof of death of the petitioner or designator, or upon the written consent of the petitioner or designator, pursuant to G.S. 35A-1373(l). (1995, c. 313, s. 1.)

§ 35A-1377. Authority concurrent to parental rights.

The commencement of the standby guardian's authority pursuant to a determination of incapacity, determination of debilitation, or written consent shall not itself divest the petitioner or designator of any parental or guardianship rights, but shall confer upon the standby guardian concurrent authority with respect to the minor child. (1995, c. 313, s. 1.)

§ 35A-1378. Powers and duties.

A standby guardian designated pursuant to G.S. 35A-1374 and a guardian of the person or general guardian appointed pursuant to this Article have all of the powers, authority, duties, and responsibilities of a guardian appointed pursuant to Subchapter II of this Chapter. (1995, c. 313, s. 1.)

§ 35A-1379. Appointment of guardian ad litem.

(a) The clerk may appoint a volunteer guardian ad litem, if available, to represent the best interests of the minor child and, where appropriate, express the wishes of the minor child.

(b) The duties of the guardian ad litem, when appointed, shall be to make an investigation to determine the facts, the needs of the minor child and the available resources within the family to meet those needs, and to protect and promote the best interests of the minor child until formally relieved of the responsibility by the clerk.

(c) The court may order the guardian ad litem to conduct an investigation to determine the fitness of the intended standby guardian and alternate standby guardian, if any, to perform the duties of standby guardian. (1995, c. 313, s. 1.)

§ 35A-1380. Bond.

The bond requirements of Article 7 of this Chapter shall apply to a guardian of the person or general guardian appointed pursuant to G.S. 35A-1373 or G.S. 35A-1374, provided that: (i) the clerk need not require a bond if the bond requirement is waived in writing by the petitioner or designator; and (ii) a general guardian appointed pursuant to G.S. 35A-1373 shall not be required to furnish a bond until a triggering event has occurred. (1995, c. 313, s. 1.)

§ 35A-1381. Accounting.

The accounting requirements of Article 10 of this Chapter apply to a general guardian appointed pursuant to this Article. (1995, c. 313, s. 1.)

§ 35A-1382. Termination.

Any standby guardianship created under this Article shall continue until the child reaches 18 years of age unless sooner terminated by order of the clerk who entered the order appointing the standby guardian, by revocation pursuant to this Article, or by renunciation pursuant to this Article. A standby guardianship shall terminate, and the authority of the standby guardian designated pursuant to G.S. 35A-1374 or of a guardian of the person or general guardian appointed pursuant to this Article shall cease, upon the entry of an order of the district court granting custody of the minor child to any other person. (1995, c. 313, s. 1.)

Chapter 36.

Trusts and Trustees.

§§ 36-1 through 36-67: Repealed by Session Laws 1977, c. 502, s. 1.

Chapter 36A.

Trusts and Trustees.

Article 1.

Investment and Deposit of Trust Funds.

§§ 36A-1 through 36A-7: Recodified as §§ 32-70 through 32-76 by Session Laws 2005-192, s. 1, effective January 1, 2006.

§§ 36A-8 through 36A-12. Reserved for future codification purposes.

Article 2.

Removal of Fiduciary Funds.

§§ 36A-13 through 36A-16: Repealed by Session Laws 2005-192, s. 1, effective January 1, 2006.

§§ 36A-17 through 36A-21. Reserved for future codification purposes.

Article 3.

Trust Administration.

§ 36A-22: Repealed by Session Laws 2001-413, s. 1, effective January 1, 2002.

§ 36A-22.1: Repealed by Session Laws 2005-192, s. 1, effective January 1, 2006.

§ 36A-23: Repealed by Session Laws 2001-413, s. 1, effective January 1, 2002.

§ 36A-23.1: Repealed by Session Laws 2005-192, s. 1, effective January 1, 2006.

§ 36A-24: Repealed by Session Laws 2001-413, s. 1.

§ 36A-24.1: Repealed by Session Laws 2005-192, s. 1, effective January 1, 2006.

§ 36A-25: Repealed by Session Laws, 2001-413, s. 1.

§ 36A-25.1: Repealed by Session Laws 2005-192, s. 1, effective January 1, 2006.

§ 36A-26: Repealed by Session Laws 2001-413, s. 1.

§ 36A-26.1: Repealed by Session Laws 2005-192, s. 1, effective January 1, 2006.

§ 36A-26.2: Repealed by Session Laws 2005-192, s. 1, effective January 1, 2006.

§ 36A-26.3: Repealed by Session Laws 2005-192, s. 1, effective January 1, 2006.

§ 36A-27: Repealed by Session Laws 2005-192, s. 1, effective January 1, 2006.

§ 36A-28: Repealed by Session Laws 1999-216., s. 2.

§ 36A-29: Repealed by Session Laws 2005-192, s. 1, effective January 1, 2006.

§ 36A-30: Repealed by Session Laws 2001-413, s. 1.

§ 36A-31: Repealed by Session Laws 2005-192, s. 1, effective January 1, 2006.

§ 36A-32: Repealed by Session Laws 2005-192, s. 1, effective January 1, 2006.

§ 36A-33: Repealed by Session Laws 2005-192, s. 1, effective January 1, 2006.

§§ 36A-34 through 36A-35: Repealed by Session Laws 2001-413, s. 1, effective January 1, 2002.

§ 36A-36: Repealed by Session Laws 2005-192, s. 1, effective January 1, 2006.

§ 36A-37: Repealed by Session Laws 2005-192, s. 1, effective January 1, 2006.

§ 36A-38: Repealed by Session Laws 2001-413, s. 1.

§ 36A-39: Repealed by Session Laws 2005-192, s. 1, effective January 1, 2006.

§ 36A-40: Repealed by Session Laws 2005-192, s. 1, effective January 1, 2006.

§ 36A-41: Repealed by Session Laws 2001-413, s. 1.

§§ 36A-42 through 36A-46. Reserved for future codification purposes.

Article 4.

Charitable Trusts.

§§ 36A-47 through 36A-54: Repealed by Session Laws 2005-192, s. 1, effective January 1, 2006.

§§ 36A-55 through 36A-59. Reserved for future codification purposes.

Article 4A.

Charitable Remainder Trusts Administration Act.

§§ 36A-59.1 through 36A-59.7: Repealed by Session Laws 2005-192, s. 1, effective January 1, 2006.

§ 36A-59.8. Reserved for future codification purposes.

§ 36A-59.9. Reserved for future codification purposes.

Article 4B.

North Carolina Community Trust Act.

§§ 36A-59.10 through 36A-59.20: Repealed by Session Laws 2005-192, s. 1, effective January 1, 2006.

§ 36A-59.21: Repealed by Session Laws 1991 (Regular Session, 1992), c. 1044, s. 48(a).

Article 5.

Uniform Trusts Act.

§§ 36A-60 through 36A-62: Repealed by Session Laws 2005-192, s. 1, effective January 1, 2006.

§ 36A-63: Recodified as § 53-163.1 by Session Laws 2005-192, s. 1, effective January 1, 2006.

§§ 36A-64 through 36A-66: Repealed by Session Laws 2005-192, s. 1, effective January 1, 2006.

§ 36A-66.1: Recodified as § 53-163.2 by Session Laws 2005-192, s. 1, effective January 1, 2006.

§§ 36A-66.2 through 36A-84: Repealed by Session Laws 2005-192, s. 1, effective January 1, 2006.

§§ 36A-85 through 36A-89. Reserved for future codification purposes.

Article 6.

Uniform Common Trust Fund Act.

§§ 36A-90 through 36A-94: Recodified as §§ 53-163.5 through 53-163.9 by Session Laws 2005-192, s. 1, effective January 1, 2006.

§§ 36A-95 through 36A-99. Reserved for future codification purposes.

Article 7.

Trusts of Death Benefits.

§§ 36A-100, 36A-101: Repealed by Session Laws 2005-192, s. 1, effective January 1, 2006.

§§ 36A-102 through 36A-106. Reserved for future codification purposes.

Article 8.

Testamentary Trustees.

§§ 36A-107, 36A-108: Repealed by Session Laws 2005-192, s. 1, effective January 1, 2006.

§§ 36A-109 through 36A-114. Reserved for future codification purposes.

Article 9.

Alienability of Beneficial Interest; Spendthrift Trust.

§ 36A-115: Repealed by Session Laws 2005-192, s. 1, effective January 1, 2006.

§§ 36A-116 through 36A-119. Reserved for future codification purposes.

Article 10.

Trust Accounts in Financial Institutions.

§ 36A-120: Repealed by Session Laws 2005-192, s. 1, effective January 1, 2006.

§§ 36A-121 through 36A-124. Reserved for future codification purposes.

Article 11.

Termination of Small Trusts.

§ 36A-125: Repealed by Session Laws 1999-266, s. 1, effective January 1, 2000.

Article 11A.

Modification and Termination of Irrevocable Trusts.

§§ 36A-125.1 through 36A-125.12: Repealed by Session Laws 2005-192, s. 1, effective January 1, 2006.

§§ 36A-126 through 36A-129. Reserved for future codification purposes.

Article 12.

Marital Deduction Trusts.

§ 36A-130: Repealed by Session Laws 2005-192, s. 1, effective January 1, 2006.

§§ 36A-131 through 36A-134. Reserved for future codification purposes.

Article 13.

Powers of Trustees.

§§ 36A-135 through 36A-141: Repealed by Session Laws 2005-192, s. 1, effective January 1, 2006.

§§ 36A-142 through 36A-144. Reserved for future codification purposes.

Article 14.

Honorary Trusts; Trusts for Pets; Trusts for Cemetery Lots.

§§ 36A-145 through 36A-148: Repealed by Session Laws 2005-192, s. 1, effective January 1, 2006.

§§ 36A-149 through 36A-160. Reserved for future codification purposes.

Article 15.

North Carolina Uniform Prudent Investor Act.

§§ 36A-161 through 36A-173: Repealed by Session Laws 2005-192, s. 1, effective January 1, 2006.

§§ 36A-174 through 36A-178. Reserved for future codification purposes.

Chapter 36B.

Uniform Management of Institutional Funds Act.

§ 36B-1: Repealed by Session Laws 2009-8, s. 1, effective March 19, 2009.

§ 36B-2: Repealed by Session Laws 2009-8, s. 1, effective March 19, 2009.

§ 36B-3: Repealed by Session Laws 2009-8, s. 1, effective March 19, 2009.

§ 36B-4: Repealed by Session Laws 2009-8, s. 1, effective March 19, 2009.

§ 36B-5: Repealed by Session Laws 2009-8, s. 1, effective March 19, 2009.

§ 36B-6: Repealed by Session Laws 2009-8, s. 1, effective March 19, 2009.

§ 36B-7: Repealed by Session Laws 2009-8, s. 1, effective March 19, 2009.

§ 36B-8: Repealed by Session Laws 2009-8, s. 1, effective March 19, 2009.

§ 36B-9: Repealed by Session Laws 2009-8, s. 1, effective March 19, 2009.

§ 36B-10: Repealed by Session Laws 2009-8, s. 1, effective March 19, 2009.

Chapter 36C.

North Carolina Uniform Trust Code.

Article 1.

General Provisions and Definitions.

§ 36C-1-101. Short title.

This Chapter may be cited as the North Carolina Uniform Trust Code. (2005-192, s. 2.)

§ 36C-1-102. Scope.

This Chapter applies to any express trust, private or charitable, with additions to the trust, wherever and however created. The term "express trust" includes both testamentary and inter vivos trusts, regardless of whether the trustee is required to account to the clerk of superior court. This Chapter also applies to any trust created for or determined by judgment or decree under which the trust is to be administered in the manner of an express trust. This Chapter does not apply to constructive trusts, resulting trusts, conservatorships, estates, Payable on Death accounts as defined in G.S. 53C-6-7, 54-109.57, 54B-130, and 54C-166, trust funds subject to G.S. 90-210.61, custodial arrangements under Chapter 33A of the General Statutes and Chapter 33B of the General Statutes, business trusts providing for certificates to be issued to beneficiaries, common trust funds, voting trusts, security arrangements, liquidation trusts, and trusts for the primary purpose of paying debts, dividends, interest, salaries, wages, profits, pensions, or employee benefits of any kind, or any arrangement under which a person is nominee or escrowee for another. (2005-192, s. 2; 2012-56, s. 8.)

§ 36C-1-103. Definitions.

The following definitions apply in this Chapter:

(1)	Action. - When applicable to an act of a trustee, includes a failure to act.

(2)	Ascertainable standard. - A standard relating to an individual's health, education, support, or maintenance within the meaning of section 2041(b)(1)(A) or 2514(c)(1) of the Internal Revenue Code.

(3)	Beneficiary. - A person who:

a.	Has a present or future beneficial interest in a trust, vested or contingent, including the owner of an interest by assignment or transfer, but excluding a permissible appointee of a power of appointment; or

b.	In a capacity other than that of trustee, holds a power of appointment over trust property.

(4)	Charitable trust. - A trust, including a split-interest trust as described in section 4947 of the Internal Revenue Code, created for a charitable purpose described in G.S. 36C-4-405(a).

(5)	Environmental law. - A federal, state, or local law, rule, regulation, or ordinance relating to protection of the environment.

(6)	General guardian. - As defined in G.S. 35A-1202(7).

(7) Guardian of the estate. - As defined in G.S. 35A-1202(9).

(8) Guardian of the person. - As defined in G.S. 35A-1202(10).

(9) Interests of the beneficiaries. - The beneficial interests provided in the terms of the trust.

(10) Internal Revenue Code. - The Internal Revenue Code of 1986, as amended from time to time. Each reference to a provision of the Internal Revenue Code shall include any successor to that provision.

(11) Jurisdiction. - When applicable to a geographic area, includes a state or country.

(12) Person. - An individual, corporation, business trust, estate, trust, partnership, limited liability company, association, joint venture, government; governmental subdivision, agency, or instrumentality; public corporation, or any other legal or commercial entity.

(13) Power of withdrawal. - A presently exercisable general power of appointment other than a power:

a. Exercisable by a trustee and limited by an ascertainable standard; or

b. Exercisable by another person only upon consent of the trustee or a person holding an adverse interest.

(13a) Principal place of administration. - The trustee's usual place of business where the records pertaining to the trust are kept or the trustee's residence if the trustee has no usual place of business. In the case of cotrustees, the principal place of administration is one of the following:

a. The usual place of business of the corporate trustee if there is a corporate cotrustee.

b. The usual place of business or residence of any of the cotrustees if there is no corporate cotrustee.

(14) Property. - Anything that may be the subject of ownership, whether real or personal, legal or equitable, or any interest therein.

(15) Qualified beneficiary. - A living beneficiary to whom, on the date the beneficiary's qualification is determined, any of the following apply:

a. Is a distributee or permissible distributee of trust income or principal.

b. Would be a distributee or permissible distributee of trust income or principal if the interests of the distributees described in sub-subdivision a. of this subdivision terminated on that date without causing the trust to terminate.

c. Would be a distributee or permissible distributee of trust income or principal if the trust terminated on that date.

(16) Revocable. - When applicable to a trust, means revocable by the settlor without the consent of the trustee or a person holding an adverse interest.

(17) Settlor. - A person, including a testator, who creates, or contributes property to, a trust. If more than one person creates or contributes property to a trust, each person is a settlor of the portion of the trust property attributable to that person's contribution except to the extent another person has the power to revoke or withdraw that portion.

(18) Spendthrift provision. - A term of a trust that restrains both voluntary and involuntary transfer of a beneficiary's interest.

(19) State. - A state of the United States, the District of Columbia, Puerto Rico, the United States Virgin Islands, or any territory or insular possession subject to the jurisdiction of the United States. The term includes an Indian tribe or band recognized by federal law or formally acknowledged by a state.

(20) Terms of a trust. - The manifestation of the settlor's intent regarding a trust's provisions as expressed in the trust instrument or established in a judicial proceeding.

(21) Trust instrument. - An instrument executed by the settlor that contains terms of the trust, including any amendments to the instrument, and any modifications permitted by court order.

(22) Trustee. - Includes an original, additional, and successor trustee, and a cotrustee, whether or not appointed or confirmed by a court. The term does not include trustees in mortgages and deeds of trusts. (2001-413, s. 1; 2005-192, s. 2; 2007-106, s. 2; 2009-222, s. 1.)

§ 36C-1-104. Knowledge.

(a) Subject to subsection (b) of this section, a person has knowledge of a fact if the person:

(1) Has actual knowledge of it;

(2) Has received notice or notification of it; or

(3) From all the facts and circumstances known to the person at the time in question, has reason to know it.

(b) An organization that conducts activities through employees has notice or knowledge of a fact involving a trust only from the time the information was received by an employee having responsibility to act for the trust, or would have been brought to the employee's attention if the organization had exercised reasonable diligence. An organization exercises reasonable diligence if it maintains reasonable routines for communicating significant information to the employee having responsibility to act for the trust and there is reasonable compliance with the routines. Reasonable diligence does not require an employee of the organization to communicate information unless the communication is part of the employee's regular duties or the employee knows a matter involving the trust would be materially affected by the information. (2005-192, s. 2.)

§ 36C-1-105. Default and mandatory rules.

(a) Except as otherwise provided in the terms of the trust, this Chapter governs the duties and powers of a trustee, relations among trustees, and the rights and interests of a beneficiary.

(b) The terms of a trust prevail over any provision of this Chapter except:

(1) The requirements for creating a trust.

(2) The duty of a trustee to act in good faith and in accordance with the terms and purposes of the trust and the interests of the beneficiaries.

(3) The requirement that a trust and its terms be for the benefit of its beneficiaries, and that the trust have a purpose that is lawful, not contrary to public policy, and possible to achieve.

(4) The power of the court to modify or terminate a trust under G.S. 36C-4-410 through G.S. 36C-4-416.

(5) The effect of a spendthrift provision and the rights of certain creditors and assignees to reach a trust as provided in Article 5 of this Chapter.

(6) The effect of an exculpatory term under G.S. 36C-10-1008.

(7) The rights under G.S. 36C-10-1010 through G.S. 36C-10-1013 of a person other than a trustee or beneficiary.

(8) Periods of limitation for commencing a judicial proceeding.

(9) The power of the court to take any action and exercise any jurisdiction as may be necessary in the interests of justice.

(10) The subject-matter jurisdiction of the court and venue for commencing a proceeding as provided in G.S. 36C-2-203 and G.S. 36C-2-204.

(11) The requirement that the exercise of the powers described in G.S. 36C-6-602.1(a) shall not alter the designation of beneficiaries to receive property on the settlor's death under that settlor's existing estate plan.

(12) The power of a trustee to renounce an interest in or power over property under G.S. 36C-8-816(32). (2005-192, s. 2; 2007-106, s. 3; 2009-48, s. 15.)

§ 36C-1-106. Common law of trusts; principles of equity.

The common law of trusts and principles of equity supplement this Chapter, except to the extent modified by this Chapter or another statute of this State. (2005-192, s. 2.)

§ 36C-1-107. Governing law.

(a) The meaning and effect of the terms of a trust are determined by any of the following:

(1) The law of the jurisdiction designated in the terms unless the designation of that jurisdiction's law is contrary to a strong public policy of the jurisdiction having the most significant relationship to the matter at issue.

(2) In the absence of a controlling designation in the terms of the trust, the law of the jurisdiction having the most significant relationship to the matter at issue.

(b) Notwithstanding subsection (a) of this section, the rights of a person other than a trustee or beneficiary are governed by G.S. 36C-10-1010 through G.S. 36C-10-1013. (2005-192, s. 2; 2007-106, s. 4.)

§ 36C-1-108. Principal place of administration.

(a) Without precluding other means for establishing a sufficient connection with the designated jurisdiction, terms of a trust designating the principal place of administration are valid and controlling if:

(1) A trustee's principal place of business is located in, or a trustee is a resident of, the designated jurisdiction; or

(2) All or part of the administration occurs in the designated jurisdiction.

(b) Without precluding the right of the court to order, approve, or disapprove a transfer, the trustee may transfer the trust's principal place of administration to another jurisdiction in accordance with this subsection:

(1) If the trustee is transferring the trust's principal place of administration to another state, the trustee must provide written notice of the proposed transfer to the qualified beneficiaries of the trust not less than 60 days before initiating the transfer. If no qualified beneficiary notifies the trustee of an objection to the proposed transfer on or before the date specified in the notice, the trustee may

make the transfer. If a qualified beneficiary notifies the trustee of an objection to the proposed transfer on or before the date specified in the notice, the authority of the trustee to transfer the trust's principal place of administration in accordance with this section terminates.

(2) If the trustee is transferring the trust's principal place of administration to a jurisdiction outside of the United States, the trustee must provide written notice of the proposed transfer to the qualified beneficiaries of the trust, and the transfer cannot be made until the written consent of all the qualified beneficiaries is obtained.

(c) Anytime a trustee is required to provide a qualified beneficiary with written notice of a proposed transfer of a trust's principal place of administration, the notice of proposed transfer must include:

(1) The name of the jurisdiction to which the principal place of administration is to be transferred;

(2) The address and telephone number at the new location at which the trustee can be contacted;

(3) An explanation of the reasons for the proposed transfer;

(4) The date on which the proposed transfer is anticipated to occur; and

(5) If the proposed transfer is to another state, the date, not less than 60 days after the giving of the notice, by which the qualified beneficiary must notify the trustee of an objection to the proposed transfer.

(d) In connection with a transfer of the trust's principal place of administration, the trustee may transfer some or all of the trust property to a successor trustee designated in the terms of the trust or appointed under G.S. 36C-7-704. (2005-192, s. 2.)

§ 36C-1-109. Methods and waiver of notice.

(a) Subject to subsection (d) of this section, notice to a person under this Chapter or the sending of a document to a person under this Chapter must be accomplished in a manner reasonably suitable under the circumstances and likely to result in receipt of the notice or document.

(1)   Permissible methods of notice or methods for sending a document include first-class mail, personal delivery, delivery to the person's last known place of residence or place of business, or a properly directed electronic message.

(2)   Notice shall be deemed to be given upon the occurrence of any of the following:

  a.   When personally delivered by hand to the person.

  b.   When transmitted by facsimile.

  c.   When placed in the hands of a nationally recognized courier service for delivery.

  d.   When received by the person if sent by registered or certified United States mail, return receipt requested.

  e.   Three days after depositing the notice in a regularly maintained receptacle for the deposit of United States mail if sent by regular United States mail.

(3)   Notice by any means other than those described in subdivision (2) of this subsection shall be deemed to be given for all purposes upon the date of actual receipt.

(b)   Notice otherwise required under this Chapter, or a document otherwise required to be sent under this Chapter, need not be provided to a person whose identity or location is unknown to and not reasonably ascertainable by the trustee.

(c)   The person to be notified or to be sent a document may waive notice under this Chapter.

(d)   Notice of a judicial proceeding must be given as provided in Article 2 of this Chapter. (2005-192, s. 2; 2007-106, s. 5.)

§ 36C-1-110. Others treated as qualified beneficiaries.

(a)   A charitable organization expressly designated to receive distributions under the terms of a charitable trust has the rights of a qualified beneficiary under this Chapter if the charitable organization, on the date the charitable organization's qualification is being determined:

(1)   Is a distributee or permissible distributee of trust income or principal;

(2)   Would be a distributee or permissible distributee of trust income or principal upon the termination of the interest of other distributees or permissible distributees then receiving or eligible to receive distributions, but the termination of those interests would not cause the trust to terminate; or

(3)   Would be a distributee or permissible distributee of trust income or principal if the trust terminated on that date.

(b)   A person appointed to enforce a trust created for the care of an animal or another noncharitable purpose as provided in G.S. 36C-4-408 or G.S. 36C-4-409 has the rights of a qualified beneficiary under this Chapter. (2005-192, s. 2.)

§ 36C-1-111. Nonjudicial settlement agreements.

(a)   For purposes of this section, "interested persons" means persons whose consent would be required in order to achieve a binding settlement were the settlement to be approved by the court.

(b)   Interested persons may enter into a binding nonjudicial settlement agreement with respect to any of the following matters involving a trust:

(1)   The approval of a trustee's report or accounting;

(2)   Direction to a trustee to perform or refrain from performing a particular administrative act or the grant to a trustee of any necessary or desirable administrative power, including a power granted under G.S. 36C-8-816;

(3)   The resignation or appointment of a trustee and the determination of a trustee's compensation;

(4) Transfer of a trust's principal place of administration; and

(5) Liability of a trustee for any action taken under subdivisions (1) through (4) of this subsection.

(c) A nonjudicial settlement agreement is valid only to the extent it does not violate a material purpose of the trust and includes terms and conditions that could be properly approved by the court under this Chapter or other applicable law.

(d) Any interested person may request the court to approve a nonjudicial settlement agreement, to determine whether the representation as provided in Article 3 of this Chapter was adequate, and to determine whether the agreement contains terms and conditions the court could have properly approved. (2005-192, s. 2.)

§ 36C-1-112. Rules of construction.

The rules of construction that apply in this State to the interpretation of and disposition of property by will also apply as appropriate to the interpretation of the terms of a trust and the disposition of the trust property. (2005-192, s. 2.)

§ 36C-1-113. Construction of certain formula clauses applicable to estates of decedents dying in calendar year 2010.

(a) Purpose. - The federal estate tax and generation-skipping transfer tax expired January 1, 2010, for one year. To carry out the intent of decedents in the construction of wills and trusts and to promote judicial economy in the administration of trusts and estates, this section construes certain formula clauses that reference federal estate and generation-skipping transfer tax laws and that are used in trust instruments or amendments to trust instruments created by settlors who die in or before calendar year 2010.

(b) Applicability. - This section applies to the following:

(1) To a trust instrument or an amendment to a trust instrument executed by a settlor before December 31, 2009, that contains a formula provision described in subsection (c) of this section if the settlor dies after December 31, 2009, and before the earlier of January 1, 2011, and the effective date of the reinstatement of the federal estate tax and generation-skipping transfer tax, unless the instrument or amendment clearly manifests an intent that a rule contrary to the rule of construction described in subsection (c) of this section applies.

(2) To the terms of a trust instrument or an amendment to a trust instrument executed by a settlor who dies before December 31, 2009, providing for a disposition of property that contains a formula provision described in subsection (c) of this section and occurs as a result of the death of another individual who dies after December 31, 2009, and before the earlier of January 1, 2011, and the effective date of the reinstatement of the federal estate tax and generation-skipping transfer tax, unless the terms of the instrument or amendment clearly manifests an intent that a rule contrary to the rule of construction described in subsection (c) of this section applies.

(c) Construction. - A trust instrument or an amendment to a trust instrument subject to this section is considered to refer to the federal estate and generation-skipping transfer tax laws as they applied with respect to estates of decedents dying on December 31, 2009, if the trust instrument or the amendment to the trust instrument contains a formula that meets one or more of the following conditions:

(1) The formula refers to any of the following: "applicable credit amount," "applicable exclusion amount," "applicable exemption amount," "applicable fraction," "estate tax exemption," "generation-skipping transfer tax exemption," "GST exemption," "inclusion ratio," "marital deduction," "maximum marital deduction," "unified credit," or "unlimited marital deduction."

(2) The formula measures a share of a trust based on the amount that can pass free of federal estate taxes or the amount that can pass free of federal generation-skipping transfer taxes.

(3) The formula is otherwise based on a provision of federal estate tax or federal generation-skipping transfer tax law similar to the provisions in subdivision (1) or (2) of this subsection.

(d) Judicial Determination. - The trustee of the trust or an affected beneficiary under the trust may commence a proceeding to determine whether the settlor intended that the references under subsection (c) of this section be construed with respect to the federal law as it existed after December 31, 2009. The proceeding must be commenced within 12 months following the death of the settlor. (2010-126, s. 2.)

§ 36C-1-114. Insurable interest of trustee.

(a) As used in this section, the term "settlor" means a person that executes a trust instrument. The term includes a person for whom a fiduciary or agent is acting.

(b) A trustee of a trust has an insurable interest in the life of an individual insured under a life insurance policy that is trust property if, as of the date the policy is issued:

(1) The insured is either of the following:

a. A settlor of the trust.

b. An individual in whom a settlor of the trust has, or would have had if living at the time the policy was issued, an insurable interest.

(2) The life insurance proceeds are primarily for the benefit of one or more trust beneficiaries that have an insurable interest in the life of the insured.

(c) This section does not limit or abridge any insurable interest or right to insure now existing at common law or by statute and shall be construed liberally to sustain insurable interests, whether as a declaration of existing law or as an extension of or addition to existing law. (2013-91, s. 2(a).)

Article 2.

Judicial Proceedings.

§ 36C-2-201. Role of court in administration of trust.

(a) The court may intervene in the administration of a trust to the extent its jurisdiction is invoked by a party or as provided by law.

(b) A trust is not subject to continuing judicial supervision, except as provided in G.S. 36C-2-208 and G.S. 36C-2-209, unless ordered by the court.

(c) A judicial proceeding involving a trust may relate to any matter involving the trust's administration, including a request for instructions and an action to declare rights. (2005-192, s. 2.)

§ 36C-2-202. Jurisdiction over trustee and beneficiary.

(a) By accepting the trusteeship of a trust having its principal place of administration in this State, or by moving the principal place of administration to this State, the trustee submits personally to the jurisdiction of the courts of this State regarding any matter involving the trust.

(b) With respect to their interests in the trust, the beneficiaries of a trust having its principal place of administration in this State are subject to the jurisdiction of the courts of this State regarding any matter involving the trust. By accepting a distribution from such a trust, the recipient submits personally to the jurisdiction of the courts of this State regarding any matter involving the trust.

(c) This section does not preclude other methods of obtaining jurisdiction over a trustee, beneficiary, or other person receiving property from the trust. (2005-192, s. 2.)

§ 36C-2-203. Subject matter jurisdiction.

(a) The clerks of superior court of this State have original jurisdiction over all proceedings concerning the internal affairs of trusts. Except as provided in subdivision (9) of this subsection, the clerk of superior court's jurisdiction is exclusive. Proceedings concerning the internal affairs of the trust are those concerning the administration and distribution of trusts, the declaration of rights, and the determination of other matters involving trustees and trust beneficiaries, to the extent that those matters are not otherwise provided for in the governing instrument. These include proceedings:

(1) To appoint or remove a trustee, including the appointment and removal of a trustee pursuant to G.S. 36C-4-414(b).

(2) To approve the resignation of a trustee.

(3) To review trustees' fees under Article 6 of Chapter 32 of the General Statutes and review and settle interim or final accounts.

(4) To (i) convert an income trust to a total return unitrust, (ii) reconvert a total return unitrust to an income trust, or (iii) change the percentage used to calculate the unitrust amount or the method used to determine the fair market value of the trust as provided in G.S. 37A-1-104.3.

(5) To transfer a trust's principal place of administration.

(6) To require a trustee to provide bond and determine the amount of the bond, excuse a requirement of bond, reduce the amount of bond, release the surety, or permit the substitution of another bond with the same or different sureties.

(7) To make orders with respect to a trust for the care of animals as provided in G.S. 36C-4-408.

(8) To make orders with respect to a noncharitable trust without an ascertainable beneficiary as provided in G.S. 36C-4-409.

(9) To ascertain beneficiaries, to determine any question arising in the administration or distribution of any trust, including questions of construction of trust instruments, to create a trust, and to determine the existence or nonexistence of trusts created other than by will and the existence or nonexistence of any immunity, power, privilege, duty, or right. Any party may file a notice of transfer of a proceeding pursuant to this subdivision to the superior court division of the General Court of Justice as provided in G.S. 36C-2-205(g1). In the absence of a transfer to Superior Court, Article 26 of Chapter 1 of the General Statutes shall apply to a trust proceeding pending before the clerk of superior court to the extent consistent with this Article.

(b) Nothing in this section shall be construed (i) to confer upon the clerk of superior court any authority to regulate or supervise the actions of a trustee except to the extent that the trustee's actions are inconsistent with the governing instrument or of State law; or (ii) to confer upon any party any additional right, remedy, or cause of action not otherwise conferred by law.

(c) Nothing in this section affects the right of a person to file an action in the superior court division of the General Court of Justice for declaratory relief under Article 26 of Chapter 1 of the General Statutes.

(d) The clerk of superior court shall not, over the objection of a party, entertain proceedings under this section involving a trust having its principal place of administration in another state, except:

(1) When all appropriate parties could not be bound by litigation in the courts of the state in which the trust had its principal place of administration; or

(2) When the interests of justice otherwise would be seriously impaired.

The clerk of superior court may condition a stay or dismissal of a proceeding under this section on the consent of any party to jurisdiction of the state in which the trust has its principal place of administration, or the clerk of superior court may grant a continuance or enter any other appropriate order.

(e) Any party to a proceeding before the clerk of superior court may appeal from the decision of the clerk to a superior court judge as provided for estate matters in G.S. 1-301.3.

(f) Without otherwise limiting the jurisdiction of the superior court division of the General Court of Justice, proceedings concerning the internal affairs of trusts shall not include, and, therefore, the clerk of superior court shall not have jurisdiction under subsection (a) of this section of any of the following:

(1) Actions to reform, terminate, or modify a trust as provided by G.S. 36C-4-410 through G.S. 36C-4-416.

(2) Actions by or against creditors or debtors of a trust.

(3) Actions involving claims for monetary damages, including claims for breach of fiduciary duty, fraud, and negligence.

(4) Actions to enforce a charitable trust under G.S. 36C-4-405.1.

(5) Actions to amend or reform a charitable trust under G.S. 36C-4A-1.

(6) Actions involving the exercise of the trustee's special power to appoint to a second trust pursuant to G.S. 36C-8-816.1.

(7) Actions to construe a formula contained in a trust subject to G.S. 36C-1-113. (1911, c. 39, s. 4; C.S. s. 4027; 1977, c. 502, s. 2; 1999-216, s. 8; 2001-413, s. 1; 2005-192, s. 2; 2007-106, ss. 6, 7; 2009-267, s. 1; 2009-318, s. 2; 2010-126, s. 3.)

§ 36C-2-204. Venue.

In any trust proceeding, whether brought before the clerk of superior court or the superior court division of the General Court of Justice, the following rules apply notwithstanding any other applicable Rule of Civil Procedure or provision of Chapter 1 of the General Statutes:

(1) If the trustee is required to account to the clerk of superior court, then unless the terms of the governing instrument provide otherwise, venue for proceedings under G.S. 36C-2-203 involving trusts is the place where the accountings are filed.

(2) If the trustee is not required to account to the clerk of superior court, then unless the terms of the governing instrument provide otherwise, venue for proceedings under G.S. 36C-2-203 involving trusts is either of the following:

a. In the case of an inter vivos trust, in any county of this State in which the trust has its principal place of administration or where any beneficiary resides.

b. In the case of a testamentary trust, in any county of this State in which the trust has its principal place of administration, where any beneficiary resides, or in which the testator's estate was administered.

(3) Repealed by Session Laws 2007-106, s. 8, effective October 1, 2007.

(4) If a trust has no trustee, venue for a judicial proceeding for the appointment of a trustee is in any county of this State in which a beneficiary

resides, in any county in which trust property is located, in the county of this State specified in the trust instrument, if any county is so specified, or in the case of a testamentary trust, in the county in which the decedent's estate was or is being administered. (2001-413, s. 1; 2003-261, s. 2; 2005-192, s. 2; 2007-106, s. 8.)

§ 36C-2-205. Commencement of proceedings, pleadings, consolidation, and joinder.

(a) Contested Proceedings. - Trust proceedings before the clerk of superior court brought against adverse parties shall be commenced as is prescribed for civil actions. Upon the filing of the petition or complaint, the clerk of superior court shall docket the cause as an estate matter. All parties not joined as petitioners shall be joined as respondents. The clerk of superior court shall issue the summons for the respondents. The clerk of superior court may order that additional persons be joined as respondents and shall issue the summons for the additional persons. The summons shall notify the respondents to appear and answer the petition within 10 days after its service upon the respondents. The summons shall comply with the requirements set forth in G.S. 1-394 for a special proceeding summons except that the clerk of superior court shall indicate on the summons by appropriate words that the summons is issued in an estate matter and not in a special proceeding or in a civil action and shall be served upon the respondents in accordance with Rule 4 of the Rules of Civil Procedure. After the time for responding to the petition or complaint has expired, any party or the clerk of superior court may give notice to all parties of a hearing.

(b) Uncontested Proceedings. - Trust proceedings before the clerk of superior court in which all the parties join in the proceeding shall be commenced by the filing of a petition, setting forth the facts entitling the petitioners to relief and the nature of the relief demanded. In these proceedings, the clerk of superior court may hear and decide the petition summarily.

(c) Pleadings. - The petition or complaint filed in a trust proceeding before the clerk of superior court shall contain a short and plain statement of the claim which is sufficiently particular to give the court and the parties notice of the transactions, occurrences, or series of transactions, intended to be proved showing that the pleaders entitled to relief, and a demand for judgment for the relief to which the pleader is entitled. Each averment of a pleading should be simple, concise, and direct. No technical forms of pleadings or motions are required. A party may set forth two or more statements of a claim or defense alternatively or hypothetically. The signature of an attorney or party constitutes a certificate by that attorney or party that (i) the attorney or party has read the pleading, motion, or other paper; (ii) to the best of the attorney's or party's knowledge, information, and belief formed after reasonable inquiry, it is well grounded in fact and is warranted by existing law or a good faith argument for the extension, modification, or reversal of existing law; and (iii) it is not interposed for any improper purpose, such as to harass or to cause unnecessary delay or needless increase in the cost of litigation. All pleadings shall be so construed as to do substantial justice.

(d) Extensions of Time. - The clerk of superior court, for cause shown at any time in the clerk's discretion, with or without motion or notice, may enter an order enlarging the period of time within which an act is required or permitted by this Article, by any applicable Rules of Civil Procedure or by order of the court, if the request is made before the expiration of the period originally prescribed, but not to exceed 10 days, except to the extent that the court finds that justice requires that the time be enlarged for a period of greater than 10 days. Upon motion made after the expiration of the specified period, the clerk of superior court may permit the act where the failure to act was the result of excusable neglect. Notwithstanding any other provision of this subsection, the parties to a proceeding may enter into binding stipulations, without approval of the clerk of superior court, enlarging the time within which an act is required or permitted by this Article, by any applicable Rules of Civil Procedure or by order of the court, not to exceed 30 days.

(e) Rules of Civil Procedure. - Unless the clerk of superior court otherwise directs, G.S. 1A-1, Rules 4, 5, 6(a), 6(d), 6(e), 18, 19, 20, 21, 24, 45, 56, and 65 of the Rules of Civil Procedure shall apply to trust proceedings. Upon motion of a party or the clerk of superior court, the clerk may further direct that any or all of the remaining Rules of Civil Procedure, shall apply, including, without limitation, discovery rules; however, nothing in Rule 17 requires the appointment of a guardian ad litem for a party represented except as provided under G.S. 36C-2-206. In applying these Rules to a trust proceeding pending before the clerk of superior court, the term "judge" shall be construed as "clerk of superior court."

(f) Consolidation. - When a trust proceeding pending before the clerk of superior court and a civil action pending before the superior court division of the General Court of Justice involve a common question of law or fact, upon the court's motion or motion of a party to either the trust proceeding or the civil action, a superior court judge may order a consolidation of the trust proceeding and civil action, and the judge may make orders concerning proceedings therein as may tend to avoid unnecessary costs or delay. Upon the entry of an order consolidating a trust proceeding and civil action, the jurisdiction for all matters pending in both the trust proceeding and the civil action shall be vested in the superior court.

(g) Joinder. - In any civil action pending before a superior court division of the General Court of Justice, a party asserting a claim for relief as an original claim, counterclaim, cross-claim, or third-party claim, may join, either as independent or as alternate claims, as many claims, legal or equitable, as that party has against an opposing party notwithstanding the fact that the claims may otherwise be within the exclusive jurisdiction of the clerk of superior court.

(g1) Notice of Transfer. - A notice to transfer a trust proceeding brought pursuant to G.S. 36C-2-203(a)(9) must be served within 30 days after the moving party is served with a copy of the pleading requesting relief pursuant to G.S. 36C-2-203(a)(9). Failure to timely serve a notice of transfer of a trust proceeding is a waiver of any objection to the clerk of superior court's exercise of jurisdiction over the trust proceeding then pending before the clerk. When a notice of transfer is duly served and filed, the clerk shall transfer the proceeding to the appropriate court. The proceeding after the transfer is subject to the provisions of the General Statutes and to the rules that apply to actions initially filed in the court to which the proceeding was transferred.

(h) Orders Upon Consolidation/Joinder/Transfer. - Upon the consolidation of a trust proceeding and a civil action, joinder of claims under subsection (f) or (g) of this section, or transfer to the Superior Court Division of the General Court of Justice pursuant to subsection (g1) of this section, the clerk of superior court or the judge may make appropriate orders to protect the interests of the parties and to avoid unnecessary costs or delay. Notwithstanding the consolidation, joinder of claims under subsection (f) or (g) of this section, or transfer to the Superior Court Division of the General Court of Justice under subsection (g1) of this section, the clerk of superior court's exclusive jurisdiction as set forth in G.S. 36C-2-203(a)(1) through (8) shall not be stayed unless so ordered by the court.

(i) Notice to Attorney General. - In every trust proceeding with respect to a charitable trust, the Attorney General shall be notified and given an opportunity to be heard. (2005-192, s. 2; 2007-106, ss. 9, 9.1, 10; 2011-344, ss. 11, 12; 2012-18, s. 3.11.)

§ 36C-2-206. Representation of parties.

(a)   Notwithstanding any other applicable rule of the Rules of Civil Procedure or provision of Chapter 1 of the General Statutes, in any trust proceeding, whether brought before the clerk of superior court or in the superior court division of the General Court of Justice, the parties shall be represented as provided in Article 3 of this Chapter.

(b)   In the case of any party represented by another as provided in subsection (a) of this section, service of process shall be made by serving such representative. (2005-192, s. 2; 2006-259, s. 13(a).)

§ 36C-2-207. Waiver of notice.

A party, or the representative of the party as provided in G.S. 36C-2-206, may waive notice by a writing signed by the party, the representative, or the attorney of the party or the representative, and filed in the proceeding. (2001-413, s. 1; 2005-192, s. 2.)

§ 36C-2-208. Accounting to clerk.

(a)   No trustee, including a trustee appointed by the clerk of superior court, is required to account to the clerk of superior court unless the trust instrument directs that the trustee is required to account to the clerk of superior court or unless the trustee is otherwise required by law to account to the clerk of superior court.

(b)   If the trustee is required to account to the clerk of superior court, the trustee shall not be permitted to resign as trustee until a final account of the trust estate is filed with the clerk of superior court and until the court is satisfied that the account is true and correct, unless the terms of the trust instrument provide otherwise.

(c) Notwithstanding subsections (a) and (b) of this section, under a proceeding brought under G.S. 36C-4-405.1, the clerk of superior court may require a trustee of a charitable trust to account to the clerk of superior court. (1911, c. 39, s. 6; C.S., s. 4029; 1977, c. 502, s. 2; 2001-413, s. 1; 2003-261, s. 4; 2005-192, s. 2.)

§ 36C-2-209. Qualification and accounting of trustee of a testamentary trust.

(a) For any testamentary trust created under a will of a decedent executed before January 1, 2004, the trustee shall first qualify under the laws applicable to executors, and shall file in the office of the clerk of superior court of the county where the will is probated inventories of the assets that come into the trustee's hands and annual and final accounts of the trust that are the same as required of executors and administrators. The power of the clerk of superior court to enforce the filing and the clerk's duties to audit and approve the trustee's inventories and accounts is the same as the clerk's powers and duties with respect to the inventories and accounts of executors and administrators. This subsection shall not apply to the extent that the will makes a different provision.

(b) For any testamentary trust created under a will of a decedent executed on or after January 1, 2004, that directs the trustee to account to the clerk of superior court, the trustee shall first qualify under the laws applicable to executors and shall file in the office of the clerk of superior court of the county where the will is probated inventories of the assets that come into the trustee's hands and annual and final accounts of the trust that are the same as are required of executors and administrators. The power of the clerk of superior court to enforce the filing and the clerk's duties to audit and approve the trustee's inventories and accounts is the same as the clerk's powers and duties with respect to the inventories and accounts of executors and administrators. No trustee, including a trustee appointed by the clerk of superior court, is required to account to the clerk of superior court unless the will directs that the trustee is required to account to the clerk of superior court or unless otherwise required by law.

(c) The Administrative Office of the Courts may adopt rules regulating the registration or indexing of testamentary trusts. (1907, c. 804; C.S., s. 51; 1961, c. 519; 1965, c. 1176, s. 1; 1973, c. 1329, s. 4; 1977, c. 502, s. 2; 1985, c. 377, s. 1, 2; 2003-261, s. 7(j); 2005-192, s. 2.)

Article 3.

Representation.

§ 36C-3-301. Representation: basic effect.

(a) Notice to a person who may represent and bind another person under this Article has the same effect as if notice were given directly to the other person.

(b) The consent of a person who may represent and bind another person under this Article is binding on the person represented unless the person represented objects to the representation before the consent would otherwise have become effective.

(c) Except as otherwise provided in G.S. 36C-4-411 and G.S. 36C-6-602, a person who under this Article may represent a settlor who lacks capacity may receive notice and give a binding consent on the settlor's behalf.

(d) A settlor may not represent and bind a beneficiary under this Article with respect to the termination or modification of trust under G.S. 36C-4-411(a). (2005-192, s. 2.)

§ 36C-3-302. Representation by holder of power of revocation or general power of appointment.

The sole holder or all coholders of a power of revocation or a presently exercisable or testamentary general power of appointment, including one in the form of a power of amendment, shall represent and bind other persons to the extent that their interests, as takers in default, are subject to the power. (2005-192, s. 2; 2009-222, s. 2; 2010-96, s. 8.)

§ 36C-3-303. Representation by fiduciaries, parents, and other persons.

To the extent that there is no conflict of interest between the representative and the person represented or among those being represented with respect to a particular question or dispute involving a trust:

(1) A general guardian or a guardian of the estate may represent and bind the estate that the guardian controls.

(2) Repealed by Session Laws 2007-106, s. 11, effective October 1, 2007.

(3) An agent under a power of attorney having authority to act with respect to the particular question or dispute may represent and bind the principal.

(4) A trustee may represent and bind the beneficiaries of the trust unless the question or dispute involves the internal affairs of the trust.

(5) A personal representative of a decedent's estate may represent and bind persons interested in the estate.

(6) A parent may represent and bind the parent's minor child if a general guardian or guardian of the estate for the child has not been appointed. If a disagreement arises between parents seeking to represent the same minor child, the parent who is a beneficiary of the trust that is the subject of the representation is entitled to represent the minor child or, if no parent is a beneficiary of the trust that is the subject of the representation, a parent who is a lineal descendant of the settlor is entitled to represent the minor child, or if no parent is a lineal descendant of the settlor, a guardian ad litem shall be appointed to represent the minor child.

(7) A person may represent and bind that person's unborn issue. (2005-192, s. 2; 2007-106, s. 11.)

§ 36C-3-304. Representation by person having substantially identical interest.

Unless otherwise represented under this Article, a minor, an incompetent or unborn individual, or a person whose identity or location is unknown and not reasonably ascertainable, may be represented by and bound by another having a substantially identical interest with respect to the particular question or dispute, but only to the extent that there is no conflict of interest between the representative and the person represented with respect to the particular question or dispute. (2005-192, s. 2; 2007-106, s. 12.)

§ 36C-3-305. Appointment of representative; scope of representation.

(a) If the court determines that an interest is not represented under this Article, or that the otherwise available representation might be inadequate, the court may appoint a guardian ad litem to receive notice, give consent, and otherwise represent, bind, and act on behalf of a minor, an incompetent or unborn individual, or a person whose identity or location is unknown. A guardian ad litem may be appointed to represent several persons or interests.

(b) Any representative under this Article may act on behalf of the individual represented with respect to any matter arising under this Chapter, whether or not a judicial proceeding concerning the trust is pending.

(c) In making decisions, a representative, including a guardian ad litem, may base a decision to consent to an action upon a finding that living members of the individual's family would generally benefit from that action. (2005-192, s. 2; 2007-106, s. 13.)

Article 4.

Creation, Validity, Modification, and Termination of Trust.

§ 36C-4-401. Methods of creating trust.

A trust may be created by any of the following methods:

(1) Transfer of property by a settlor to a person as trustee during the settlor's lifetime or by will or other disposition taking effect upon the settlor's death including either of the following:

a. The devise to the trustee of the trust as provided in G.S. 31-47.

b. The designation of the trust as beneficiary of life insurance or other death benefits as provided in G.S. 36C-4-401.1.

(2) Declaration by the owner of property that the owner holds identifiable property as trustee unless the transfer of title of that property is otherwise required by law.

(3) Exercise of a power of appointment in favor of a trustee.

(4) A court by judgment, order, or decree, including the establishment of a trust pursuant to section 1396p(d)(4) of Title 42 of the United States Code. (2005-192, s. 2; 2007-106, s. 14; 2009-267, s. 2; 2011-284, s. 45.)

§ 36C-4-401.1. Interest of trustee as beneficiary of life insurance or other death benefit sufficient to support inter vivos or testamentary trust.

(a) The interest of a trustee as the beneficiary of a life insurance policy is a sufficient property interest or res to support the creation of an inter vivos or testamentary trust notwithstanding the fact that the insured or any other person or persons reserves or has the right to exercise any one or more of the following rights or powers:

(1) To change the beneficiary;

(2) To surrender the policy and receive the cash surrender value;

(3) To borrow from the insurance company issuing the policy or elsewhere using the policy as collateral security;

(4) To assign the policy; or

(5) To exercise any other right in connection with the policy commonly known as an incident of ownership of that policy.

The term "life insurance policy" includes life, annuity, and endowment contracts, or any variation or combination of those contracts, and any agreement entered into by an insurance company in connection with life, annuity, or endowments contracts.

(b) The interest of a trustee as the beneficiary of a death benefit under an employee benefit plan or group life insurance policy is a sufficient property interest or res to support the creation of an inter vivos or testamentary trust notwithstanding the fact that the insured, employer, insurer or administrator of the plan reserves or has the right to revoke or otherwise defeat the designation or assignment or to exercise any one or more of the rights or powers incident to employee benefit plans or group life insurance policies.

The term "employee benefit plan" includes pension, retirement, death benefit, deferred compensation, employment, agency, retirement annuity, stock bonus, profit-sharing or employees' savings contracts, plans, systems or trusts; and trusts, securities or accounts established or held under the federal Self-Employed Individuals Tax Retirement Act of 1962, the federal Employee Retirement Income Security Act of 1974, or similar legislation. The term "group life insurance policy" includes group life, industrial life, accident, and health insurance policies having death benefits.

(c) A testator having the right to designate the beneficiary under a life insurance policy, employee benefit plan, or group life insurance policy described in subsection (a) or (b) of this section may designate as that beneficiary a trustee named or to be named in the testator's will whether or not the will is in existence at the time of the designation. The proceeds received by the trustee shall be held and disposed of as part of the trust estate under the terms of the will as they exist at the death of the testator. If no trustee makes claim to the proceeds within six months after the death of the testator, payments shall be made to the personal representative of the estate of the testator unless it is otherwise provided by an alternative designation or by the policy or plan. The proceeds received by the trustee is not subject to claims against the estate of the testator to estate or inheritance taxes to any greater extent than if the proceeds were payable directly to the beneficiary or beneficiaries named in the trust. The proceeds may be commingled with any other assets that may properly become part of the trust, but the proceeds shall not become part of the testator's estate for purposes of trust administration unless the will expressly so provides. (1957, c. 1444, s. 1; 1977, c. 502, s. 2; 1999-337, s. 7(j); 2005-192, s. 2.)

§ 36C-4-401.2. Creation of trust by a court.

A court may create or establish a trust by judgment or decree, including a trust pursuant to section 1396p(d)(4) of Title 42 of the United States Code, upon petition of an interested party in accordance with the provisions of this Chapter or in any other matter properly before the court. (2009-267, s. 3; 2010-97, s. 5(a).)

§ 36C-4-402. Requirements for creation.

(a)   A trust is created only if:

(1)   The settlor has capacity to create a trust;

(2)   The settlor indicates an intention to create the trust;

(3)   The trust has a definite beneficiary or is:

a.   A charitable trust;

b.   A trust for the care of an animal, as provided in G.S. 36C-4-408; or

c.   A trust for a noncharitable purpose, as provided in G.S. 36C-4-409;

(4)   The trustee has duties to perform; and

(5)   The same person is not the sole trustee and sole beneficiary.

(b)   A beneficiary is definite if the beneficiary can be ascertained now or in the future, subject to any applicable rule against perpetuities.

(c)   A power in a trustee to select a beneficiary from an indefinite class is valid. If the power is not exercised within a reasonable time, the power fails, and the property subject to the power passes to the persons who would have taken the property had the power not been conferred. (2005-192, s. 2.)

§ 36C-4-403. Trusts created in other jurisdictions.

A trust not created by will is validly created if its creation complies with the law of the jurisdiction in which the trust instrument was executed, or the law of the jurisdiction in which, at the time of creation:

(1) The settlor was domiciled, had a place of abode, or was a national;

(2) A trustee was domiciled or had a place of business; or

(3) Any trust property was located. (2005-192, s. 2.)

§ 36C-4-404. Trust purposes.

A trust may be created only to the extent that its purposes are lawful, not contrary to public policy, and possible to achieve. A trust and its terms must be for the benefit of its beneficiaries. (2005-192, s. 2.)

§ 36C-4-405. Charitable purposes.

(a) A charitable trust may be created for the relief of poverty, the advancement of education or religion, the promotion of health, scientific, benevolent, literary, governmental, or municipal purposes, or other purposes the achievement of which is beneficial to the community.

(b) It is the policy of the State that a gift for charitable purposes, whether in trust or otherwise, is valid, notwithstanding the fact that the gift is made in general terms, and this section shall be construed liberally to effect this policy.

(c) No gift for charitable purposes, whether in trust or otherwise, is void or invalid because:

(1) The gift is in general terms or is uncertain as to the specific charitable purposes;

(2) When the gift is made in trust, the trustee is granted discretionary powers in the selection and designation of the beneficiaries of that charitable trust or in carrying out the purpose of that trust;

(3) The trustee or other recipient of the gift is given no specific instructions, powers, or duties as to the manner or means of carrying out those charitable purposes; or

(4) The gift contravenes any statute or rule against perpetuities.

(d) When any gift is made in general terms, the trustee or other recipient of the gift may:

(1) Select from time to time one or more specific charitable beneficiaries or purposes for which any trust or property or income is held and administered; and

(2) Determine the means to accomplish those charitable purposes, unless otherwise provided, including the creation of corporations or other legal entities for those purposes.

(e) For purposes of this section, the reference to a "gift" includes both inter vivos and testamentary gifts, grants, and other transfers. (2005-192, s. 2.)

§ 36C-4-405.1. Enforcement of charitable gift or trust.

(a) The settlor of a charitable trust, the Attorney General, the district attorney, a beneficiary, or any other interested party may maintain a proceeding to enforce a charitable trust, including the following:

(1) A proceeding to require a trustee to make a selection as may be necessary to establish the charitable beneficiaries or purposes for which the trust was established, as provided in subdivisions (d)(1) and (d)(2) of G.S. 36C-4-405;

(2) A proceeding for breach of fiduciary duty if there is reason to believe that the trust property has been mismanaged through negligence or fraud; and

(3) A proceeding for an accounting of the trustee's administration of the trust.

(b) The donor of a charitable gift, the Attorney General, the district attorney, or any other interested party may maintain a proceeding to enforce the gift, including a proceeding to require the recipient of the gift to make a selection as may be necessary to establish the charitable beneficiaries or purposes for which the gift was intended, as provided in subdivisions (d)(1) and (d)(2) of G.S. 36C-4-405. (2005-192, s. 2.)

§ 36C-4-405.2. Spending rules applicable to charitable trusts.

Subject to the intent of a settlor specifically expressed in a trust instrument, including a document making a gift to a charitable trust after it is established, a trustee of a charitable trust may appropriate for expenditure or accumulate so much of the trust property as the trustee determines is prudent for the uses, benefits, purposes, and duration for which that charitable trust is established. In making a determination to appropriate or accumulate trust property, a trustee shall act in good faith, with the care that an ordinarily prudent person in a like position would exercise under similar circumstances, and shall consider, if relevant, the following factors:

(1) The duration and preservation of the trust;

(2) The purposes of the trust;

(3) General economic conditions;

(4) The possible effect of inflation or deflation;

(5) The expected total return from income and the appreciation of investments;

(6) Other resources of the trust; and

(7) The investment policy of the trust. (2009-8, s. 3.)

§ 36C-4-406. Creation of trust induced by fraud, duress, or undue influence.

A trust is voidable to the extent that its creation was induced by fraud, duress, or undue influence. (2005-192, s. 2.)

§ 36C-4-407. Evidence of oral trust.

Except as required by a State statute other than this Chapter, a trust need not be evidenced by a trust instrument, but the creation of an oral trust, and its terms may be established only by clear and convincing evidence. (2005-192, s. 2.)

§ 36C-4-408. Trust for care of animal.

(a) Subject to this section, a trust for the care of one or more designated domestic or pet animals alive at the time of creation of the trust is valid.

(b) Except as expressly provided otherwise in the trust instrument, no portion of the principal or income may be converted to the use of the trustee or to any use other than for the benefit of the designated animal or animals.

(c) The trust terminates at the death of the animal or last surviving animal. Upon termination, the trustee shall transfer the unexpended trust property in the following order:

(1) As directed in the trust instrument.

(2) If the trust was created in a preresiduary clause in the settlor's will or in a codicil to the settlor's will, under the residuary clause in the settlor's will.

(3) If no taker is produced by the application of subdivision (1) or (2) of this subsection, to the settlor, if then living, otherwise to the settlor's heirs determined as of the date of the settlor's death under Chapter 29 of the General Statutes.

(d) The intended use of the principal or income can be enforced by a person designated for that purpose in the trust instrument or, if none, by a person appointed by the clerk of superior court having jurisdiction over the trust upon application to the clerk of superior court by a person.

(e) Except as ordered by the clerk of superior court or required by the trust instrument, no filing, report, registration, periodic accounting, separate maintenance of funds, appointment, bond, or fee is required by reason of the existence of the fiduciary relationship of the trustee.

(f) A governing instrument shall be liberally construed to bring the transfer within this section, to presume against the merely precatory or honorary nature of the disposition, and to carry out the general intent of the settlor. Extrinsic evidence is admissible in determining the settlor's intent.

(g) The clerk of superior court may reduce the amount of the property transferred, if the clerk of superior court determines that the amount substantially exceeds the amount required for the intended use. The amount of the reduction, if any, passes as unexpended trust property under subsection (c) of this section.

(h) If no trustee is designated or if no designated trustee agrees to serve or is able to serve, the clerk of superior court must name a trustee. The clerk of superior court may order the transfer of the property to another trustee, if required to assure that the intended use is carried out and if no successor trustee is designated in the trust instrument or if no designated successor trustee agrees to serve or is able to serve. The clerk of superior court may also make other orders and determinations as are advisable to carry out the intent of the settlor and the purpose of this section. (1995, c. 225, s. 1; 2005-192, s. 2; 2006-259, s. 13(b).)

§ 36C-4-409. Noncharitable trust without ascertainable beneficiary.

Except as otherwise provided in G.S. 36C-4-408 or by another statute, the following rules apply:

(1) A trust may be created for a noncharitable purpose without a definite or definitely ascertainable beneficiary or for a noncharitable but otherwise valid purpose to be selected by the trustee. The trust may not be enforced for more than 21 years. If the trust is still in existence after 21 years, the trust shall terminate. The unexpended trust property shall be transferred in the following order:

a. As directed in the trust instrument.

b. If the trust was created in a preresiduary clause in the settlor's will or in a codicil to the settlor's will, under the residuary clause in the settlor's will.

c. If no taker is produced by the application of sub-subdivisions a. or b. of this subdivision, to the settlor, if then living, otherwise to the settlor's heirs as determined under Chapter 29 of the General Statutes as of the date of the settlor's death.

(2) A trust authorized by this section may be enforced by a person appointed in the terms of the trust or, if no person is so appointed, by a person appointed by the court.

(3) Property of a trust authorized by this section may be applied only to its intended use, except to the extent that the court determines that the value of the trust property exceeds the amount required for the intended use. The property not required for the intended use shall be distributed under subdivision (1) of this section.

(4) Notwithstanding subdivisions (1) through (3) of this section, a trust, contract, or other arrangement to provide for the care of a cemetery lot, grave, crypt, niche, mausoleum, columbarium, grave marker, or monument is valid without regard to remoteness of vesting, duration of the arrangement, or lack of definite beneficiaries to enforce the trust, provided that the trust, contract, or other arrangement meets the requirements of G.S. 28A-19-10, Article 4 of Chapter 65 of the General Statutes, Article 9 of Chapter 65 of the General Statutes, or other applicable law. This section does not repeal or supersede G.S. 36C-4-413. (1995, c. 225, s. 1; 2005-192, s. 2; 2007-106, s. 15.)

§ 36C-4-410. Modification or termination of trust; proceedings for approval or disapproval.

(a) In addition to the methods of termination prescribed by G.S. 36C-4-411 through G.S. 36C-4-414, a trust terminates to the extent that the trust is revoked or expires under its terms, no purpose of the trust remains to be achieved, or the purposes of the trust have become unlawful, contrary to public policy, or impossible to achieve.

(b) A trustee or beneficiary may commence a proceeding to approve or disapprove a proposed modification or termination under G.S. 36C-4-411 through G.S. 36C-4-416. A settlor may commence a proceeding to approve or disapprove a proposed modification or termination under G.S. 36C-4-411. The settlor of a charitable trust may maintain a proceeding to modify the trust under

G.S. 36C-4-413. A trustee is a necessary party to any proceeding under this Article.

(c) Repealed by Session Laws 2006-259, s. 13(c), effective October 1, 2006. (2005-192, s. 2; 2006-259, s. 13(c); 2007-106, s. 16.)

§ 36C-4-411. Modification or termination of noncharitable irrevocable trust by consent.

(a) If the settlor and all beneficiaries of a noncharitable irrevocable trust consent, they may compel the modification or termination of the trust without the approval of the court even if the modification or termination is inconsistent with a material purpose of the trust. If any beneficiary (i) is a minor or incompetent or a person who is unborn or whose identity or location is unknown and (ii) is unable to be represented under Article 3 of this Chapter, the settlor or any competent adult beneficiary or the representative of any beneficiary properly represented under Article 3 of this Chapter may institute a proceeding before the court to appoint a guardian ad litem. The court shall allow the modification or termination if the court finds that, following the appointment of a guardian ad litem, all beneficiaries or their representatives have consented. A settlor's power to consent to a trust's modification or termination may be exercised by:

(1) An agent under a power of attorney only to the extent expressly authorized by the power of attorney or the terms of the trust.

(2) The settlor's general guardian or the guardian of the estate with the approval of the court supervising the guardianship.

(b) A noncharitable irrevocable trust may be terminated upon consent of all of the beneficiaries if the court concludes that continuance of the trust is not necessary to achieve any material purpose of the trust. A noncharitable irrevocable trust may be modified upon consent of all of the beneficiaries, if the court concludes that modification is consistent with a material purpose of the trust.

(c) Where the beneficiaries of an a noncharitable irrevocable trust seek to compel a termination of the trust and the continuance of the trust is necessary to carry out a material purpose of the trust, or where the beneficiaries seek to compel a modification of the trust in a manner that is inconsistent with its material purpose, the trust may be modified or terminated, in the discretion of the court, only if the court determines that the reason for modifying or terminating the trust under the circumstances substantially outweighs the interest in accomplishing a material purpose of the trust.

(d) If not all of the beneficiaries consent to a proposed modification or termination of the trust under subsection (a), (b), or (c) of this section, the modification or termination may be approved by the court if the court is satisfied that all of the following apply:

(1) If all of the beneficiaries had consented, the trust could have been modified or terminated under this section.

(2) The interests of a beneficiary who does not consent will be adequately protected.

(e) Repealed by Session Laws 2006-259, s. 13(d), effective October 1, 2006.

(f) In determining the class of beneficiaries whose consent is necessary to modify or terminate a trust under this section, the presumption of fertility is rebuttable.

(g) If a trust instrument provides for the disposition of property to a class of persons described only as "heirs" or "next of kin" of any person or uses other words that describe the class of all persons who would take under the rules of intestacy, the court may limit the class of beneficiaries whose consent is needed to compel the modification or termination of the trust to the beneficiaries who are reasonably likely to take under the circumstances. (2005-192, s. 2; 2006-259, s. 13(d); 2007-106, s. 17.)

§ 36C-4-412. Modification or termination because of unanticipated circumstances or inability to administer trust effectively.

(a) The court may modify the administrative or dispositive terms of a trust or terminate the trust if, because of circumstances not anticipated by the settlor, modification or termination will further the purposes of the trust. To the extent practicable, the modification must be made in accordance with the settlor's probable intention.

(b) The court may modify the administrative terms of a trust if continuation of the trust on its existing terms would be impracticable or wasteful or impair the trust's administration.

(c) Repealed by Session Laws 2006-259, s. 13(e), effective October 1, 2006. (2005-192, s. 2; 2006-259, s. 13(e).)

§ 36C-4-413. Cy pres.

(a) Except as otherwise provided in subsections (c1) and (d) of this section, if a charitable trust becomes unlawful, impracticable, impossible to achieve, or wasteful:

(1) The trust does not fail, in whole or in part;

(2) The trust property does not revert to the settlor or the settlor's successors in interest; and

(3) The court may apply cy pres to modify or terminate the trust by directing that the trust property be applied or distributed, in whole or in part, in a manner consistent with the settlor's charitable purposes.

(b) The settlor or a trustee of a charitable trust, the Attorney General, a beneficiary, or any other interested party may maintain a cy pres proceeding under Article 2 of this Chapter.

(c) Repealed by Session Laws 2007-106, s. 17.1, effective October 1, 2007.

(c1) If a trustee of a charitable trust determines that a restriction contained in the trust instrument, including a document making a gift to a charitable trust after it is established, relating to the management, investment, or purpose of the trust or gift is unlawful, impracticable, impossible to achieve, or wasteful, the trustee may release or modify the restriction, in whole or part, if:

(1) The trust property to which the restriction applies has a total value of less than one hundred thousand dollars ($100,000);

(2) More than 10 years have elapsed since the trust property to which the restriction applies was given to the charitable trust; and

(3) The trustee uses the trust property in a manner consistent with the charitable purposes expressed in the applicable trust instrument.

The trustee must provide written notice of the proposed release or modification of the restriction to the Attorney General not less than 60 days before releasing or modifying the restriction. The Attorney General may make application to the court to contest the trustee's determination that the restriction should be released or modified within 60 days of receipt of the trustee's written notice.

(d) This section is not applicable if the settlor has provided, either directly or indirectly, for an alternative plan in the event that the charitable trust is or becomes unlawful, impracticable, impossible to achieve, or wasteful. However, if the alternative plan is also a charitable trust and that trust fails, the intention shown in the original plan shall prevail in the application of this section. (2005-192, s. 2; 2007-106, s. 17.1; 2009-8, s. 4.)

§ 36C-4-414. Modification or termination of uneconomic trust.

(a) After notice to the qualified beneficiaries, the trustee of a trust consisting of trust property having a total value of less than fifty thousand dollars ($50,000) may terminate the trust if the trustee concludes that the value of the trust property is insufficient to justify the cost of administration. The trustee may enter into an agreement or make other provisions that the trustee deems necessary or appropriate to protect the interests of the beneficiaries and to carry out the intent and purpose of the trust. This subsection shall not apply where the instrument creating the trust, by specific reference to this section, or to former G.S. 36A-125.6, provides that it shall not apply. The trustee shall not be liable for that termination and distribution notwithstanding the existence or potential existence of other beneficiaries who are not sui juris. Any beneficiary receiving a distribution from a trust terminated under this section shall incur no liability and shall not be required to account to anyone for such distribution.

(b) The court may modify or terminate a trust or remove the trustee and appoint a different trustee if the court determines that the value of the trust property is insufficient to justify the cost of administration.

(c) This section does not apply to an easement for conservation or preservation.

(d) Repealed by Session Laws 2006-259, s. 13(f), effective October 1, 2006. (2005-192, s. 2; 2006-259, s. 13(f).)

§ 36C-4-415. Reformation to correct mistakes.

The court may reform the terms of a trust, even if unambiguous, to conform the terms to the settlor's intention if it is proved by clear and convincing evidence that both the settlor's intent and the terms of the trust were affected by a mistake of fact or law, whether in expression or inducement. Jurisdiction of a proceeding brought under this section shall be as provided in G.S. 36C-2-203. (2005-192, s. 2.)

§ 36C-4-416. Modification to achieve settlor's tax objectives.

To achieve a settlor's tax objectives, the court may modify the terms of a trust in a manner that is not contrary to the settlor's probable intention. The court may provide that the modification has retroactive effect. (2005-192, s. 2; 2006-259, s. 13(g).)

§ 36C-4-417. Combination and division of trusts.

(a) Unless otherwise provided in the trust instrument, a trustee may do any of the following:

(1) Consolidate the assets of more than one trust and administer the assets as one trust under the terms of one of the trusts if the terms of the trusts are substantially similar and the beneficiaries of the trusts are identical.

(2) Divide one trust into two or more separate trusts if the new trusts provide in the aggregate for the same succession of interests and beneficiaries as are provided in the original trust.

(b) In dividing a trust into two or more separate trusts, a trustee shall accomplish the division by severing the trusts on a fractional basis and funding the separate trusts either (i) with a pro rata portion of each asset held by the undivided trust; or (ii) on a non-pro rata basis based on either the fair market value of the assets on the date of funding or in a manner that fairly reflects the net appreciation or depreciation in the value of the assets measured from the valuation date to the date of funding.

(c) In any case where two separate identical trusts are created under this section, one of which is fully exempt from the federal generation-skipping transfer tax and one of which is fully subject to that tax, the trustee may thereafter, to the extent possible consistent with the terms of the trust, determine the value of any mandatory or discretionary distributions to trust beneficiaries on the basis of the combined value of both trusts, but may satisfy those distributions by a method other than pro rata from the separate trusts in a manner designed to minimize the current and potential generation-skipping transfer tax. (2005-192, s. 2; 2006-259, s. 13(h).)

§ 36C-4-418. Distribution upon termination of trust.

Upon termination of a trust under G.S. 36C-4-411(a), the trustee shall distribute the trust property as agreed by the beneficiaries. Upon termination of a trust under G.S. 36C-4-411(b) or (c), the trustee shall distribute the trust property in accordance with the order entered by the court. Upon termination of a trust under G.S. 36C-4-412(a) or G.S. 36C-4-414, the trustee shall distribute the trust property in a manner consistent with the purposes of the trust. (1999-266, s. 2; 2005-192, s. 2; 2007-106, s. 18.)

§ 36C-4-419. Effect of inalienable interest on modification or termination.

The court, in exercising its discretion to modify or terminate an irrevocable trust under G.S. 36C-4-411, 36C-4-412, or 36C-4-414 shall consider provisions making the interest of a beneficiary inalienable, including those described in Article 5, but the court is not precluded from the exercise of that discretion solely because of such provisions. (2005-192, s. 2; 2006-259, s. 13(i).)

Article 4A.

Tax Status of Charitable Trusts.

§ 36C-4A-1. Prohibited transactions.

(a) Notwithstanding any provisions in the laws of this State or in the governing instrument to the contrary unless otherwise decreed by a court of competent jurisdiction except as provided in subsection (b) of this section, the trust instrument of each trust that is a private foundation described in section 509 of the Internal Revenue Code (including each nonexempt charitable trust described in section 4947(a)(1) of the Internal Revenue Code that is treated as a private foundation) and the trust instrument of each nonexempt split-interest trust described in section 4947(a)(2) of the Internal Revenue Code (but only to the extent that section 508(e) of the Internal Revenue Code is applicable to the nonexempt split-interest trust under section 4947(a)(2) of the Internal Revenue Code) is considered to contain the following provisions: "The trust shall make distributions at any time and in any manner as not to subject it to tax under section 4942 of the Internal Revenue Code; the trust shall not engage in any act of self-dealing which would subject it to tax under section 4941 of the Internal Revenue Code; the trust shall not retain any excess business holdings that would subject it to tax under section 4943 of the Internal Revenue Code; the trust shall not make any investments that would subject it to tax under section 4944 of the Internal Revenue Code; and the trust shall not make any taxable expenditures that would subject it to tax under section 4945 of the Internal Revenue Code." With respect to any trust created before January 1, 1970, this section shall apply only for its taxable years beginning on or after January 1, 1972.

(b) Notwithstanding any provisions in the laws of this State or in the governing instrument to the contrary, unless otherwise decreed by a court of competent jurisdiction except as provided in subsection (a) of this section, the governing instrument of each trust that is a nonexempt charitable trust described in section 4947(a)(1) of the Internal Revenue Code is considered to contain the following provisions:

(1) The trust shall be operated exclusively for charitable, educational, religious, and scientific purposes within the meaning of section 501(c)(3) and section 170(c)(2) of the Internal Revenue Code.

(2) Upon any dissolution, winding up, or liquidation of the trust, its assets shall be distributed for one or more exempt purposes within the meaning of section 501(c)(3) of the Internal Revenue Code, or shall be distributed to the federal government, or a state or local government for a public purpose.

(c) The trustee of any trust described in this section may do one of the following:

(1) Without judicial proceedings, amend the trust to expressly exclude the application of this section by executing a written amendment to the trust instrument and filing a duplicate original of the amendment with the Attorney General. Upon filing of the amendment, this section shall not apply to that trust.

(2) Institute a proceeding under Article 2 of this Chapter seeking reformation of the trust instrument. (1971, c. 1136, s. 4; 1977, c. 502, s. 2; 1981 (Reg. Sess., 1982), c. 1210, ss. 1-3; 2005-192, s. 2.)

§ 36C-4A-2. Reformation of charitable remainder trust.

If a federal estate tax deduction is not allowable at the time of a decedent's death because of the failure of an interest in property that passes from the decedent under a will or trust to a person, or for a use, described in section 2055(a) of the Internal Revenue Code, to meet the requirements of subsections 2055(e)(2)(A) or (B) of the Internal Revenue Code, then in order that the deduction shall nevertheless be allowable under section 2055(e)(3) of the Internal Revenue Code, the court may, on application of any trustee or interested party with either (i) the written consent of the qualified beneficiaries, or (ii) a finding that the interest of those beneficiaries is substantially preserved, order an amendment to the trust so that the remainder interest is in a trust that is a charitable remainder annuity trust, a charitable remainder unitrust (as those terms are described in section 664 of the Internal Revenue Code), or a pooled income fund (as that term is described in section 642(c)(5) of the Internal Revenue Code), or so that any other interest of a charitable beneficiary is in the form of a guaranteed annuity or is a fixed percentage distributed yearly of the fair market value of the property (to be determined yearly), in accordance with section 2055(e)(2)(B) of the Internal Revenue Code. In every proceeding under this section, the Attorney General shall be notified, and given an opportunity to be heard. (1971, c. 1136, s. 4; 1977, c. 502, s. 2; 1981 (Reg. Sess., 1982), c. 1210, ss. 1-3; 2005-192, s. 2.)

Article 4B.

Charitable Remainder Trust Administration Act.

§ 36C-4B-1. Short title.

This Article shall be known as the Charitable Remainder Administration Trust Act. (1981 (Reg. Sess., 1982), c. 1252, s. 1; 2005-192, s. 2.)

§ 36C-4B-2. General rule.

Notwithstanding any provisions in the laws of this State or in the governing instruments to the contrary, any charitable remainder annuity trust and any charitable remainder unitrust that cannot qualify for a deduction for federal tax purposes under section 2055 or section 2522 of the Internal Revenue Code in the absence of this Article shall be administered in accordance with this Article. (1981 (Reg. Sess., 1982), c. 1252, s. 1; 2005-192, s. 2.)

§ 36C-4B-3. Definitions.

The following definitions apply to this Article unless the context clearly requires otherwise:

(1) "Charitable remainder trust" means a trust that provides for a specified distribution at least annually for either life or a term of years to one or more beneficiaries, at least one of which is not a charity (hereinafter referred to as "beneficiaries"), with an irrevocable remainder interest to be held for the benefit of, or paid over to, charity. For purposes of this Article, only a charitable remainder annuity trust or a charitable remainder unitrust is considered a charitable remainder trust.

(2) "Charitable remainder annuity trust" means a charitable remainder trust:

a. From which a sum certain (that is not less than five percent (5%) of the initial net fair market value of all property placed in trust) is to be paid at least annually to one or more persons (at least one of which is not an organization described in section 170(c) of the Internal Revenue Code and, in the case of individuals, only to an individual who was living at the time of the creation of the trust) for a term of years (not in excess of 20 years) or for the life or lives of that individual or those individuals; however, in the case of an individual, the amount to be paid to that individual may be subject to a qualified contingency according to the terms of the governing instrument;

b. From which no amount other than the payments described in sub-subdivision a. of this subdivision may be paid to or for or both to and for the use of anyone other than an organization that is or was described in section 170(c) of the Internal Revenue Code; and

c. Following the termination of the payments described in sub-subdivision a. of this subdivision, the remainder interest in the trust is to be transferred to, or for the use of, an organization that is or was described in section 170(c) of the Internal Revenue Code or is to be retained by the trust for that use.

(3) "Charitable remainder unitrust" means a charitable remainder trust:

a. From which a fixed percentage (that is not less than five percent (5%)) of the net fair market value of its assets, valued annually, is to be paid at least annually to one or more persons (at least one of which is not an organization described in section 170(c) of the Internal Revenue Code and, in the case of individuals, only to an individual who was living at the time of the creation of the trust) for a term of years (not in excess of 20 years) or for the life or lives of that individual or those individuals; however, in the case of an individual, the amount to be paid to that individual may be made subject to a qualified contingency according to the terms of the governing instrument;

b. From which no amount other than the payments described in sub-subdivision a. of this subdivision may be paid to or for the use of anyone other than an organization that is or was an organization described in section 170(c) of the Internal Revenue Code; and

c. Following the termination of the payments described in sub-subdivision a. of this subdivision, the remainder interest in the trust is to be transferred to, or for the use of, an organization that is or was described in section 170(c) of the Internal Revenue Code, or is to be retained by the trust for such a use.

Notwithstanding sub-subdivisions a. and b. of this subdivision, the trust instrument may provide that the trustee shall pay to the income beneficiary for any year (i) the amount of the trust income if that amount is less than the amount required to be distributed under sub-subdivision a. of this subdivision, and (ii) any amount of the trust income that exceeds the amount required to be distributed under sub-subdivision a. of this subdivision to the extent that (by reason of sub-subdivision a.) the aggregate of the amounts paid in prior years is less than the aggregate of the required amounts.

(4) "Qualified contingency" means any provision of the governing instrument that provides that, upon the happening of a contingency, the payments made to an individual noncharitable beneficiary of a charitable remainder trust will terminate not later than those payments would otherwise terminate under the governing instrument. (1981 (Reg. Sess., 1982), c. 1252, s. 1; 1985, c. 406, ss. 1-3; 2005-192, s. 2.)

§ 36C-4B-4. Administrative provisions applicable to both charitable remainder annuity trusts and charitable remainder unitrusts.

(a) Creation of Remainder Interests in Charity. - Upon the termination of the noncharitable interests, the trustee shall distribute all of the then principal and income of the trust, other than any amount due the noncharitable beneficiary or beneficiaries, to the designated charity or charities, or shall hold the property in trust for the designated charity or charities in accordance with the terms of the trust document.

(b) Selection of Alternate Charitable Beneficiary if Remaindermen Do Not Qualify Under Section 170(c) of the Internal Revenue Code at Time of Distribution. - If the designated charity is not an organization described in section 170(c) of the Internal Revenue Code at the time when any principal or income of the trust is to be distributed to it, the trustee must distribute the principal or income to one or more organizations then described in section 170(c) of the Internal Revenue Code selected in accordance with the terms of the trust instrument. If the trust instrument does not provide for a method of selecting alternate charitable beneficiaries that are then qualified under section 170(c) of the Internal Revenue Code, the trustee must, in the trustee's sole discretion, select alternate trust beneficiaries that are qualified under section 170(c) of the Internal Revenue Code.

(c) Selection of Alternative Charitable Beneficiary if Remaindermen Do Not Qualify Under Section 170(b)(1)(A) of the Internal Revenue Code at Time of Distribution. - Notwithstanding subsection (b) of this section, if the designated charity is, at the time of the creation of the trust, an organization described in both section 170(b)(1)(A) and section 170(c) of the Internal Revenue Code, and if the designated charity is not an organization described in both section 170(b)(1)(A) and section 170(c) of the Internal Revenue Code when any principal or income of the trust is to be distributed to it, the trustee must distribute the principal or income to one or more organizations then described in both section 170(b)(1)(A) and section 170(c) of the Internal Revenue Code selected in accordance with the terms of the governing instrument; however, in the event that the governing instrument does not provide a method of selecting alternative charitable beneficiaries that are then described in both section 170(b)(1)(A) and section 170(c) of the Internal Revenue Code, the trustee shall, in his sole discretion, select one or more alternative charitable beneficiaries that are described in both section 170(b)(1)(A) and section 170(c) of the Internal Revenue Code and must distribute the principal or income to the organization or organizations so selected in shares as the trustee, in the trustee's sole discretion, shall determine.

(d) Prohibitions Governing Trustees. - Except for payment of the annuity amount or the unitrust amount to the beneficiaries, whichever is applicable, the trustee is prohibited from engaging in any act of self-dealing as defined in section 4941(d) of the Internal Revenue Code, retaining any excess business holdings as defined in section 4943(c) of the Internal Revenue Code that would subject the trust to tax under section 4943 of the Code, making any investments that would subject the trust to tax under section 4944 of the Internal Revenue Code, and making any taxable expenditures as defined in section 4945(d) of the Code. The trustee shall make distributions at a time and in a manner as not to subject the trust to tax under section 4942 of the Internal Revenue Code.

(e) Distribution to Charity During Term of Noncharitable Interests and Distributions in Kind. - If the governing instrument of the trust provides for distribution to charity during the term of the noncharitable interests, the trustee may pay to the designated charity the amounts specified in the governing instrument that exceed the annuity amount or the unitrust amount payable to any of the beneficiaries for the taxable year of the trust in which the income is earned. If the governing instrument of the trust provides for distribution to charity in kind, the adjusted basis for federal income tax purposes of any trust property the trustee distributes in kind to charity during the term of the noncharitable interests must be fairly representative of the adjusted basis for those purposes of all trust property available for distribution on the date of distribution.

(f) Investment Restrictions on Trustee. - Nothing in the trust instrument shall be construed to restrict the trustee from investing the trust assets in a manner that could result in the annual realization of a reasonable amount of income or gain from the sale or disposition of trust assets.

(g) Distribution From Trust Used to Administer an Estate to Charitable Remainder Trust. - If the governing instrument of a revocable inter vivos trust provides that the revocable inter vivos trust will be used partially to administer the estate of the settlor or for some other purpose, and further provides the assets will then be distributed to another trust that is a charitable remainder trust, upon the death of the settlor, or upon the occurrence of any event that causes the trust to become irrevocable, then the trust shall become irrevocable, and the trustee of this trust shall perform any remaining duties or obligations provided for in the trust instrument and then transfer the property specified in the governing instrument to the trustee of the charitable remainder trust to be held, administered, and distributed in the manner and according to the terms and conditions provided by the charitable remainder trust.

(h) Payment of Taxes by Noncharitable Beneficiary. - In the case of any inter vivos charitable remainder trust that is liable to pay, from trust property, any federal estate, state inheritance, or other similar death taxes by reason of the death of the settlor of the trust, the interest of any noncharitable beneficiary of the trust shall terminate upon the death of the settlor unless the noncharitable beneficiary furnishes to the trust sufficient funds for payment of all those taxes attributable to the interest of the noncharitable beneficiary in the trust property, and the termination shall be deemed as the occurrence of a qualified contingency. (1981 (Reg. Sess., 1982), c. 1252, s. 1; 1985, c. 406, ss. 4, 5; 2005-192, s. 2.)

§ 36C-4B-5. Administrative provisions applicable to charitable remainder trusts only.

(a) Creation of Annuity Amount for Period of Years or Life. - In each taxable year of the trust, the trustee shall pay the annuity amount designated in the trust instrument to the beneficiaries named in the trust instrument during their lives or, if the governing instrument so provides, for a period of 20 years or less. The annuity amount shall be paid annually or in more frequent equal or unequal installments if the governing instrument so provides. The annuity amount shall be paid from income and, to the extent that income is not sufficient, from principal. Any income of the trust for a taxable year in excess of the annuity amount shall be added to principal.

The total amount payable at least annually to a person or persons named in the trust document, at least one of which is not an organization described in section 170(c) of the Internal Revenue Code, may not be less than five percent (5%) of the initial net fair market value of the property placed in trust as finally determined for federal tax purposes, except as provided in subsection (g) of this section.

(b) Computation of Annuity Amount in Short and Final Taxable Years. - For a short taxable year and for the taxable year in which the noncharitable beneficiary's interest terminates by death or otherwise, the trustee shall prorate the annuity amount on a daily basis.

(c) Prohibition of Additional Contributions. - No additional contributions shall be made to the trust after the initial contribution.

(d) Deferral of Annuity Amount During Period of Administration or Settlement. - When property passes to the trust at the death of the settlor, the obligation to pay the annuity amount commences with the date of death of the settlor, but payment of the annuity amount may be deferred from the date of the settlor's death to the end of the taxable year in which complete funding of the trust occurs. Within a reasonable time after the end of the taxable year in which the complete funding of the trust occurs, the trustee must pay to the beneficiary, in the case of an underpayment, or must receive from the beneficiary, in the case of an overpayment, the difference between:

(1) Any annuity amounts actually paid, plus interest on those amounts computed at ten percent (10%) a year, compounded annually; and

(2) The annuity amounts payable, determined under the method described in Section 1.664-1(a)(5) of the federal income tax regulations, plus interest on those amounts computed at ten percent (10%) a year, compounded annually.

Notwithstanding the foregoing sentence, in computing any underpayment or overpayment of the annuity amounts, if the governing instrument was executed or last amended before August 9, 1984, and if the governing instrument does not specify that a ten percent (10%) rate of interest shall be used, the underpayment or overpayment of the annuity amounts must be computed using an interest rate at six percent (6%) a year, compounded annually.

(e) Dollar Amount Annuity May Be Stated as Fraction or Percentage. - If the governing instrument of the trust states the amount of the annuity as a fraction or a percentage, the trustee must pay to the beneficiaries in each taxable year of the trust during their lives an annuity amount equal to a percentage (that percentage being stipulated in the governing instrument of the trust and, in any event, being five percent (5%) or greater) of the initial net fair market value of the assets constituting the trust. In determining this amount, assets shall be valued at their values as finally determined for federal tax purposes. If the fiduciary incorrectly determines the initial net fair market value of the assets constituting the trust, then, within a reasonable period after a final determination, the trustee shall pay to the beneficiaries, in the case of an undervaluation or shall receive from the beneficiaries, in the case of an overvaluation, an amount equal to the difference between the annuity amount properly payable and the annuity amount actually paid.

(f) Annuity Amount May Be Allocated Among Class of Noncharitable Beneficiaries in Discretion of Trustee. - If the governing instrument of the trust provides that the annuity trust amount may be allocated among a class of noncharitable beneficiaries in the discretion of the trustee, then the trustee must pay the annuity amount, which is defined in the governing instrument of the trust, in each taxable year of the trust, to the member or members of the class of noncharitable beneficiaries in an amount and proportions as the trustee in the trustee's absolute discretion shall from time to time determine until the last of the noncharitable beneficiaries dies. The trustee may pay the entire annuity amount to one member of this class or may apportion it among the various members in a manner as the trustee from time to time considers advisable as long as the power to allocate does not cause any person to be treated as the owner of any part of the trust under the rules of section 671 through section 678 of the Internal Revenue Code. If the class provided for in the governing instrument is open, then the distribution must be for a period of years not to exceed 20 years, notwithstanding a provision to the contrary in the trust instrument. If the class provided for in the governing instrument is closed at the creation of the trust, and all members of the class are ascertainable, the distribution may be for the lives of the members of the class or for a period not exceeding 20 years. The trustee shall pay the entire annuity amount for each taxable year annually and may not delay payment of the annuity amount.

(g) Reduction of Annuity Amount If Part of Corpus Is Paid to Charity at Expiration of Term of Years or on Death of Recipient. - If the governing instrument of the trust provides for the reduction of the annuity amount if part of the corpus is paid to charity at the expiration of a term of years or upon the death of a recipient, then during the term of years or during the joint lives of the noncharitable beneficiaries, the trustee shall, in each taxable year of the trust, pay a total annuity amount of at least five percent (5%) of the initial net fair market value of the assets placed in trust. Upon the expiration of the term of years or the death of a beneficiary, the trustee shall distribute an amount or percentage of the trust assets, as provided in the governing instrument of the trust, to the charity named in the governing instrument, and thereafter the trustee shall pay, annually or in more frequent installments, to the survivors for their lives, an annuity amount that in each taxable year of the trust, bears the same ratio to five percent (5%) of the initial net fair market value of the trust assets as the net fair market value of the trust assets valued as of the date of distribution, less the amount or percentage of trust assets distributed to the charity, bears to the net fair market value of the trust assets as of the date of distribution.

(h) Termination of Annuity Amount on Payment Date Preceding Termination of Noncharitable Interest. - If the governing instrument of the trust provides that payment of the annuity amount may terminate with the regular payment preceding the termination of all noncharitable interests, then the trustee must pay to the noncharitable beneficiary during the term of the noncharitable interest the annuity amount, defined in the trust document, in each taxable year of the trust. The obligation of the trustee to pay the annuity amount shall terminate with the payment preceding the death of the noncharitable beneficiary or other event that terminates the noncharitable interest.

(i) Retention of Testamentary Power to Revoke Noncharitable Interest. - If the governing instrument of the trust provides that the settlor of the trust retains the power, exercisable only by will, to revoke or terminate the interest of any recipient other than an organization described in section 170(c) of the Internal Revenue Code, then the trustee shall pay to the settlor during the settlor's life the annuity amount, as defined in the governing instrument of the trust and, upon the death of the settlor, if the noncharitable beneficiary survives the settlor, the trustee must pay to the noncharitable beneficiary during that beneficiary's life the annuity amount equal to the amount paid to the settlor. The settlor shall have the power, exercisable only by will, to revoke and terminate the interest of the noncharitable beneficiary under the trust. Upon the first to occur of (i) the death of the survivor of the settlor and noncharitable beneficiary; or (ii) the death of the settlor if the settlor effectively exercised the settlor's testamentary power to revoke and terminate the interest of the noncharitable beneficiary, the trustee must distribute all of the then principal and income of the trust, other than any amount due the settlor or noncharitable beneficiary, to the charity named in the trust document or, if the governing instrument so provides, the trustee must continue to hold the principal and income in trust for the charity or for the charitable purposes specified in the trust. No other retained power to terminate an interest in the trust is effective. (1981 (Reg. Sess., 1982), c. 1252, s. 1; 1985, c. 406, s. 6; 2005-192, s. 2.)

§ 36C-4B-6. Administrative provisions applicable to charitable remainder unitrusts only.

(a) Creation of Unitrust Amount for a Period of Years or Life. - The trustee shall pay to the beneficiaries named in the trust investment in each taxable year of the trust during their lives or, if the governing instrument so provides, for a period not exceeding 20 years, a unitrust amount equal to a fixed percentage, as stated in the governing instrument of the trust, of the net fair market value of the trust assets valued annually on the date or by the method designated in the governing instrument of the trust or, if no date or method is specified, on the date or by the method selected by the trustee in the trustee's discretion, so long as the same valuation date or dates or valuation methods are used each year. The unitrust amount is paid annually or in more frequent equal or unequal installments if the governing instrument so provides. The unitrust amount is paid from income and, to the extent that income is not sufficient, from principal. Any income of the trust for a taxable year in excess of the unitrust amount is added to principal. The fixed percentage to be paid at least annually to all beneficiaries cannot be less than five percent (5%).

(b) Unitrust Amount Expressed as the Lesser of Income or a Fixed Percentage. - If the governing instrument of the trust provides that the trustee shall pay, instead of a regular unitrust amount (the fixed percentage of the net fair market value of the trust assets, determined annually), the amount of trust income for the taxable year to the extent that this amount is not greater than the amount required to be distributed as a regular unitrust amount for that taxable year or the amount of the trust income for the taxable year that exceeds the regular unitrust amount for that taxable year to the extent that the aggregate of the amounts paid in prior years is less than the aggregate of the regular unitrust amount for those prior years, then the trustee must pay to the beneficiaries in each taxable year of the trust during their lives, or for a period not exceeding 20 years if the trust agreement so provides, an amount equal to the lesser of (i) the trust income for the taxable year, as defined in section 643(b) of the Internal Revenue Code and the regulations under that section, and (ii) the percentage, as stated in the governing instrument, of the net fair market value of the trust assets valued as of the taxable year decreased as elsewhere provided if the taxable year is a short taxable year or is the taxable year in which the noncharitable interest terminates by death or otherwise, and increased as elsewhere provided if additional contributions are made in the taxable year.

If the governing instrument of the trust so provides and if the trust income for any taxable year exceeds the amount determined under (ii) above, the payment to beneficiaries also must include the excess income to the extent that the aggregate of the amounts paid to beneficiaries in prior years is less than the percentage of the aggregate net fair market value of the trust assets, which percentage is defined in the governing instrument of the trust, for these years. Payments to beneficiaries must be made annually or in more frequent equal or unequal installments if the governing instrument so provides. Any income of the trust in excess of these payments must be added to principal.

(c) Adjustment for Incorrect Valuation. - If the fiduciary incorrectly determines the net fair market value of the trust assets for any taxable year, the trustee must, within a reasonable period after the final determination of the correct value, pay to the beneficiaries, in the case of an undervaluation, or receive from the beneficiaries, in the case of an overvaluation, an amount equal to the difference between the unitrust amount properly payable and the unitrust amount actually paid.

(d) Computation of Unitrust Amount in Short and Final Taxable Years. - For a short taxable year and for the taxable year in which the noncharitable beneficiary's interest terminates by death or otherwise, the trustee shall prorate the unitrust amount on a daily basis. If a trust provides for a valuation date other than the first day of the taxable year, and the valuation date does not occur in a taxable year of the trust because the taxable year is either a short taxable year or is the taxable year in which the noncharitable interests terminate, the trust assets must be valued as of the last day of the short taxable year or the day on which the noncharitable interests terminate, as appropriate.

(e) Additional Contributions. - If the governing instrument does not prohibit additional contributions and additional contributions are made to the trust after the initial contribution in the trust, the unitrust amount for the taxable year in which the additional contributions are made must be a fixed percentage, as stated in the governing instrument of the trust, of the sum of (i) the net fair market value of trust assets, excluding the additional contributions and any income from or appreciation of these contributions and (ii) that proportion of the value of the additional contributions excluded under (i) which the number of days in the period beginning with the date of contribution and ending with the earlier of the last day of the taxable year or the day the noncharitable beneficiary's interest terminated bears to the number of days in the period beginning on the first day of the taxable year and ending with the earlier of the last day in the taxable year or the day the noncharitable beneficiary's interest terminated. If no valuation date occurs after the contributions are made, the assets so added are valued as of the time of contribution.

(f) Deferral of Unitrust Amount During Period of Administration or Settlement. - When property passes to the trust at the death of the settlor, the obligation to pay the unitrust amount commences with the date of the settlor's death, but payment of the unitrust amount may be deferred from the date of the settlor's death to the end of the taxable year of the trust in which complete funding of the trust occurs. Within a reasonable time after the end of the taxable year in which the complete funding of the trust occurs, the trustee must pay to the beneficiary, in the case of an underpayment, or must receive from the beneficiary, in the case of an overpayment, the difference between:

(1) Any unitrust amounts actually paid, plus interest on those amounts computed at ten percent (10%) a year, compounded annually; and

(2) The unitrust amounts payable, determined under the method described in section 1.664-1(a)(5) of the federal income tax regulations, plus interest on those amounts computed at ten percent (10%) a year, compounded annually.

Notwithstanding the foregoing sentence, in computing any underpayment or overpayment of the unitrust amounts, if the governing instrument was executed or last amended before August 9, 1984, and if the governing instrument does not specify that a ten percent (10%) rate of interest shall be used, the underpayment or overpayment of the unitrust amounts shall be computed using an interest rate of six percent (6%) a year, compounded annually.

(g) Unitrust Amount May Be Allocated Among Class of Noncharitable Beneficiaries in Discretion of Trustee. - If the governing instrument of the trust provides that the unitrust amount may be allocated to a class of noncharitable beneficiaries in the discretion of the trustee, then the trustee must pay, in each taxable year of the trust, the unitrust amount to the member or members of the class of noncharitable beneficiaries in amounts and proportions as the trustee in the trustee's absolute discretion shall from time to time determine until the last of the noncharitable beneficiaries dies. The trustee may pay the unitrust amount to any one member of the class or may apportion it among the various members in a manner that the trustee shall from time to time consider advisable as long as the power to allocate does not cause any person to be treated as the owner of any part of the trust under the rules of section 671 through section 678 of the Internal Revenue Code. If the class provided for in the governing instrument is open, the distribution must be for a period not exceeding 20 years, notwithstanding a provision to the contrary in the trust instrument. If the class provided for in the governing instrument is closed at the creation of the trust, and all members of the class are ascertainable, the distribution may be for the lives of the members of the class or for a period not exceeding 20 years. The trustee shall pay the entire unitrust amount for each taxable year annually and may not delay payment of the unitrust amount.

(h) Reduction of Unitrust Amount if Part of Corpus Is Paid to Charity at Expiration of Term of Years or on Death of a Recipient. - If the governing instrument of the trust provides for the reduction of the unitrust amount if part of the corpus is paid to charity at the expiration of a term of years or upon the death of a recipient, then during the term of years or during the joint lives of the noncharitable beneficiaries the trustee shall, in each taxable year of the trust, pay the total unitrust amount equal to a percentage of the net fair market value of the trust assets valued annually, which shall not be less than five percent (5%). Upon expiration of the term of years or the death of a recipient, the trustee shall distribute an amount or percentage of the trust assets, as provided in the governing instrument of the trust, to the charity named in the governing instrument, and thereafter the trustee shall pay to the survivors for their lives a unitrust amount in each taxable year of the trust equal to at least five percent (5%)(the actual percentage being defined in the trust instrument) of the net fair market value of the remaining trust assets valued annually.

(i) Termination of Unitrust Amount on Payment Date Preceding Termination of Noncharitable Interests. - If the governing instrument of the trust provides that payment of the unitrust amount may terminate with the regular payment preceding the termination of all noncharitable interests, then the trustee must pay the unitrust amount to the noncharitable beneficiary in each taxable year of the trust during the term of the noncharitable interest. The obligation of the trustee to pay the unitrust amount terminates with the payment preceding the termination of the noncharitable interest by death or otherwise.

The five percent (5%) requirement provided in subsection (a) of this section shall be met until the termination of all payments of the unitrust amount.

(j) Retention of Testamentary Power to Revoke Noncharitable Interest. - If the governing instrument of the trust provides that the settlor of the trust shall retain the power, exercisable only by will, to revoke or terminate the interest of any recipient other than an organization described in section 170(c) of the Internal Revenue Code, then the trustee must pay the unitrust amount to the settlor during the settlor's life and, upon the death of the settlor, shall pay the unitrust amount to the noncharitable beneficiary during the charitable beneficiary's life, provided the noncharitable beneficiary survives the settlor. The settlor shall have the power, exercisable only by will, to revoke and terminate the interest of the noncharitable beneficiary under the trust. Upon the first to occur of (i) the death of the survivor of the settlor and the noncharitable beneficiary; or (ii) the death of the settlor if the settlor effectively exercised the testamentary power to revoke and terminate the interest of the noncharitable beneficiary, the trustee shall distribute all of the then principal and income of the trust, other than any amount due the noncharitable beneficiaries, to the charity named in the trust document or, if the governing instrument so provides, the trustee shall continue to hold the principal and income in trust for the charity or for the charitable purposes specified in the trust. No other retained power to terminate an interest in the trust is effective. (1981 (Reg. Sess., 1982), c. 1252, s. 1; 1985, c. 406, s. 7; 2005-192, s. 2.)

§ 36C-4B-7. Interpretation.

This Article shall be interpreted and construed to effectuate its general purpose to cause all charitable remainder annuity trusts and all charitable remainder unitrusts to be administered in accordance with section 2055 and section 2522 of the Internal Revenue Code and the regulations under those sections. (1981 (Reg. Sess., 1982), c. 1252, s. 1; 2005-192, s. 2.)

Article 5.

Creditors' Claims; Spendthrift and Discretionary Trusts.

§ 36C-5-501. Rights of beneficiary's creditor or assignee.

(a) Except as provided in subsection (b) of this section, the court may authorize a creditor or assignee of the beneficiary to reach the beneficiary's interest by attachment of present or future distributions to or for the benefit of the beneficiary or other means. The court may limit the award to that relief as is appropriate under the circumstances.

(b) Subsection (a) of this section shall not apply, and a trustee shall have no liability to any creditor of a beneficiary for any distributions made to or for the benefit of the beneficiary, to the extent that a beneficiary's interest is protected or restricted by any of the following:

(1) A spendthrift provision.

(2) A discretionary trust interest as defined in G.S. 36C-5-504(a)(2).

(3) A protective trust interest as described in G.S. 36C-5-508. (2005-192, s. 2; 2007-106, s. 19.)

§ 36C-5-502. Spendthrift provision.

(a) A spendthrift provision is valid only if it restrains both voluntary and involuntary transfer of a beneficiary's interest.

(b) A term of a trust providing that the interest of a beneficiary is held subject to a "spendthrift trust", or words of similar import, is sufficient to restrain both voluntary and involuntary transfer of the beneficiary's interest.

(c) A beneficiary may not transfer an interest in a trust in violation of a valid spendthrift provision and, except as otherwise provided in this Article, a creditor or assignee of the beneficiary may not reach the interest or a distribution by the trustee before its receipt by the beneficiary. (2005-192, s. 2.)

§ 36C-5-503. Exceptions to spendthrift provision.

(a) As used in this section, the term "child" includes any person for whom an order or judgment for child support has been entered in this or another state.

(b) Even if a trust contains a spendthrift provision, or if the beneficiary's interest is a discretionary trust interest as defined in G.S. 36C-5-504(a)(2) or a protective trust interest as defined in G.S. 36C-5-508, a beneficiary's child who has a judgment or court order against the beneficiary for support or maintenance may obtain from a court an order attaching present or future distributions to or for the benefit of the beneficiary. The court may limit the award to relief that is appropriate under the circumstances. (2005-192, s. 2.)

§ 36C-5-504. Discretionary trusts; effect of standard.

(a) In this section:

(1) "Child" includes any person for whom an order or judgment for child support has been entered in this or another state.

(2) "Discretionary trust interest" means an interest in a trust that is subject to the trustee's discretion, whether or not the discretion is expressed in the form of a standard of distribution. A discretionary trust interest shall include an interest in any one or any combination of the following:

a. A trust in which the amount to be received by the beneficiary, including whether or not the beneficiary, or a class of beneficiaries, is to receive anything at all, is within the discretion of the trustee.

b. A trust in which the trustee has no duty to pay or distribute any particular amount to the beneficiary, but has only a duty to pay or distribute to the beneficiary, or apply on behalf of the beneficiary, those sums that the trustee, in the trustee's discretion, determines are appropriate for the support, education, or maintenance of the beneficiary.

(b) The beneficiary may not transfer a discretionary trust interest. Except as otherwise provided in this Article, a creditor or assignee of a beneficiary may not reach a discretionary trust interest or a distribution by the trustee before its receipt by the beneficiary.

(c) Except as provided in subsection (d) of this section, a creditor of a beneficiary may not compel a distribution from a trust in which the beneficiary has a discretionary trust interest even if the trustee has abused the trustee's discretion.

(d) To the extent that a trustee has not complied with a standard of distribution or has abused a discretion:

(1) A distribution may be ordered by the court to satisfy a judgment or court order against the beneficiary for support or maintenance of the beneficiary's child; and

(2) The court shall direct the trustee to pay to the child an amount that is equitable under the circumstances but not more than the amount the trustee would have been required to distribute to or for the benefit of the beneficiary had the trustee complied with the standard or not abused the discretion.

(e) This section does not limit the right of a beneficiary to maintain a judicial proceeding against a trustee for an abuse of discretion or failure to comply with a standard for distribution.

(f) A creditor may not reach the interest of a beneficiary who is also a trustee or cotrustee, or otherwise compel a distribution, if the trustee's discretion to make distributions for the trustee's own benefit is limited by an ascertainable standard. (2005-192, s. 2.)

§ 36C-5-505. Creditor's claim against settlor.

(a) Subject to the other applicable law, whether or not the terms of a trust contain a spendthrift provision or the interest in the trust is a discretionary trust interest as defined in G.S. 36C-504(a)(2) or a protective trust interest as defined in G.S. 36C-5-508, the following rules apply:

(1) During the lifetime of the settlor, the property of a revocable trust is subject to claims of the settlor's creditors.

(2) With respect to an irrevocable trust, a creditor or assignee of the settlor may reach the maximum amount that can be distributed to or for the settlor's benefit. If a trust has more than one settlor, the amount the creditor or assignee of a particular settlor may reach may not exceed the settlor's interest in the portion of the trust attributable to that settlor's contribution.

(2a) Notwithstanding subdivision (2) of this subsection, the trustee's discretionary authority to pay directly to the taxing authorities or to reimburse the settlor for any tax on trust income or trust principal that is payable by the settlor under the law imposing the tax shall not be considered to be an amount that can be distributed to or for the settlor's benefit, and a creditor or assignee of the settlor shall not be entitled to reach any amount.

(3) After the death of a settlor, and subject to the settlor's right to direct the source from which liabilities will be paid, the property of a trust that was revocable at the settlor's death is subject to claims of the settlor's creditors, costs of administration of the settlor's estate, the expenses of the settlor's funeral and disposal of remains, and statutory allowances to a surviving spouse and children to the extent that the settlor's probate estate is inadequate to satisfy those claims, costs, expenses, and allowances, unless barred by applicable law.

(b) For purposes of this section, with respect to a power of withdrawal over property of a trust exercisable by a holder of the power other than the settlor of the trust, both of the following shall apply:

(1) The property subject to the exercise of the power shall be subject to the claims of the creditors of the holder only when and to the extent that the holder exercises the power.

(2) The lapse, release, or waiver of a power shall not be deemed to be an exercise of the power and shall not cause the holder to be treated as a settlor of the trust.

(c) Subject to Article 3A of Chapter 39 of the General Statutes, for purposes of this section, if the settlor is a beneficiary of the following trusts after the death of the settlor's spouse, the property of the trusts shall, after the death of the settlor's spouse, be deemed to have been contributed by the settlor's spouse and not by the settlor:

(1) An irrevocable intervivos marital trust that is treated as a general power of appointment trust described in section 2523(e) of the Internal Revenue Code.

(2) An irrevocable intervivos marital trust that is treated as qualified terminable interest property under section 2523(f) of the Internal Revenue Code.

(3) An irrevocable intervivos trust of which the settlor's spouse is the sole beneficiary during the lifetime of the settlor's spouse but which does not qualify for the federal gift tax marital deduction.

(4) Another trust, to the extent that the property of the other trust is attributable to property passing from a trust described in subdivision (1), (2), or (3) of this subsection.

For purposes of this subsection, the settlor is a beneficiary whether so named under the initial trust instrument or through the exercise of a limited or general power of appointment, and the "settlor's spouse" refers to the person to whom the settlor was married at the time the irrevocable intervivos trust was created, notwithstanding a subsequent dissolution of the marriage. (2005-192, s. 2; 2007-106, s. 20; 2011-339, s. 2; 2013-91, s. 2(b).)

§ 36C-5-506. Overdue distribution.

(a) In this section, "mandatory distribution" means a distribution of income or principal that the trustee is required to make to a beneficiary under the terms of the trust, including a distribution upon termination of the trust. The term excludes a distribution subject to the exercise of the trustee's discretion, regardless of whether the terms of the trust (i) include a support or other standard to guide the trustee in making distribution decisions; or (ii) provide that the trustee "may" or "shall" make discretionary distributions, including distributions under a support or other standard.

(b) Whether or not a trust contains a spendthrift provision, a creditor or assignee of a beneficiary may reach a mandatory distribution of income or principal, including a distribution upon termination of the trust, if the trustee has not made the distribution to the beneficiary within a reasonable time after the designated distribution date. (2005-192, s. 2.)

§ 36C-5-507. Personal obligations of trustee.

Trust property is not subject to personal obligations of the trustee, even if the trustee becomes insolvent or bankrupt. (2005-192, s. 2.)

§ 36C-5-508. Protective trusts.

Except with respect to an interest retained by the settlor, a "protective trust interest" means an interest in a trust in which the terms of the trust provide that the interest terminates or becomes discretionary if:

(1) The beneficiary alienates or attempts to alienate that interest; or

(2) Any creditor attempts to reach the beneficiary's interest by attachment, levy, or otherwise; or

(3) The beneficiary becomes insolvent or bankrupt. (2005-192, s. 2.)

Article 6.

Revocable Trusts.

§ 36C-6-601. Capacity of settlor of revocable trust.

The capacity required to create, amend, revoke, or add property to a revocable trust, or to direct the actions of the trustee of a revocable trust, is the same as that required to make a will. (2005-192, s. 2.)

§ 36C-6-602. Revocation or amendment of revocable trust.

(a) Unless the terms of a trust expressly provide that the trust is irrevocable, the settlor may revoke or amend the trust without regard to the actual capacity of the settlor. This subsection does not apply to a trust created under an instrument executed before the effective date of this Chapter.

(b) If a revocable trust is created or funded by more than one settlor:

(1) To the extent the trust consists of community property, the trust may be revoked by either spouse acting alone but may be amended only by joint action of both spouses; and

(2) To the extent the trust consists of property other than community property, each settlor may revoke or amend the trust with regard to the portion of the trust property attributable to that settlor's contribution.

(c) The settlor may revoke or amend a revocable trust:

(1) By substantial compliance with a method provided in the terms of the trust; or

(2) If the terms of the trust do not provide a method or the method provided in the terms is not expressly made exclusive, by:

a. A later will or codicil that expressly refers to the trust or specifically devises property that would otherwise have passed according to the terms of the trust; or

b. By oral statement to the trustee if the trust was created orally; or

c. Any other written method delivered to the trustee manifesting clear and convincing evidence of the settlor's intent.

(d) Upon revocation of a revocable trust, the trustee shall deliver the trust property as the settlor directs.

(e) Repealed by Session Laws 2007-106, s. 21, effective October 1, 2007.

(f) Repealed by Session Laws 2007-106, s. 22, effective October 1, 2007.

(g) A trustee who does not know that a trust has been revoked or amended is not liable to the settlor or settlor's successors in interest for distributions made and other actions taken on the assumption that the trust had not been amended or revoked. (2005-192, s. 2; 2007-106, ss. 21, 22.)

§ 36C-6-602.1. Exercise of settlor's powers with respect to revocable trust by agent or guardian.

(a) An agent acting under a power of attorney may exercise any of the following powers of the settlor with respect to a revocable trust only to the extent expressly authorized by the terms of the trust or the power of attorney:

(1) Revocation of the trust.

(2) Amendment of the trust.

(3) Additions to the trust.

(4) Direction to dispose of property of the trust.

(5) The creation of the trust, notwithstanding G.S. 36C-4-402(a)(1) and (2).

The exercise of the powers described in this subsection shall not alter the designation of beneficiaries to receive property on the settlor's death under that settlor's existing estate plan.

(b) A general guardian or a guardian of the estate of the settlor may exercise the powers of the settlor with respect to a revocable trust as provided in G.S. 35A-1251(24). (2007-106, s. 23.)

§ 36C-6-603. Settlor's control of revocable trust.

(a) While a trust is revocable, rights of the beneficiaries are subject to the control of, and the duties of the trustee are owed exclusively to, the settlor. If a trustee is a settlor, the trustee's actions are presumed to be taken at the direction of the settlor.

(b) If a revocable trust has more than one settlor, the duties of the trustee are owed to all of the settlors. (2005-192, s. 2; 2007-106, s. 24.)

§ 36C-6-604. Limitation on action contesting validity of revocable trust; distribution of trust property.

(a) A person may commence a judicial proceeding to contest the validity of a trust that was revocable at the settlor's death within the earlier of:

(1) Three years after the settlor's death; or

(2) 120 days after the trustee sent the person a copy of the trust instrument and written notice pursuant to G.S. 1A-1, Rule 4 of the Rules of Civil Procedure, informing the person of the trust's existence, of the trustee's name and address, and of the time allowed for commencing a proceeding.

(b) Upon the death of the settlor of a trust that was revocable at the settlor's death, the trustee may proceed to distribute the trust property in accordance with the terms of the trust. The trustee is not subject to liability for doing so unless:

(1) The trustee knows of a pending judicial proceeding contesting the validity of the trust; or

(2) A potential contestant has notified the trustee of a possible judicial proceeding to contest the trust, and a judicial proceeding is commenced within 60 days after the contestant sent the notification.

(c) A beneficiary of a trust that is determined to have been invalid is liable to return any distribution received. (2005-192, s. 2; 2011-344, s. 13; 2012-18, s. 3.11.)

§ 36C-6-605. Failure of disposition of property of a trust by lapse or otherwise.

(a) If a beneficiary under a revocable trust predeceases the execution of the trust or the settlor or is treated as having predeceased the settlor, and if the beneficiary is a grandparent of or a descendant of a grandparent of the settlor, then the issue of the predeceased beneficiary who survive the settlor shall take in place of the deceased beneficiary. The deceased beneficiary's issue shall take the deceased beneficiary's share in the same manner that the issue would take as heirs of the deceased beneficiary under the intestacy provisions in effect at the time of the settlor's death. The provisions of this section apply whether the disposition of property is to an individual, to a class, or is a part of the residue of the trust. In the case of the disposition to a class, the issue shall take whatever share the deceased beneficiary would have taken had the deceased beneficiary survived the settlor. In the event the deceased class member leaves no issue, the deceased beneficiary's share shall devolve upon the members of the class who survived the settlor and the issue of any deceased members taking by substitution.

(b)   If the provisions of subsection (a) of this section do not apply to the disposition of property that fails, the property shall pass to the beneficiaries in proportion to their share of the residue of the trust. If the disposition is part of the residue of the trust, it shall augment the shares of the other residuary beneficiaries, including the shares of any substitute takers under subsection (a) of this section. If there are no residuary beneficiaries, then the property shall pass by intestacy. (2007-106, s. 25.)

§ 36C-6-606. Revocation of provisions in revocable trust by divorce or annulment; revival.

Dissolution of the settlor's marriage by absolute divorce or annulment after executing a revocable trust revokes all provisions in the trust in favor of the settlor's former spouse, including, but not by way of limitation, any provision conferring a general or special power of appointment on the former spouse and any appointment of the former spouse as trustee. Property prevented from passing to the former spouse because of revocation by divorce or absolute annulment passes as if the former spouse failed to survive the settlor, and other provisions conferring some power or office on the former spouse are interpreted as if the former spouse failed to survive the settlor. If provisions are revoked solely by this section, they are revived by the settlor's remarriage to the former spouse. The reference to "former spouse" in this section includes a purported former spouse. (2007-106, s. 26.)

§ 36C-6-607. Modification or termination of a revocable trust.

(a)   A revocable trust may be modified or terminated by the court pursuant to any of the methods for modification or termination of an irrevocable trust set forth in G.S. 36C-4-411(b) or (c), 36C-4-412, 36C-4-415, or 36C-4-416.

(b)   The settlor is a necessary party to any proceeding brought to modify or terminate a revocable trust. (2007-106, s. 26.1.)

Article 7.

Office of Trustee.

§ 36C-7-701. Accepting or declining trusteeship.

(a) Except as otherwise provided in subsection (c) of this section, a person designated as trustee accepts the trusteeship:

(1) By substantially complying with a method of acceptance provided in the terms of the trust; or

(2) If the terms of the trust do not provide a method or the method provided in the terms is not expressly made exclusive, by accepting delivery of the trust property, exercising powers or performing duties as trustee, or otherwise indicating acceptance of the trusteeship.

(b) A person designated as trustee who has not yet accepted the trusteeship may reject the trusteeship. A designated trustee who does not accept the trusteeship within 120 days after written notice to accept the trusteeship is provided is considered to have rejected the trusteeship.

(c) A person designated as trustee, without accepting the trusteeship, may:

(1) Act to preserve the trust property if, within a reasonable time after acting, the person sends a rejection of the trusteeship to the settlor or, if the settlor is dead or lacks capacity, to a qualified beneficiary; and

(2) Inspect or investigate trust property to determine potential liability under environmental or other law or for any other purpose. (2005-192, s. 2; 2006-259, s. 13(j).)

§ 36C-7-702. Trustee's bond.

(a) A trustee shall provide bond to secure the performance of the trustee's duties if:

(1) The trust instrument was executed before January 1, 2006, unless the terms of the trust instrument provide otherwise;

(2) The trust instrument was executed on or after January 1, 2006, but only if the terms of the trust instrument require the trustee to provide bond;

(3) A beneficiary requests the trustee to provide bond, and the court finds the request to be reasonable; or

(4) The court finds that it is necessary for the trustee to provide bond in order to protect the interests of beneficiaries who are not able to protect themselves and whose interests otherwise are not adequately represented.

However, in no event shall bond be required of a trustee if the governing instrument directs otherwise.

(b) If bond is required, it shall be in a sum of double the value of the personal property to come into the trustee's hands if bond is executed by a personal surety, and in an amount not less than one and one-fourth times the value of all personal property of the trust estate if the bond is secured by a suretyship bond executed by a corporate surety company authorized by the Commissioner of Insurance to do business in this State, provided that the court, when the value of the personal property exceeds one hundred thousand dollars ($100,000), may accept bond in an amount equal to the value of the personal property plus ten percent (10%) of that value, conditioned upon the faithful performance of the trustee's duties and for the payment to the persons entitled to receive property that may come into the trustee's hands. All bonds executed under this Article shall be filed with the clerk of superior court.

(c) On petition of the trustee or a qualified beneficiary, the court may excuse a requirement of bond, reduce the amount of the bond, release the surety, or permit the substitution of another bond with the same or different sureties.

(d) As provided in G.S. 53-159 and G.S. 53-366(a)(10), banks and trust companies licensed to do trust business in this State need not give bond, even if required by the terms of the trust. (1911, c. 39, s. 7; C.S., s. 4031; 1951, c. 264; 1965, c. 1177, s. 1; 1977, c. 502, s. 2; 2001-413, s. 1; 2003-261, s. 5; 2005-192, s. 2.)

§ 36C-7-703. Cotrustees.

(a)   Cotrustees who are unable to reach a unanimous decision may act by majority decision if more than two are serving. Unanimity is required when only two cotrustees are serving.

(b)   If a vacancy occurs in a cotrusteeship, the remaining cotrustees may act for the trust and exercise all trustee powers, except those powers that the remaining trustees are prohibited from exercising under the trust instrument or by law.

(c)   A cotrustee must participate in the performance of a trustee's function unless the cotrustee is unavailable to perform the function because of absence, illness, disqualification under other law, or other temporary incapacity, or the cotrustee has properly delegated the performance of the function to another trustee.

(d)   If a cotrustee is unavailable to perform duties because of absence, illness, disqualification under other law, or other temporary incapacity, and prompt action is necessary to achieve the purposes of the trust or to avoid injury to the trust property, the remaining cotrustee or a majority of the remaining cotrustees may act for the trust.

(e)   A trustee may delegate to a cotrustee with the consent of the cotrustee the performance of any function other than those the settlor reasonably expected the trustees to perform jointly. The following functions are not considered to be those that the settlor reasonably expected the trustees to perform jointly:

(1)   Establish and maintain bank accounts for the trust and issue checks for the trust.

(2)   Maintain inventories, accountings, and income and expense records of the trust.

(3)   Enter any safety deposit box rented by the trust.

(4)   Employ persons as advisors or assistants in the performance of administrative duties, including agents, attorneys, accountants, brokers, appraisers, and custodians.

(5)   List trust property for taxes and prepare and file tax returns for the trust.

(6)   Collect and give receipts for claims and debts of the trust.

(7)   Pay debts, claims, costs of administration, and taxes of the trust.

(8)   Compromise, adjust, or otherwise settle any claim by or against the trust and release, in whole or in part, a claim belonging to the trust.

(9)   Have custody of the trust property.

(10)   Perform any function relating to investment of trust assets.

The list of functions contained in this subsection is not intended to be exclusive of others that may be delegated to a cotrustee in accordance with this subsection.

(e1)   If the terms of a trust confer upon a cotrustee, to the exclusion of another cotrustee, the power to take certain actions with respect to the trust, including the power to direct or prevent certain actions of the trustees, the following apply:

(1)   The duty and liability of the excluded trustee is as follows:

a.   If the terms of a trust confer upon the cotrustee the power to direct certain actions of the excluded trustee, the excluded trustee must act in accordance with the direction and is not liable, individually or as a fiduciary, for any loss resulting directly or indirectly from compliance with the direction unless compliance with the direction constitutes intentional misconduct on the part of the directed cotrustee.

b.   If the terms of the trust confer upon the cotrustee any other power, the excluded trustee is not liable, individually or as a fiduciary, for any loss resulting directly or indirectly from the action taken by the cotrustee.

c.   The excluded trustee has no duty to monitor the conduct of the cotrustee, provide advice to the cotrustee, or consult with or request directions from the cotrustee. The excluded trustee is not required to give notice to any beneficiary of any action taken or not taken by the cotrustee whether or not the excluded trustee agrees with the result. Administrative actions taken by the excluded trustee for the purpose of implementing directions of the cotrustee, including confirming that the directions of the cotrustee have been carried out, do not constitute monitoring of the cotrustee nor do they constitute participation in decisions within the scope of the cotrustee's authority.

(2) Except as otherwise provided in sub-subdivision a. of subdivision (1) of this subsection, the cotrustee holding the power to take certain actions with respect to the trust shall be liable to the beneficiaries with respect to the exercise of the power as if the excluded trustee were not in office and has the exclusive obligation to account to the beneficiaries and defend any action brought by the beneficiaries with respect to the exercise of the power.

(f) Repealed by Session Laws 2007-106, s. 27, effective October 1, 2007.

(g) A trustee shall exercise reasonable care in connection with matters for which the trustee is given authority under the terms of a trust to:

(1) Avoid enabling a cotrustee to commit a serious breach of trust; and

(2) Compel a cotrustee to redress a serious breach of trust.

(h) Notwithstanding subsection (g) of this section, a cotrustee is not liable for the action of a majority of the other trustees if either of the following apply:

(1) The trustee does not join in an action approved by a majority of the other trustees.

(2) The dissenting trustee joins in an action necessary to carry out the decision of the majority of the trustees and notifies in writing the cotrustees of the dissent at or before joining in the action, unless the trustee had knowledge that the action taken involved intentional misconduct or was taken with an intention to directly or indirectly provide an improper personal benefit to one or more trustees approving the action.

(i) Notwithstanding any other provision of this section to the contrary, if two or more trustees own shares of corporate stock or other securities, their acts with respect to voting shall have the following effect:

(1) If only one votes, in person or by proxy, the act binds all;

(2) If more than one vote, in person or by proxy, the act binds all; and

(3) If more than one vote, in person or by proxy, but the vote is evenly split on any particular matter, each faction is entitled to vote the stock or other securities in question proportionately. (2005-192, s. 2; 2007-106, ss. 27, 28, 29; 2012-18, s. 3.2.)

§ 36C-7-704. Vacancy in trusteeship; appointment of successor.

(a) A vacancy in a trusteeship occurs if:

(1) A person designated as trustee rejects the trusteeship;

(2) A person designated as trustee cannot be identified or does not exist;

(3) A trustee resigns;

(4) A trustee is disqualified or removed;

(5) A trustee dies; or

(6) A general guardian, guardian of the estate, or guardian of the person is appointed for an individual serving as trustee.

(b) If one or more cotrustees remain in office, a vacancy in a trusteeship need not be filled. A vacancy in a trusteeship must be filled if the trust has no remaining trustee.

(c) A vacancy in a trusteeship of a noncharitable trust that is required to be filled must be filled in the following order of priority:

(1) By a person designated in the terms of the trust or appointed under the terms of the trust to act as successor trustee;

(2) By a person appointed by unanimous agreement of the qualified beneficiaries; or

(3) By a person appointed by the court.

(d) A vacancy in a trusteeship of a charitable trust that is required to be filled must be filled in the following order of priority:

(1) By a person designated in the terms of the trust or appointed under the terms of the trust to act as successor trustee;

(2) By a person selected by majority agreement of the qualified beneficiaries, if the trust is a split-interest charitable trust;

(2a) By a person selected by majority agreement of the charitable organizations expressly designated to receive distributions under the terms of the trust; or

(3) By a person appointed by the court.

(e) Whether or not a vacancy in a trusteeship exists or is required to be filled, the court may appoint an additional trustee or special fiduciary whenever the court considers the appointment necessary for the administration of the trust.

(f) A successor trustee shall succeed to all the rights, powers, and privileges, and is subject to all the duties, liabilities, and responsibilities that were imposed upon the original trustee, unless a contrary intent appears from the governing instrument or unless the order appointing the successor trustee provides otherwise. A successor trustee shall be vested with the title to property of the former trustee. (1911, c. 39, s. 8; C.S., s. 4032; 1977, c. 502, s. 2; 2001-413, s. 1; 2003-261, s. 6; 2005-192, s. 2; 2007-106, s. 30; 2011-339, s. 3.)

§ 36C-7-705. Resignation of trustee.

(a) A trustee may resign:

(1) Upon at least 30 days' notice in writing to the qualified beneficiaries, the settlor, if living, and all cotrustees; or

(2) With the approval of the court.

(b) In approving a resignation, the court may issue orders and impose conditions reasonably necessary for the protection of the trust property.

(c) Any liability of a resigning trustee or of any sureties on the trustee's bond for acts or omissions of the trustee is not discharged or affected by the trustee's resignation. (2005-192, s. 2.)

§ 36C-7-706. Removal of trustee.

(a) For the reasons set forth in subsection (b) of this section, the settlor of an irrevocable trust, a cotrustee of an irrevocable trust, or a beneficiary of an irrevocable trust may request the court to remove a trustee, or a trustee may be removed by the court on its own initiative.

(b) The court may remove a trustee if:

(1) The trustee has committed a serious breach of trust;

(2) Lack of cooperation among cotrustees substantially impairs the administration of the trust;

(3) Because of unfitness, unwillingness, or persistent failure of the trustee to administer the trust effectively, the court determines that removal of the trustee best serves the interests of the beneficiaries; or

(4) There has been a substantial change of circumstances, the court finds that removal of the trustee best serves the interests of all of the beneficiaries and is consistent with a material purpose of the trust, and a suitable cotrustee or successor trustee is available.

(c) Pending a final decision on a request to remove a trustee, or in lieu of or in addition to removing a trustee, the court may order appropriate relief under G.S. 36C-10-1001(b) as may be necessary to protect the trust property or the interests of the beneficiaries. (2005-192, s. 2.)

§ 36C-7-707. Delivery of property by former trustee.

(a) Unless a cotrustee remains in office or the court otherwise orders, and until the trust property is delivered to a successor trustee or other person entitled to it, a trustee who has resigned or been removed has the duties of a trustee and the powers necessary to protect the trust property.

(b) A trustee who has resigned or been removed shall proceed expeditiously to deliver the trust property within the trustee's possession to the cotrustee, successor trustee, or other person entitled to it. A former trustee shall execute those documents acknowledging the transfer of title to trust property as may be reasonably requested by the cotrustee, successor trustee, or other person entitled to it to facilitate administration of the trust, and in the event that the former trustee fails to do so, the clerk of superior court may order the former trustee to execute those documents. (2005-192, s. 2; 2012-18, s. 3.5.)

§ 36C-7-708. Compensation of trustee.

(a) If the terms of a trust do not specify the trustee's compensation, a trustee is entitled to compensation determined in accordance with Article 6 of Chapter 32 of the General Statutes.

(b) If the terms of a trust specify the trustee's compensation, the trustee is entitled to be compensated as specified. (2005-192, s. 2.)

§ 36C-7-709. Reimbursement of expenses.

A trustee is entitled to be reimbursed out of the trust property for expenses properly incurred in the administration of the trust as provided in G.S. 32-58. (2005-192, s. 2.)

Article 8.

Duties and Powers of Trustee.

§ 36C-8-801. Duty to administer trust.

Upon acceptance of a trusteeship, a trustee shall administer the trust in good faith, in accordance with its terms and purposes and the interests of the beneficiaries, and in accordance with this Chapter. (2005-192, s. 2.)

§ 36C-8-802. Duty of loyalty.

(a)   A trustee shall administer the trust solely in the interests of the beneficiaries.

(b)   Subject to the rights of persons dealing with or assisting the trustee as provided in G.S. 36C-10-1012, a sale, encumbrance, or other transaction involving the investment or management of trust property entered into by the trustee for the trustee's own personal account, or that is otherwise affected by a conflict between the trustee's fiduciary and personal interests, is voidable by a beneficiary affected by the transaction, without regard to whether the transaction is fair to the beneficiary, unless:

(1)   The terms of the trust authorized the transaction;

(2)   The court approved the transaction;

(3)   The beneficiary did not commence a judicial proceeding within the time allowed by G.S. 36C-10-1005;

(4)   The beneficiary consented to the trustee's conduct, ratified the transaction, or released the trustee in compliance with G.S. 36C-10-1009; or

(5)   The transaction involves a contract entered into, or claim acquired by, the trustee before the person became or contemplated becoming trustee.

(c)   In determining whether a sale, encumbrance, or other transaction involving the investment or management of trust property is affected by a conflict of interest between the trustee's fiduciary and personal interests, the transaction is rebuttably presumed to be affected by a conflict of interest if the trustee enters into the transaction with:

(1)   The trustee's spouse or a parent of the trustee's spouse;

(2) The trustee's descendants, siblings, ancestors, or their spouses;

(3) An agent, attorney, employee, officer, director, member, manager, or partner of the trustee, or an entity that controls, is controlled by, or is under common control with the trustee; or

(4) Any other person or entity in which the trustee, or a person that owns a significant interest in the trust, has an interest or relationship that might affect the trustee's best judgment.

(d) A transaction between a trustee and a beneficiary that does not concern trust property, but that occurs during the existence of the trust or while the trustee retains significant influence over the beneficiary, and from which the trustee obtains an advantage and which is outside the ordinary course of the trustee's business or on terms and conditions substantially less favorable than those the trustee generally offers similarly situated customers, is voidable by the beneficiary unless the trustee establishes that the transaction was fair to the beneficiary.

(e) A transaction not concerning trust property in which the trustee engages in the trustee's individual capacity involves a conflict between personal and fiduciary interests if the transaction concerns an opportunity properly belonging to the trust.

(f) Notwithstanding subsection (c) of this section:

(1) An investment by a trustee in securities of an investment company, investment trust, or pooled investment vehicle in which the trustee or its affiliate has an investment, or to which the trustee, or its affiliate, provides services for compensation, is not presumed to be affected by a conflict between personal and fiduciary interests if the investment otherwise complies with the prudent investor rule of Article 9 of this Chapter. The investment company, investment trust, or pooled investment vehicle may compensate the trustee for providing those services out of fees charged to the trust if the trustee at least annually notifies the persons entitled under G.S. 36C-8-813 to receive a copy of the trustee's annual report of the rate and method by which the compensation was determined; and

(2) Payment made by a trustee to an attorney, broker, accountant, or agent for services performed on behalf of the trust in the ordinary course of business

is not considered to be affected by a conflict between the trustee's personal and fiduciary interests if the payment is consistent with payments generally made for the same or similar services.

(g) In voting shares of stock or in exercising powers of control over similar interests in other forms of enterprise, the trustee shall act in the best interests of the beneficiaries. If the trust is the sole owner of a corporation or other form of enterprise, the trustee shall elect to appoint directors or other managers who will manage the corporation or enterprise in the best interests of the beneficiaries.

(h) This section does not preclude any of the following transactions:

(1) An agreement between a trustee and a beneficiary relating to the appointment or compensation of the trustee.

(2) Payment of compensation to which the trustee is entitled under G.S. 36C-7-708.

(3) A transaction that is fair to the beneficiaries between a trust and another trust, decedent's estate, or guardianship, or similar relationship of which the trustee is a fiduciary or in which a beneficiary has an interest.

(4) A deposit of trust money in a regulated financial-service institution operated by the trustee or an affiliate of the trustee.

(5) An advance by the trustee of money for the protection of the trust.

(i) The court may appoint a special fiduciary to make a decision with respect to any proposed transaction that might violate this section if entered into by the trustee. (1999-215, s. 1; 2005-192, s. 2; 2007-106, ss. 31, 32, 33.)

§ 36C-8-803. Impartiality.

If a trust has two or more beneficiaries, the trustee shall act impartially in investing, managing, and distributing the trust property, giving due regard to the beneficiaries' respective interests. (1999-215, s. 1; 2005-192, s. 2.)

§ 36C-8-804. Prudent administration.

A trustee shall administer the trust as a prudent person would, by considering the purposes, terms, distributional requirements, and other circumstances of the trust. In satisfying this standard, the trustee shall exercise reasonable care, skill, and caution. (2005-192, s. 2.)

§ 36C-8-805. Cost of administration.

In administering a trust, the trustee may incur only costs that are reasonable in relation to the trust property, the purposes of the trust, and the skills of the trustee. (1999-215, s. 1; 2005-192, s. 2.)

§ 36C-8-806. Trustee's skills.

A trustee who has special skills or expertise, or is named trustee in reliance upon the trustee's representation that the trustee has special skills or expertise, shall use those special skills or expertise. (1999-215, s. 1; 2005-192, s. 2.)

§ 36C-8-807. Delegation by trustee.

(a)   A trustee may delegate duties and powers that a prudent trustee of comparable skills could properly delegate under the circumstances. The trustee shall exercise reasonable care, skill, and caution in:

(1)   Selecting an agent;

(2)   Establishing the scope and terms of the delegation, consistent with the purposes and terms of the trust; and

(3)   Periodically reviewing the agent's actions in order to monitor the agent's performance and compliance with the terms of the delegation.

(b)   In performing a delegated function, an agent owes a duty to the trust to exercise reasonable care to comply with the terms of the delegation.

(c) A trustee who complies with subsection (a) of this section is not liable to the beneficiaries or to the trust for an action of the agent to whom the function was delegated.

(d) By accepting a delegation of powers or duties from the trustee of a trust that is subject to the law of this State, an agent submits to the jurisdiction of the courts of this State. (2005-192, s. 2.)

§ 36C-8-808. Powers of a settlor to take certain actions with respect to the trust.

While a trust is revocable, the settlor of a revocable trust has, at all times, the power to direct or consent to the actions of the trustee whether or not the power is conferred upon the settlor by the terms of the trust. The duty and liability of the trustee subject to the direction and consent of the settlor is as follows:

(1) The trustee may follow a direction of the settlor that is not authorized by or is contrary to the terms of the trust, even if by doing so (i) the trustee exceeds the authority granted to the trustee under the terms of the trust, or (ii) the trustee would otherwise violate a duty the trustee owes under the trust.

(2) The trustee is not liable, individually or as a fiduciary, for any loss resulting directly or indirectly from compliance with the direction. If the settlor requires the settlor's consent to certain actions of the trustee, and the settlor does not provide consent within a reasonable time after the trustee has made a timely request for the settlor's consent, the trustee is not liable, individually or as a fiduciary, for any loss resulting directly or indirectly from the trustee's failure to take any action that required the settlor's consent. (2005-192, s. 2; 2007-106, s. 34; 2012-18, s. 3.1.)

§ 36C-8-809. Control and protection of trust property.

A trustee shall take reasonable steps to take control of and protect the trust property. (2005-192, s. 2.)

§ 36C-8-810. Record keeping and identification of trust property.

(a)   A trustee shall keep adequate records of the administration of the trust.

(b)   A trustee shall keep trust property separate from the trustee's own property.

(c)   Except as otherwise provided in subsection (d) of this section, a trustee shall cause the trust property to be designated so that the interest of the trust, to the extent feasible, appears in records maintained by a party other than a trustee or beneficiary.

(d)   If the trustee maintains records clearly indicating the respective interests, a trustee may invest and administer as a whole the property of two or more separate trusts. (2005-192, s. 2; 2007-106, s. 34.1.)

§ 36C-8-811. Enforcement and defense of claims.

A trustee shall take reasonable steps to enforce claims of the trust and to defend claims against the trust. (2005-192, s. 2.)

§ 36C-8-812. Collecting trust property.

A trustee shall take reasonable steps to compel a former trustee or other person to deliver trust property to the trustee and to redress a breach of trust known to the trustee to have been committed by a former trustee. (2005-192, s. 2.)

§ 36C-8-813. Duty to inform and report.

(a)   The trustee is under a duty to do all of the following:

(1)   Provide reasonably complete and accurate information as to the nature and amount of the trust property, at reasonable intervals, to any qualified

beneficiary who is a distributee or permissible distributee of trust income or principal.

(2)   In response to a reasonable request of any qualified beneficiary:

a.   Provide a copy of the trust instrument.

b.   Provide reasonably complete and accurate information as to the nature and amount of the trust property.

c.   Allow reasonable inspections of the subject matter of the trust and the accounts and other documents relating to the trust.

(b)   Notwithstanding subsection (a) of this section:

(1)   The duty of the trustee under subsection (a) of this section shall not include informing any beneficiary in advance of transactions relating to the trust property.

(2)   A trustee is considered to have discharged the trustee's duty under subdivision (1) of subsection (a) of this section as to a qualified beneficiary for matters disclosed by a report sent at least annually and at termination of the trust to the beneficiary that describes the trust property, liabilities, receipts, and disbursements, including the source and amount of the trustee's compensation, and lists the trust assets and their respective market values, including estimated values of assets with uncertain values. No presumption shall arise that a trustee who does not comply with this subdivision failed to discharge the trustee's duty under subdivision (1) of subsection (a) of this section.

(c)   A qualified beneficiary may waive the right to a trustee's report or other information otherwise required to be furnished under this section. With respect to future reports and other information, a beneficiary may withdraw a waiver previously given.

(d)   Repealed by Session Laws 2007-106, s. 35, effective October 1, 2007. (2005-192, s. 2; 2007-106, s. 35.)

§ 36C-8-814. Discretionary powers; tax savings.

(a) Notwithstanding the breadth of discretion granted to a trustee in the terms of the trust, including the use of terms such as "absolute", "sole", or "uncontrolled", a trustee abuses the trustee's discretion in exercising or failing to exercise a discretionary power if the trustee acts with bad faith, acts dishonestly, acts with an improper motive, even though not a dishonest motive, or if the trustee fails to use the trustee's judgment in accordance with the terms and purposes of the trust and the interests of the beneficiaries.

(b) Subject to subsection (d) of this section, and unless the terms of the trust indicate by an express reference to this subsection that a rule in this subsection does not apply:

(1) A person other than a settlor who is a beneficiary and trustee of a trust that confers on the trustee a power that would, except for this subsection, constitute in whole or in part a general power of appointment may not exercise that power in favor of the trustee/beneficiary, the trustee/beneficiary's estate, the trustee/beneficiary's creditors, or the creditors of the trustee/beneficiary's estate.

(2) Notwithstanding subdivision (1) of this subsection, if the trust confers on the trustee the power to make discretionary distributions to or for the trustee's personal benefit that would, except for this subsection, constitute in whole or in part a general power of appointment, the trustee may exercise the power in accordance with an ascertainable standard.

(3) The trustee may not exercise a power to make discretionary distributions to satisfy a legal obligation of support that the trustee personally owes another person.

(4) Any power conferred upon the trustee in the trustee's capacity as a trustee to allocate receipts and expenses as between income and principal in the trustee's own favor must be exercised in accordance with the provisions of Chapter 37A of the General Statutes, the Uniform Principal and Income Act of 2003.

For purposes of this subsection, a "general power of appointment" means any power that would cause the income to be taxed to the trustee in his individual capacity under section 678 of the Internal Revenue Code and any power that would be a general power of appointment, in whole or in part, under section 2041(b)(1) or section 2514(c) of the Internal Revenue Code.

(c) A power whose exercise is limited or prohibited by subsection (b) of this section may be exercised by a majority of the remaining trustees whose exercise of the power is not so limited or prohibited. If the power of all trustees is so limited or prohibited, the court may appoint a special fiduciary with authority to exercise the power.

(d) Subsection (b) of this section does not apply to:

(1) A power held by the settlor's spouse who is the trustee of a trust for which a marital deduction, as defined in section 2056(b)(5) or section 2523(e) of the Internal Revenue Code, was previously allowed;

(2) Any trust during any period that the trust may be revoked or amended by its settlor; or

(3) A trust, if contributions to the trust qualify for the annual exclusion under section 2503(c) of the Internal Revenue Code.

(e) If a trust created under a will or trust instrument for the benefit of the spouse of the settlor of the trust, other than a trust that provides that upon the termination of the income interest that the entire remaining trust estate be paid to the estate of the spouse, requires that all the income of the trust be paid not less frequently than annually to the spouse and a federal estate or gift tax marital deduction is claimed with respect to the trust, then, unless the trust instrument specifically provides otherwise by reference to this section, any investment in or retention of unproductive property as an asset of the trust is subject to the power of the spouse to require either that the asset be made productive of income, or that it be converted to assets productive of income, within a reasonable period of time. (1991, c. 736, s. 2; 2003-232, s. 5a; 2005-192, s. 2; 2007-106, s. 36.)

§ 36C-8-815. General powers of trustee.

(a) A trustee, without authorization by the court, may exercise any of the following:

(1) Powers conferred by the terms of the trust.

(2) Except as limited by the terms of the trust:

a. All powers over the trust property that an unmarried competent owner has over individually owned property;

b. Any other powers appropriate to achieve the proper investment, management, administration, or distribution of the trust property; and

c. Any other powers conferred by this Chapter.

(b) No provision of this section shall relieve a trustee of the fiduciary duties under this Article. (2005-192, s. 2; 2006-259, s. 13(k).)

§ 36C-8-816. Specific powers of trustee.

Without limiting the authority conferred by G.S. 36C-8-815, a trustee may:

(1) Collect and control trust property and accept or reject additions to the trust property from a settlor or any other person;

(2) Invest and reinvest trust property as the trustee considers advisable in accordance with the trust, and to acquire or sell property, for cash or on credit, at public or private sale;

(3) Exchange, partition, or otherwise change the character of trust property;

(4) Deposit trust money in an account in a regulated financial services institution, including an institution operated by the trustee or an affiliate of the trustee upon compliance with any applicable requirements for the deposit;

(5) Borrow money, with or without security, including from a corporate trustee's lending department, renew or modify loans, and mortgage or pledge trust property for a period within or extending beyond the duration of the trust;

(6) With respect to an interest in a proprietorship, partnership, limited liability company, business trust, corporation, venture, agricultural operation, or other form of business or enterprise, form and transfer, assign, and convey to that form of business or enterprise all or any part of the trust property in exchange for the stock, securities, or obligations of that form of business or enterprise, continue any business or other enterprise, and take any action that

may be taken by shareholders, members, or property owners, including merging, dissolving, or otherwise changing the form of business organization, or contributing additional capital;

(7) With respect to stocks or other securities, exercise the rights of an absolute owner, including the right to:

a. Vote, or give general or limited proxies to vote, with or without power of substitution, or enter into or continue a voting trust agreement, or execute waivers, consents, or objections with respect to those securities;

b. Hold a security in the name of a nominee or in other form without disclosure of the trust so that title may pass by delivery;

c. Pay calls, assessments, and other sums chargeable or accruing against the securities, and sell or exercise stock subscription or conversion rights;

d. Deposit the securities with a depositary or other regulated financial service institution; and

e. Consent, directly or through a committee or other agent, to the merger, consolidation, reorganization, readjustment of capital or financial structure, lease, sale, dissolution, or liquidation of a business enterprise, and elect whether to participate as a member of a class in any litigation involving the securities;

(8) With respect to an interest in real property, construct, or make ordinary or extraordinary repairs to, alterations to, or improvements in, buildings or other structures, demolish improvements, raze existing party walls or buildings or erect new party walls or buildings, subdivide or develop land, dedicate land to public use or grant public or private easements, and make or vacate plats and adjust boundaries, make contracts, licenses, leases, conveyances, or grants of every nature and kind with respect to crops, gravel, sand, oil, gas, timber and forest products, other usufructs or natural resources, and other benefits or incidents of the real property;

(9) Enter into a lease for any purpose as lessor or lessee, including a lease or other arrangement for exploration and removal of natural resources, with or without the option to purchase or renew, for a period within or extending beyond the duration of the trust;

(10) Grant an option involving a sale, lease, or other disposition of trust property or acquire an option for the acquisition of property, including an option exercisable beyond the duration of the trust, and exercise an option so acquired;

(11) Insure the property of the trust against damage or loss and insure the trustee, the trustee's agents, and beneficiaries against liability arising from the administration of the trust at the expense of the trust;

(12) Abandon, relinquish any or all rights to, or decline to administer property of no value or of insufficient benefit or value to the trust to justify its collection or continued administration;

(13) With respect to possible liability for violation of environmental law:

a. Inspect or investigate property the trustee holds or has been asked to hold, or property owned or operated by an organization in which the trustee holds or has been asked to hold an interest, for the purpose of determining the application of environmental law with respect to the property;

b. Take action to prevent, abate, or otherwise remedy any actual or potential violation of any environmental law affecting property held directly or indirectly by the trustee, whether taken before or after the assertion of a claim or the initiation of governmental enforcement;

c. Repealed by Session Laws 2009-48, s. 17, effective October 1, 2009, and applicable to renunciations and powers of attorney executed on or after that date.

d. Compromise claims against the trust that may be asserted for an alleged violation of environmental law; and

e. Pay the expense of any inspection, review, abatement, or remedial action to comply with environmental law;

(14) Pay or contest any claim, compromise, adjust or otherwise settle a claim by or against the trust, and release, in whole or in part, a claim belonging to the trust;

(15) Pay from the trust property taxes, assessments, compensation of the trustee and of employees and agents of the trust, and other expenses incurred in the administration of the trust and the protection of the trust property;

(16) Exercise elections with respect to federal, state, and local taxes including, but not limited to, considering discretionary distributions to a beneficiary as being made from capital gains realized during the year;

(17) Select a mode of payment under any employee benefit or retirement plan, annuity, or life insurance payable to the trustee, exercise rights under that plan, annuity, or life insurance, including exercise of the right to indemnification for expenses and against liabilities, and take appropriate action to collect the proceeds;

(18) Make loans out of trust property, including loans to a beneficiary on terms and conditions the trustee considers to be fair and reasonable under the circumstances, and acquire a lien on future distributions for repayment of those loans;

(19) Pledge trust property to guarantee loans made to any beneficiary;

(19a) Guarantee loans made to any beneficiary;

(19b) Pledge trust property to guarantee loans made to any proprietorship, partnership, limited liability company, business trust, corporation, venture, agricultural operation, or other form of business or enterprise in which the trust or any beneficiary has an ownership interest.

(19c) Guarantee loans made to any proprietorship, partnership, limited liability company, business trust, corporation, venture, agricultural operation, or other form of business or enterprise in which the trust or any beneficiary has an ownership interest.

(20) Appoint a trustee to act in another jurisdiction with respect to trust property located in the other jurisdiction, confer upon the appointed trustee all of the powers and duties of the appointing trustee, limit those powers the appointed trustee may exercise and the duties for which the appointed trustee is responsible, require that the appointed trustee furnish security, and remove any trustee so appointed;

(21) Pay an amount distributable to a beneficiary regardless of whether the beneficiary is a minor or incompetent or whether the trustee reasonably believes the beneficiary to be incompetent, by paying it directly to the beneficiary or

applying it for the beneficiary's benefit, or if the beneficiary is a minor or incompetent or a person the trustee reasonably believes to be incompetent, by:

a. Paying it to the beneficiary's general guardian or the guardian of the beneficiary's estate;

b. Paying it to a custodian under a uniform transfer to minors act or custodial trustee under a uniform custodial trust act and, for that purpose, creating a custodianship or custodial trust for the benefit of the beneficiary;

c. Paying it to an adult relative or other person having legal or physical care or custody of the beneficiary, to be expended on the beneficiary's behalf; or

d. Managing it as a separate fund on the beneficiary's behalf.

A trustee making payments under this subdivision does not have any duty to see to the application of the payments so made, if the trustee exercised due care in the selection of the person, including a minor or incompetent, to whom the payments were made, and the receipt of that person shall be full acquittance to the trustee. Notwithstanding the foregoing, if a mandatory distribution is to be paid to a beneficiary who is not a minor or incompetent or a person the trustee reasonably believes to be incompetent, the distribution may be applied for the beneficiary's benefit only with the beneficiary's consent;

(22) On distribution of trust property or the division or termination of a trust, make distributions in divided or undivided interests, allocate particular assets in proportionate or disproportionate shares without regard to the income tax basis or other special tax attributes of the assets, as the trustee finds to be most practicable and for the best interests of the distributees, value the trust property for those purposes, and adjust for resulting differences in valuation; and to distribute trust property in kind or in cash, or partially in kind and partially in cash, in divided or undivided interests;

(23) Resolve a dispute concerning the interpretation of the trust or its administration by mediation, arbitration, or other procedure for alternative dispute resolution;

(24) Prosecute or defend an action, claim, or judicial proceeding in any jurisdiction to protect trust property and the trustee in the performance of the trustee's duties;

(25) Make, execute, and deliver contracts and other instruments, including instruments under seal, that are useful to achieve or facilitate the exercise of the trustee's powers;

(26) On termination of the trust, exercise all of the powers otherwise exercisable by the trustee during the administration of the trust, including, without limitation, the trustee's investment powers, the power to sell assets, and the powers set forth in subdivision (22) of this section, and exercise the additional powers appropriate to wind up the administration of the trust and distribute the trust property to the persons entitled to it;

(27) Employ as advisors or assistants in the performance of administrative duties, or delegate administrative duties in the manner provided in G.S. 36C-8-807, to persons, firms, and corporations, including agents, auditors, accountants, brokers, attorneys-at-law, attorneys-in-fact, investment advisors, appraisers, custodians, rental agents, realtors, and tax specialists;

(28) Bid on property at a foreclosure sale, or acquire property from a mortgagor or obligor without foreclosure, and retain the property so bid on or taken over without foreclosure;

(29) Divide one trust into several trusts and make distributions from those trusts in the manner provided in G.S. 36C-4-417;

(30) Request an order from the court for the sale of real or personal property under Article 29A of Chapter 1 of the General Statutes, or for the exchange, partition, or other disposition or change in the character of, or for the grant of options or other rights in or to, such property;

(31) Distribute the assets of an inoperative trust consistent with the authority granted under G.S. 28A-22-110; and

(32) Renounce, in accordance with Chapter 31B of the General Statutes, an interest in or power over property, including property that is or may be burdened with liability for violation of environmental law. (2005-192, s. 2; 2007-106, s. 37; 2009-48, ss. 16, 17; 2009-222, s. 3; 2011-339, s. 4; 2013-91, s. 2(c).)

§ 36C-8-816.1. Trustee's special power to appoint to a second trust.

(a) For purposes of this section, the following definitions apply:

(1) Current beneficiary. - A person who is a permissible distributee of trust income or principal.

(2) Original trust. - A trust established under an irrevocable trust instrument pursuant to the terms of which a trustee has a discretionary power to distribute principal or income of the trust to or for the benefit of one or more current beneficiaries of the trust.

(3) Second trust. - A trust established under an irrevocable trust instrument, the current beneficiaries of which are one or more of the current beneficiaries of the original trust. The second trust may be a trust created under the same trust instrument as the original trust or under a different trust instrument.

(b) A trustee of an original trust may, without authorization by the court, exercise the discretionary power to distribute principal or income to or for the benefit of one or more current beneficiaries of the original trust by appointing all or part of the principal or income of the original trust subject to the power in favor of a trustee of a second trust. The trustee of the original trust may exercise this power whether or not there is a current need to distribute principal or income under any standard provided in the terms of the original trust. The trustee's special power to appoint trust principal or income in further trust under this section includes the power to create the second trust.

(c) The terms of the second trust shall be subject to all of the following:

(1) The beneficiaries of the second trust may include only beneficiaries of the original trust.

(2) A beneficiary who has only a future beneficial interest, vested or contingent, in the original trust cannot have the future beneficial interest accelerated to a present interest in the second trust.

(3) The terms of the second trust may not reduce any fixed income, annuity, or unitrust interest of a beneficiary in the assets of the original trust if that interest has come into effect with respect to the beneficiary.

(4) If any contribution to the original trust qualified for a marital or charitable deduction for federal income, gift, or estate tax purposes under the Internal Revenue Code, then the second trust shall not contain any provision that, if

included in the original trust, would have prevented the original trust from qualifying for the deduction or that would have reduced the amount of the deduction.

(5) If contributions to the original trust have been excluded from the gift tax by the application of section 2503(b) and section 2503(c) of the Internal Revenue Code, then the second trust shall provide that the beneficiary's remainder interest in the contributions shall vest and become distributable no later than the date upon which the interest would have vested and become distributable under the terms of the original trust.

(6) If any beneficiary of the original trust has a power of withdrawal over trust property, then either:

a. The terms of the second trust must provide a power of withdrawal in the second trust identical to the power of withdrawal in the original trust; or

b. Sufficient trust property must remain in the original trust to satisfy the outstanding power of withdrawal.

(7) If a trustee of an original trust exercises a power to distribute principal or income that is subject to an ascertainable standard by appointing property to a second trust, then the power to distribute income or principal in the second trust must be subject to the same ascertainable standard as in the original trust and must be exercisable in favor of the same current beneficiaries to whom such distribution could be made in the original trust.

(8) The second trust may confer a power of appointment upon a beneficiary of the original trust to whom or for the benefit of whom the trustee has the power to distribute principal or income of the original trust. The permissible appointees of the power of appointment conferred upon a beneficiary may include persons who are not beneficiaries of the original or second trust. The power of appointment conferred upon a beneficiary shall be subject to the provisions of G.S. 41-23 specifying the permissible period allowed for the suspension of the power of alienation of the original trust and the time from which that permissible period is computed.

(d) A trustee may not exercise the power to appoint principal or income under subsection (b) of this section if the trustee is a beneficiary of the original trust, but the remaining cotrustee or a majority of the remaining cotrustees may act for the trust. If all the trustees are beneficiaries of the original trust, then the court may appoint a special fiduciary with authority to exercise the power to appoint principal or income under subsection (b) of this section.

(e) The exercise of the power to appoint principal or income under subsection (b) of this section:

(1) Shall be considered the exercise of a power of appointment, other than a power to appoint to the trustee, the trustee's creditors, the trustee's estate, or the creditors of the trustee's estate; and

(2) Shall be subject to the provisions of G.S. 41-23 specifying the permissible period allowed for the suspension of the power of alienation of the original trust and the time from which that permissible period is computed; and

(3) Is not prohibited by a spendthrift provision or by a provision in the original trust instrument that prohibits amendment or revocation of the trust.

(f) To effect the exercise of the power to appoint principal or income under subsection (b) of this section, all of the following shall apply:

(1) The exercise of the power to appoint shall be made by an instrument in writing, signed and acknowledged by the trustee, setting forth the manner of the exercise of the power, including the terms of the second trust, and the effective date of the exercise of the power. The instrument shall be filed with the records of the original trust.

(2) The trustee shall give written notice to all qualified beneficiaries of the original trust, at least 60 days prior to the effective date of the exercise of the power to appoint, of the trustee's intention to exercise the power. The notice shall include a copy of the instrument described in subdivision (1) of this subsection.

(3) If all qualified beneficiaries waive the notice period by a signed written instrument delivered to the trustee, the trustee's power to appoint principal or income shall be exercisable after notice is waived by all qualified beneficiaries, notwithstanding the effective date of the exercise of the power.

(4) The trustee's notice under this subsection shall not limit the right of any beneficiary to object to the exercise of the trustee's power to appoint and bring an action for breach of trust seeking appropriate relief as provided by G.S. 36C-10-1001.

(g)   Nothing in this section shall be construed to create or imply a duty of the trustee to exercise the power to distribute principal or income, and no inference of impropriety shall be made as a result of a trustee not exercising the power to appoint principal or income conferred under subsection (b) of this section. Nothing in this section shall be construed to abridge the right of any trustee who has a power to appoint property in further trust that arises under the terms of the original trust or under any other section of this Chapter or under another provision of law or under common law.

(h)   A trustee or beneficiary may commence a proceeding to approve or disapprove a proposed exercise of the trustee's special power to appoint to a second trust pursuant to subsection (b) of this section. (2009-318, s. 1; 2010-97, s. 5(b); 2013-91, s. 2(d).)

§ 36C-8-817. Distribution upon termination.

Upon the occurrence of an event terminating or partially terminating a trust, the trustee shall proceed expeditiously to distribute the trust property to the persons entitled to it, subject to the right of the trustee to retain a reasonable reserve for the payment of debts, expenses, and taxes. (2005-192, s. 2.)

§ 36C-8-818. Notice of deceased Medicaid beneficiaries.

If a trust was established by a person who at the time of that person's death was receiving medical assistance, as defined in G.S. 108A-70.5(b)(1), and the trust was revocable at the time of that person's death, then any trustee of that trust who knows of the medical assistance within 90 days of the person's death shall provide notice of that person's death to the Department of Health and Human Services, Division of Medical Assistance, within 90 days of the person's death. This section does not apply to trustees of preneed funeral trusts established or created pursuant to Article 13D of Chapter 90 of the General Statutes. (2013-378, s. 5.)

Article 8A.

Powers, Duties, and Liability of a Power Holder Other Than a Trustee; Duty and Liability of a Trustee With Respect to Power Holder's Actions.

§ 36C-8A-1. Definition.

For purposes of this Article, the term "power holder" means a person who under the terms of a trust has the power to take certain actions with respect to a trust and who is not a trustee or a settlor with a power to direct or consent pursuant to G.S. 36C-8-808. (2012-18, s. 3.4.)

§ 36C-8A-2. Powers of a power holder.

(a) The terms of a trust may confer upon a power holder a power to direct or consent to a duty that would normally be required of a trustee, including, but not limited to, a power to direct or consent to the following:

(1) Investments, including any action relating to investment of all or any one or more of the trust assets that a trustee is authorized to take under this Chapter.

(2) Discretionary distributions of trust assets, including distributions to one or more beneficiaries, distribution of one of more trust assets, and termination of the trust by distribution of all of the trust assets.

(3) Any other matter regarding trust administration, including the transfer of the principal place of administration of the trust.

(b) The terms of a trust may also confer upon the power holder any other power, including, but not limited to, the power to do the following:

(1) Modify or amend the trust to do any of the following:

a. Achieve favorable tax status under applicable law.

b. Take advantage of laws governing restraints on alienation or other State laws restricting the terms of the trust, distribution of trust property, or the administration of the trust.

(2) Remove and appoint trustees and power holders.

(3) Increase or decrease the interests of any beneficiary.

(4) Grant a power of appointment to one or more beneficiaries of the trust or modify the terms of or terminate a power of appointment granted to a beneficiary by the governing instrument, except that a grant or modification of a power of appointment may not grant a beneficial interest to any of the following:

a. Any individual or class of individuals not specifically provided for in the trust instrument.

b. The person having the power to grant, modify, or terminate the power of appointment.

c. The estate and creditors of the person having the power to grant, modify, or terminate the power of appointment.

(5) Change the governing law of the trust. (2012-18, s. 3.4.)

§ 36C-8A-3. Duty and liability of power holder.

(a) A power holder is a fiduciary with respect to the powers conferred upon the power holder who, as such, is required to act in good faith and in accordance with the purposes and terms of a trust and the interests of the beneficiaries, except a power holder is not a fiduciary with respect to the following:

(1) A power to remove and appoint a trustee or power holder.

(2) A power that constitutes a power of appointment held by a beneficiary of a trust.

(3) A power the exercise or nonexercise of which may affect only the interests of the power holder and no other beneficiary.

(b) A power holder is liable for any loss that results from breach of fiduciary duty occurring as a result of the exercise or nonexercise of the power.

(c) The following provisions applicable to a trustee shall also be applicable to a power holder with respect to powers conferred upon the power holder as a fiduciary:

(1) The provisions of G.S. 36C-8-814 regarding discretionary powers and tax savings.

(2) The provisions of G.S. 36C-10-1001 through G.S. 36C-10-1012 regarding liability of trustees and rights of third persons dealing with trustees.

(3) The provisions of Article 9 of this Chapter regarding the uniform prudent investor rule. (2012-18, s. 3.4.)

§ 36C-8A-4. Duty and liability of trustee.

(a) If the terms of a trust confer upon a power holder the power to direct certain actions of the trustee, the trustee must act in accordance with the direction and is not liable, individually or as a fiduciary, for any loss resulting directly or indirectly from compliance with the direction unless compliance with the direction constitutes intentional misconduct on the part of the trustee.

(b) If the terms of a trust confer upon the power holder the power to consent to certain actions of the trustee, and the power holder does not provide consent within a reasonable time after the trustee has made a timely request for the power holder's consent, the trustee is not liable, individually or as a fiduciary, for any loss resulting directly or indirectly from the trustee's failure to take any action that required the power holder's consent.

(c) If the terms of a trust confer upon the person a power other than the power to direct or consent to actions of the trustee, the trustee is not liable, individually or as a fiduciary, for any loss resulting directly or indirectly from the exercise or nonexercise of the power.

(d) The trustee has no duty to monitor the conduct of the power holder, provide advice to the power holder, or consult with the power holder. The trustee is not required to give notice to any beneficiary of any action taken or not taken by the power holder whether or not the trustee agrees with the result. Administrative actions taken by the trustee for the purpose of implementing directions of the power holder, including confirming that the directions of the power holder have been carried out, do not constitute monitoring of the power holder nor do they constitute participation in decisions within the scope of the power holder's authority. (2012-18, s. 3.4.)

§ 36C-8A-5. Compensation and reimbursement of expenses of power holder.

A power holder as a fiduciary is entitled to compensation and reimbursement of expenses as provided in G.S. 32-59. (2012-18, s. 3.4.)

§ 36C-8A-6. Jurisdiction over power holder.

(a) By accepting appointment to serve as a power holder with respect to a trust having its principal place of business in this State, or by moving the principal place of administration to this State, the power holder submits personally to the jurisdiction of the courts of this State regarding any matter involving action or inaction of the power holder.

(b) This section does not preclude other methods of obtaining jurisdiction over a power holder. (2012-18, s. 3.4.)

§ 36C-8A-7. Accepting or declining the appointment as power holder.

(a) A person designated as a power holder accepts the appointment to serve as a power holder:

(1) By substantially complying with a method of acceptance provided in the terms of a trust; or

(2) If the terms of a trust do not provide a method or the method provided in the terms of a trust is not expressly made exclusive, by exercising powers or

performing duties as a power holder or otherwise indicating acceptance of the appointment to serve as a power holder.

(b)   A person designated as a power holder may reject the appointment to serve as a power holder. A trustee may give written notice to a power holder requesting acceptance of the appointment as power holder. A power holder who does not accept such appointment within 120 days after receipt of such notice is considered to have rejected the appointment to serve as a power holder. (2012-18, s. 3.4.)

§ 36C-8A-8. Powers of trustee in the absence of a power holder.

The trustee shall be vested with any fiduciary power or duty conferred upon a power holder by the terms of a trust that are described in G.S. 36C-8A-2(a) during the time when no power holder is available to exercise such power or perform such duty because of absence, illness, or other cause. (2012-18, s. 3.4.)

§ 36C-8A-9. More than one power holder.

When there is more than one power holder authorized to act, and they are unable to reach a unanimous decision, they may act by majority decision. Unanimity is required when only two are authorized to act. (2012-18, s. 3.4.)

§ 36C-8A-10. Resignation of power holder.

(a)   A power holder may resign upon either of the following conditions:

(1)   Upon at least 30 days' notice in writing to the qualified beneficiaries, the settlor, if living, and all trustees.

(2)   With the approval of the court.

(b) In approving a resignation, the court may issue orders and impose conditions reasonably necessary for the protection of the trust property. (2012-18, s. 3.4.)

§ 36C-8A-11. Removal of power holder.

(a) For the reasons set forth in subsection (b) of this section, the settlor of an irrevocable trust, a trustee of an irrevocable trust, or a beneficiary of an irrevocable trust may request the court to remove a power holder, or a power holder may be removed by the court on its own initiative.

(b) The court may remove a power holder under any of the following circumstances:

(1) The power holder has committed a serious breach of trust.

(2) Lack of cooperation with the trustee substantially impairs the administration of the trust.

(3) Because of unfitness, unwillingness, or a persistent failure of the power holder to exercise effectively the duties and powers conferred upon the power holder the court determines that removal of the power holder best serves the interests of the beneficiaries.

(4) There has been a substantial change of circumstances, the court finds that removal of the power holder best serves the interests of all of the beneficiaries and is consistent with a material purpose of the trust, and a suitable successor power holder is available.

(c) Pending a final decision on a request to remove a power holder, or in lieu of or in addition to removing a power holder, the court may order appropriate relief under G.S. 36C-10-1001(b) as may be necessary to protect the trust property or the interests of the beneficiaries. (2012-18, s. 3.4.)

Article 9.

Uniform Prudent Investor Act.

§ 36C-9-901. Prudent investor rule; applicability.

(a) Except as otherwise provided in subsection (b) of this section, a trustee who invests and manages trust assets owes a duty to the beneficiaries of the trust to comply with the prudent investor rule set forth in this Article.

(b) The prudent investor rule is a default rule and may be expanded, restricted, eliminated, or otherwise altered by the provisions of a trust that govern or direct investments in a manner inconsistent with this Article. A trustee is not liable to a beneficiary to the extent that the trustee acted in reasonable reliance on the terms of the trust.

(c) The following terms or comparable language in a trust, unless otherwise limited or modified, authorize any investment or strategy permitted under this Article: "Chapter 36A", "investments in accordance with Article 15 of Chapter 36A", "investments in accordance with Article 9 of Chapter 36C", "investments permissible by law for investment of trust funds", "legal investments", "authorized investments", "using the judgment and care under the circumstances then prevailing that persons of prudence, discretion, and intelligence exercise in the management of their own affairs, not in regard to speculation but in regard to the permanent disposition of their funds, considering the probable income as well as the probable safety of their capital", "prudent man rule", "prudent trustee rule", "prudent person rule", and "prudent investor rule". This Article also applies where a trust contains no investment standard.

(d) This Article does not apply to:

(1) Unless the trust provides otherwise by specific reference to this Article:

a. Trusts under any federal employee retirement income security statute or other retirement or pension trusts;

b. Trusts that are created by legislative act;

c. Trusts that are created by or under premarital or postmarital agreements, divorce settlements, settlements of other proceedings or disputes;

d. Transfers under a Uniform Transfers to Minors Act;

e. Transfers under a Uniform Custodial Trust Act; or

f. Honorary trusts, trusts for pets, and trusts for cemetery lots.

(2) Trusts imposed or required under another Chapter of the General Statutes or by rule in which the investment of the trust funds is regulated by the other Chapter or by rule, unless a provision of the other chapter or the rule provides otherwise by a specific reference to this Article. (1999-215, s. 1; 2001-267, s. 7; 2005-192, s. 2.)

§ 36C-9-902. Standard of care; portfolio strategy; risk and return objectives.

(a) A trustee shall invest and manage trust assets as a prudent investor would, by considering the purposes, terms, distribution requirements, and other circumstances of the trust. In satisfying this standard, the trustee shall exercise reasonable care, skill, and caution.

(b) A trustee's investment and management decisions respecting individual assets must be evaluated not in isolation but in the context of the trust portfolio as a whole and as a part of an overall investment strategy having risk and return objectives reasonably suited to the trust.

(c) Among circumstances that a trustee shall consider in investing and managing trust assets are any of the following that are relevant to the trust or its beneficiaries:

(1) General economic conditions;

(2) The possible effect of inflation or deflation;

(3) The expected tax consequences of investment decisions or strategies;

(4) The role that each investment or course of action plays within the overall trust portfolio, which may include financial assets, interests in closely held enterprises, tangible and intangible personal property, and real property;

(5) The expected total return from income and the appreciation of capital;

(6) Other resources of the beneficiaries known to the trustee;

(7) Needs for liquidity, regularity of income, and preservation or appreciation of capital; and

(8) An asset's special relationship or special value, if any, to the purposes of the trust or to one or more of the beneficiaries.

(d) A trustee shall make a reasonable effort to verify facts relevant to the investment and management of trust assets.

(e) A trustee may invest in any kind of property or type of investment consistent with the standards of this Article. (1999-215, s. 1; 2005-192, s. 2.)

§ 36C-9-903. Diversification.

A trustee shall diversify the investments of the trust unless the trustee reasonably determines that, because of special circumstances, the purposes of the trust are better served without diversifying. (1999-215, s. 1; 2005-192, s. 2.)

§ 36C-9-903.1. Duties as to life insurance.

(a) Notwithstanding the provisions of this Article, the duties of a trustee with respect to acquiring or retaining a contract of insurance upon the life of the settlor, or the lives of the settlor and the settlor's spouse, do not include a duty (i) to determine whether any such contract is or remains a proper investment; (ii) to exercise policy options, including investment options, available under any such contract; or (iii) to diversify any such contract. A trustee is not liable to the beneficiaries of the trust or to any party for any loss arising from the absence of those duties upon the trustee.

(b) The trustee of a trust described under subsection (a) of this section established prior to October 1, 1995, shall notify the settlor in writing that, unless the settlor provides written notice to the contrary to the trustee within 60 days of the trustee's notice, the provisions of subsection (a) of this section shall apply to the trust. Subsection (a) of this section shall not apply if, within 60 days of the trustee's notice, the settlor notifies the trustee that subsection (a) of this section shall not apply. (2007-106, s. 37.1.)

§ 36C-9-904. Duties at inception of trusteeship.

Within a reasonable time after accepting a trusteeship or receiving trust assets, a trustee shall review the trust assets and make and implement decisions concerning the retention and disposition of assets in order to bring the trust portfolio into compliance with the purposes, terms, distribution requirements, and other circumstances of the trust, and with the requirements of this Chapter. (1999-215, s. 1; 2005-192, s. 2.)

§ 36C-9-905. Reviewing compliance.

Compliance with the prudent investor rule is determined in light of the facts and circumstances existing at the time of a trustee's decision or action and not by hindsight. (1999-215, s. 1; 2005-192, s. 2.)

§ 36C-9-906. Effect on charitable remainder trusts.

Nothing in this Article shall prevent the application of Article 4B of this Chapter to a "charitable remainder trust" as defined in G.S. 36C-4B-3(1). (1999-215, s. 1; 2005-192, s. 2.)

§ 36C-9-907. Short title.

This Article may be cited as the "North Carolina Uniform Prudent Investor Act." (1999-215, s. 1; 2005-192, s. 2.)

Article 10.

Liability of Trustees and Rights of Persons Dealing with Trustees.

§ 36C-10-1001. Remedies for breach of trust.

(a) A violation by a trustee of a duty the trustee owes under a trust is a breach of trust.

(b) To remedy a breach of trust that has occurred or may occur, the court may:

(1) Compel the trustee to perform the trustee's duties;

(2) Enjoin the trustee from committing a breach of trust;

(3) Compel the trustee to redress a breach of trust by paying money, restoring property, or other means;

(4) Order a trustee to account;

(5) Appoint a special fiduciary to take possession of the trust property and administer the trust;

(6) Suspend the trustee;

(7) Remove the trustee as provided in G.S. 36C-7-706;

(8) Reduce or deny compensation to the trustee;

(9) Subject to G.S. 36C-10-1012, void an act of the trustee, impose a lien or a constructive trust on trust property, or trace trust property wrongfully disposed of and recover the property or its proceeds; or

(10) Order any other appropriate relief.

(c) The court may, for cause shown, relieve a trustee from liability for any breach of trust, or wholly or partly excuse a trustee who has acted honestly and reasonably from liability for a breach of trust. (2005-192, s. 2.)

§ 36C-10-1002. Damages for breach of trust.

(a) A trustee who commits a breach of trust is liable for the greater of:

(1) The amount required to restore the value of the trust property and trust distributions to what they would have been had the breach not occurred; or

(2) The profit the trustee made by reason of the breach.

(b) Except as otherwise provided in this subsection, if more than one trustee is liable to the beneficiaries for a breach of trust, a trustee is entitled to contribution from the other trustee or trustees. A trustee is not entitled to contribution if the trustee was substantially more at fault than another trustee or if the trustee committed the breach of trust in bad faith or with reckless indifference to the purposes of the trust or the interests of the beneficiaries. A trustee who received a benefit from the breach of trust is not entitled to contribution from another trustee to the extent of the benefit received. (2005-192, s. 2.)

§ 36C-10-1003. Liability in absence of breach.

(a) A trustee is accountable for any profit made by the trustee arising from the administration of the trust, even absent a breach of trust. Nothing in this section limits a trustee's right to compensation under G.S. 36C-7-708 or payments allowed under G.S. 36C-8-802(f).

(b) Absent a breach of trust, a trustee is not liable for a loss or depreciation in the value of trust property or for not having made a profit. (2005-192, s. 2.)

§ 36C-10-1004. Attorneys' fees and costs.

In a judicial proceeding involving the administration of a trust, the court may award costs and expenses, including reasonable attorneys' fees, as provided in the General Statutes. (2005-192, s. 2.)

§ 36C-10-1005. Limitation of action against trustee.

(a) No proceeding against a trustee for breach of trust may be commenced more than five years after the first to occur of: (i) the removal, resignation, or death of the trustee; (ii) the termination of the beneficiary's interest in the trust; or (iii) the termination of the trust.

(b) Except as provided in subsection (a) of this section, Chapter 1 of the General Statutes governs the limitations of actions on judicial proceedings involving trusts. (2005-192, s. 2.)

§ 36C-10-1006. Reliance on trust instrument.

A trustee who acts in reasonable reliance on the terms of the trust as expressed in a trust instrument is not liable for a breach of trust to the extent that the breach resulted from the reliance. (2005-192, s. 2.)

§ 36C-10-1007. Event affecting administration or distribution.

If the happening of an event, including marriage, divorce, performance of educational requirements, or death, affects the administration or distribution of a trust, a trustee who has exercised reasonable care to ascertain the happening of the event is not liable for a loss resulting from the trustee's lack of knowledge. (2005-192, s. 2.)

§ 36C-10-1008. Exculpation of trustee.

A term of a trust relieving a trustee of liability for breach of trust is unenforceable to the extent that it relieves the trustee of liability for breach of trust committed in bad faith or with reckless indifference to the purposes of the trust or the interests of the beneficiaries. (2005-192, s. 2.)

§ 36C-10-1009. Beneficiary's consent, release, or ratification.

(a)   A trustee is not liable to a beneficiary for breach of trust if the beneficiary consented to the conduct constituting the breach, released the trustee from liability for the breach, or ratified the transaction constituting the breach, unless:

(1)   The consent, release, or ratification of the beneficiary was induced by improper conduct of the trustee; or

(2)   At the time of the consent, release, or ratification, the beneficiary did not have knowledge of the beneficiary's rights or of the material facts relating to the breach.

(b)   No consideration is required for the consent, release, or ratification to be valid. (2005-192, s. 2.)

§ 36C-10-1010. Limitation on personal liability of trustee.

(a)   Except as otherwise provided in the contract, a trustee is not personally liable on a contract properly entered into in the trustee's fiduciary capacity in the course of administering the trust if the trustee in making the contract disclosed the fiduciary capacity. The addition of the phrase "trustee" or "as trustee" or a similar designation to the signature of a trustee on a written contract is considered prima facie evidence of a disclosure of fiduciary capacity.

(b)   A trustee is personally liable for torts committed in the course of administering a trust, or for obligations arising from ownership or control of trust property, including liability for violation of environmental law, only if the trustee is personally at fault.

(c)   A claim based on a contract entered into by a trustee in the trustee's fiduciary capacity, on an obligation arising from ownership or control of trust property, or on a tort committed in the course of administering a trust, may be asserted in a judicial proceeding against the trustee in the trustee's fiduciary capacity, whether or not the trustee is personally liable for the claim. Any judgment rendered in favor of a claimant in such a judicial proceeding against a trust may be recovered from the trust property without proof that the trustee could have obtained reimbursement from the trust if the trustee had paid the claim.

(d) A trustee is entitled to indemnity from the trust for any claim, other than a breach of trust, for which the trustee is liable:

(1) If the claim arose from a common incident of activity in which the trustee was properly engaged for the trust;

(2) If the trustee was not personally at fault; or

(3) To the extent that the trustee's actions increased the value of trust property.

(e) A decision by a trustee not to inspect property, or to decline to accept property, shall not create any inference as to liability, under any environmental law, with respect to that property. A trustee shall have no liability for a decrease in value of property in a trust by reason of the trustee's compliance with any environmental law, including reporting requirements. (2005-192, s. 2.)

§ 36C-10-1011. Interest as general partner.

(a) Except as otherwise provided in subsection (c) of this section or unless personal liability is imposed in the contract, a trustee who holds, in a fiduciary capacity, an interest as a general partner in a general or limited partnership is not personally liable on a contract entered into by the partnership if the fiduciary capacity was disclosed. The addition of the phrase "trustee" or "as trustee" or a similar designation to the signature of a trustee on a written partnership document is considered prima facie evidence of a disclosure of fiduciary capacity.

(b) A trustee who holds, in a fiduciary capacity, an interest as a general partner is not personally liable for torts committed by the partnership or for obligations arising from ownership or control of the interest unless the trustee is personally at fault. This subsection does not apply to additional ownership interests of the trustee held in a nonfiduciary capacity.

(c) If the settlor transfers an existing general partnership interest to a revocable trust, the settlor remains personally liable for partnership obligations as if the settlor were a general partner. (2005-192, s. 2.)

§ 36C-10-1012. Protection of person dealing with trustee.

(a) A person other than a beneficiary who in good faith assists a trustee, or who in good faith and for value deals with a trustee, without knowledge that the trustee is exceeding or improperly exercising the trustee's powers, is protected from liability as if the trustee properly exercised the power.

(b) A person other than a beneficiary who in good faith deals with a trustee is not required to inquire into the extent of the trustee's powers or the propriety of their exercise.

(c) A person who in good faith delivers assets to a trustee need not ensure their proper application.

(d) A person other than a beneficiary who in good faith assists a former trustee, or who in good faith and for value deals with a former trustee, without knowledge that the trusteeship has terminated is protected from liability as if the former trustee were still a trustee.

(e) Comparable protective provisions of other laws relating to commercial transactions or transfer of securities by fiduciaries prevail over the protection provided by this section.

(f) A person is not required to obtain a certification under G.S. 36C-10-1013 in order to be entitled to the protections of this section. (2005-192, s. 2.)

§ 36C-10-1013. Certification of trust.

(a) Instead of furnishing a copy of the trust instrument to a person other than a beneficiary, the trustee may furnish to the person a certification of trust containing the following information:

(1) The existence of the trust and the date the trust instrument was executed;

(2) The identity of the settlor, unless withheld under a provision in the trust instrument;

(3)   The identity and address of the currently acting trustee;

(4)   The powers of the trustee;

(5)   The revocability or irrevocability of the trust and the identity of any person holding a power to revoke the trust;

(6)   The authority of cotrustees to sign or otherwise authenticate and whether all or less than all are required in order to exercise powers of the trustee;

(7)   The trust's taxpayer identification number; and

(8)   The manner of taking title to trust property.

(b)   Any trustee may sign or otherwise authenticate a certification of trust.

(c)   A certification of trust must state that the trust has not been revoked, modified, or amended in any manner that would cause the representations contained in the certification of trust to be incorrect.

(d)   A certification of trust need not contain the dispositive terms of a trust.

(e)   A recipient of a certification of trust may require the trustee to furnish copies of those excerpts from the original trust instrument and later amendments that designate the trustee and confer upon the trustee the power to act in the pending transaction.

(f)   A person who acts in reliance upon a certification of trust without knowledge that the representations contained in the certification are incorrect is not liable to any person for so acting and may assume without inquiry the existence of the facts contained in the certification. Knowledge of the terms of the trust may not be inferred solely from the fact that the person relying upon the certification holds a copy of all or part of the trust instrument.

(g)   A person who in good faith enters into a transaction in reliance upon a certification of trust may enforce the transaction against the trust property as if the representations contained in the certification were correct.

(h) A person making a demand for the trust instrument in addition to a certification of trust or excerpts is liable for damages if the court determines that the person did not act in good faith in demanding the trust instrument.

(i) This section does not limit the right of a person to obtain a copy of the trust instrument in a judicial proceeding concerning the trust.

(j) In transactions involving real property, a person who acts in reliance upon a certification of trust may require that the certification of trust be executed and acknowledged in a manner that will permit its registration in the office of the register of deeds in the county where the real property is located. The certification of trust need not contain the trust's taxpayer identification number if that taxpayer identification number is also the social security number of a grantor. However, the trust's taxpayer identification number shall be certified by the trustee to the person acting in reliance upon the certification of trust in a manner reasonably satisfactory to that person. (2005-192, s. 2.)

Article 11.

Miscellaneous Provisions.

§ 36C-11-1101. Uniformity of application and construction.

In applying and construing this Chapter, consideration may be given to the need to promote uniformity of the law with respect to its subject matter among states that enact it. (2005-192, s. 2.)

§ 36C-11-1102. Electronic records and signatures.

The provisions of this Chapter governing the legal effect, validity, or enforceability of electronic records or electronic signatures, and of contracts formed or performed with the use of those records or signatures, conform to the requirements of section 102 of the Electronic Signatures in Global and National Commerce Act (15 U.S.C. § 7002) and supersede, modify, and limit the requirements of the Electronic Signatures in Global and National Commerce Act. (2005-192, s. 2.)

§ 36C-11-1103. Severability clause.

If any provision of this Chapter or its application to any person or circumstances is held invalid, the invalidity does not affect other provisions or applications of this Chapter that can be given effect without the invalid provision or application, and to this end the provisions of this Chapter are severable. (2005-192, s. 2.)

§ 36C-11-1104. Trustee signatures.

The signature of a trustee of a trust who signs a document for or on behalf of the trust shall be deemed to be the signature of the trustee as such. A document which identifies a trust shall be deemed to include the trustee or the trustees as such. (2007-106, s. 54.)

§ 36C-11-1105: Reserved for future codification purposes.

§ 36C-11-1106. Application to existing relationships.

(a) Except as otherwise provided in this Chapter, this Chapter applies to (i) all trusts created before, on, or after January 1, 2006; (ii) all judicial proceedings concerning trusts commenced on or after January 1, 2006; and (iii) judicial proceedings concerning trusts commenced before January 1, 2006, unless the court finds that application of a particular provision of this Chapter would substantially interfere with the effective conduct of the judicial proceedings or prejudice the rights of the parties, in which case the particular provision of this Chapter does not apply and the superseded law applies.

(b) Except as otherwise provided in this Chapter, any rule of construction or presumption provided in this Chapter applies to trust instruments executed before January 1, 2006, unless there is a clear indication of a contrary intent in the terms of the trust or unless application of that rule of construction or presumption would impair substantial rights of a beneficiary. Except as otherwise provided in this Chapter, an act done before January 1, 2006, is not affected by this Chapter. If a right is acquired, extinguished, or barred upon the expiration of a prescribed period that has commenced to run under any other statute before January 1, 2006, that statute continues to apply to the right even if it has been repealed or superseded.(2005-192, ss. 7(a), (b); 2006-226, ss. 31(a), (b).)

Vision Books Order Form

Fax Orders: 1-980-299-5965

Phone Orders: 1-704-898-0770

E-mail Orders: www.visionbooks.org

Mail Orders: Vision Books, LLC
                  P.O. Box 42406
                  Charlotte, NC 28215

Shipp To:
Name_____
Address_____
City_____State_____Zip_____
Phone_____Fax_____
Email_____@_____

Bill To: We can bill a third party on your behalf.
Name_____
Address_____
City_____State_____Zip_____
Phone____(   )_____Fax_____
Email_____@_____

Pamphlet Number ($15.00 Each)	Qty	Total Cost
_____	_____	_____
_____	_____	_____
_____	_____	_____
_____	_____	_____
_____	_____	_____
_____	_____	_____
_____	_____	_____
<u>Full Volume Set 1-92</u>	<u>92 Pamphlets</u>	<u>1,380.00</u>

Free Shipping Shipping & Handling on Full Volume Orders
Add $1.00 Shipping & Handling per pamphlet $_____

Total Cost $_____

<u>Thank You for Your Support. Management!</u>

DID YOU ENJOY THIS BOOK?

Vision Books would like to hear from you! If you or someone you know has been falsely imprisoned, we would like to hear your story. If the 'North Carolina Criminal Law and Procedure' has had an effect in your life or if you have suggestions, we would like to hear from you. Send your letters to:

Vision Books, LLC
Attn: Staff Writers
P.O. Box 42406
Charlotte, NC 28215
Email: staff@visionbooks.org

Order Additional Copies:

Fax Orders:	1-980-299-5965
Phone Orders:	1-704-898-0770
E-mail Orders:	www.visionbooks.org
Mail Orders:	Vision Books, LLC P.O. Box 42406 Charlotte, NC 28215

www.ingramcontent.com/pod-product-compliance
Lightning Source LLC
Chambersburg PA
CBHW051637170526
45167CB00001B/223